Geraniaceae

GERANIACEÆ.

THE

NATURAL ORDER

OF

GERANIA,

ILLUSTRATED BY COLOURED FIGURES & DESCRIPTIONS;

COMPRISING

THE NUMEROUS AND BEAUTIFUL MULE-VARIETIES CULTIVATED IN THE GARDENS OF GREAT BRITAIN,

WITH

DIRECTIONS FOR THEIR TREATMENT.

BY ROBERT SWEET, F.L.S.

Author of Hortus Britannicus, Botanical Cultivator, The British Flower Garden, Cistineæ, The British Warblers, &c.

VOL. III.

LONDON:

JAMES RIDGWAY, PICCADILLY.

1824—1826.

TILLING, PRINTER, CHELSEA.

BOOKS QUOTED IN THE THIRD VOLUME,

IN

ADDITION TO THOSE ENUMERATED IN THE FIRST AND SECOND.

DC. prodr. DE CANDOLLE (Augustin Pyramus.) Prodromus systematis naturalis regni vegetabilis. pars 1 et 2. *Paris.* 8vo. 1824—1825.

Desf. arb. DESFONTAINES (Renè Louiche.) Histoire des arbres et arbrisseaux qui peuvent être cultivés en pleine terre sur le sol de la France. 2 vol. in 8vo. *Paris.* 1809.

Forskahl descr. FORSKAHL (Petrus.) Flora Ægyptiaco-arabica. 1 vol. in 4to. *Hauniæ.* 1775.

Horn. sup. HORNEMANN (J. W.) Hortii regii Botanici Hafniensis supplementum, in 12mo. *Hafniæ.* 1819.

Linn. f. supp. LINNÆUS FILIUS (Carolus.) Supplementum Plantarum. 1 vol. in 8vo. *Brunsvigiæ.* 1781.

Murr. gœtt. Commentarii Societatis regiæ scientiarum Gottingensis. in 4 vol. 1751—1754—1769—1816.

Schleich. cat. SCHLEICHER. (J. C.) Catalogus hucusque absolutus omnium plantarum in Helvetia. *Camberii.* 1821.

Swt. hort. brit. Sweet's Hortus Britannicus, or a Catalogue of the plants cultivated in the gardens of Great Britain, arranged according to their natural orders, with reference to Figures, and numerous synonyms. 1 vol. 8vo. *London.* 1826.

Ten. prodr. fl. neap. TENORE (Michel.) Floræ Neapolitanæ Prodromi. Neapoli. 1811—1813.

201

Smith del. Pub by J. Ridgway 170 Piccadilly March 1. 1824. Watts sc.

PELARGONIUM calocephalon.

Pretty-headed Stork's-bill.

P. *calocephalon*, umbellis plurifloris capitatis, foliis planis cordatis subseptemlobatis hirsutis dentatis: lobis acutiusculis, stipulis acuminatis subdentatis, tubo nectarifero calyce duplo breviore.

Tull's Imperial Geranium. *Hortulanorum.*

Stem shrubby, branching; *branches* spreading, thickly clothed with long shaggy hairs, as are the petioles, peduncles, and calyx. *Leaves* flat, cordate, acute, deeply 5 or 7-lobed, thickly clothed on both sides with short hairs, sharply toothed with short unequal teeth, strongly and numerously nerved underneath: lobes a little pointed. *Petioles* shorter than the leaves, flattened and furrowed on the upper side and convex on the lower, a little widened at the base. *Stipules* lanceolate, taper pointed, fringed, sometimes toothed. *Peduncles* cylindrical, several-flowered. *Flowers* in a close compact head. *Involucre* of six or seven long lanceolate acute keeled bractes. *Pedicles* very short, scarcely half the length of the bractes. *Calyx* 5-cleft, segments very long, lanceolate, acute, spreading or slightly reflexed. *Nectariferous tube* about half the length of the calyx, flattened and furrowed on each side, villous. *Petals* 5, all obovate, of a pale blush; upper ones elegantly marked with a red spot and numerous branching lines. *Stamens* 10, united at the base, seven producing anthers which are always without pollen. *Style* long, flesh-coloured, very hairy on the lower part and smooth upwards. *Stigmas* 5, of the same colour, with curled points.

Our drawing was taken from a plant received from the Nursery of Mr. James Lee, of Hammersmith. It is of hybrid origin; and we suspect one of its parents to be P. *augustum;* the other is likely to be one of the varieties of P. *cucullatum.* It is nearer related to P. *augustum* than any other with which we are acquainted, but differs sufficiently. We have never yet seen it with perfect anthers; in all the plants that we have examined, they have been destitute of pollen. It is a fine strong-growing plant, and produces a great abundance of flowers, which continue to bloom in succession from May to November. The best soil for it is a mixture of turfy loam and peat, or any rich vegetable mould, requiring only to be protected from frost. Cuttings soon strike root, if planted under hand-glasses, or in pots placed in the greenhouse.

202.

Pub. by J. Ridgway 170 Piccadilly Mar. 1.1824. J. Watts sc.

DIMACRIA elegans.

Elegant Dimacria.

D. *elegans,* subacaule, scapo folioso, foliis pinnatifido-laciniatis canescenti-pubescentibus; segmentis oblongis obtusis integris bifidisque, umbella composita, petalis patentibus, calycibus reflexis, tubo nectarifero calyce triplo longiore.

Dimacria elegans. *Colv. catal. ed.* 2. *p.* 21. *col.* 2.

Root tuberous, branching out into other smaller tubers. *Stem* none. *Leaves* pinnatifid or laciniate: segments oblong, obtuse, entire or 2-fid, seldom toothed, thickly clothed with a short canescent pubescence. *Petioles* slender, a little flattened on the upper side and convex on the lower, thickly clothed with short silky hairs. *Stipules* lanceolate, acute, joined to the base of the petioles. *Scape* leafy, branching, and bearing many umbels of flowers. *Umbels* many-flowered. *Involucre* of numerous linear, acute, fringed bractes. *Pedicles* very short, scarcely as long as the bractes. *Calyx* 5-cleft; segments lanceolate, unequal, all reflexed. *Nectariferous tube* flattened and keeled at the back, about three times longer than the calyx. *Petals* 5, spreading, of a scarlet orangy colour; two upper ones distinct at the base, broadly spatulate, a little waved, and marked from the base with numerous dark lines, which branch in various directions; lower petals ligulate, self-coloured. *Filaments* 10, united at the base, five only bearing anthers; two lower fertile ones longest, as in the others of the genus; upper one very short; barren ones short, erect, and subulate. *Style* red, hairy at the base and smooth at the point. *Stigmas* 5, red, reflexed.

Since the Descriptions and Indices for our last Number were sent home from the press, we have received the first volume of the very extensive and interesting PRODROMUS of M. DE CANDOLLE. The learned author of the above work has adopted our subdivision of the genus *Pelargonium* as Sections or Subgenera; but we are quite certain that we cannot do better than to continue them as distinct genera; for, if we were to join them all with *Pelargonium*, it would be quite impossible to find names for them. We already find it difficult, though perhaps one fourth part of them are not yet described. M. De Candolle describes three hundred and sixty-nine; and we believe more than one thousand are cultivated in the collections of this country; and we have been informed, by various travellers from the Cape, that they are there without end. Mr. J. Niven, who was there collecting plants and seeds for several years, on his return informed me, that the shrubby species were innumerable; so much so, that he paid no attention to them: and we have heard from others, that the tuberous-rooted tribe is as numerous in other situations. Many of the latter, introduced by Mr. Niven, are now lost in our collections, as the cultivation of them at that time was not so well known as at present: amongst the rest, the beautiful P. *Grenvilleæ*, *roseum*, and *incrassatum*, have, I believe, entirely disappeared. Mr. Colvill informs me, that at that time he had another magnificent one, nearly related to those, with large panicles of golden yellow flowers: this was thrown down from a shelf by a cat when in full flower, which caused its death.

The present beautiful plant is a hybrid production, and was raised in the magnificent collection of R. Henry Jenkinson, Esq. from a seed of D. *pinnata*, that had been fertilized by P. *fulgidum*. It requires the same treatment as the other tuberous-rooted kinds, and may be increased by the little tubers from the roots. The anthers are perfect, and it ripens seeds.

203.

Smith del. Pub by J. Ridgway 170 Piccadilly March 1. 1824. Watts sc

PELARGONIUM incanescens.

Whitish-leaved Stork's-bill.

P. *incanescens,* umbellis subquinquefloris, foliis cordatis, profunde quinquelobis dentatis canescenti-pubescentibus, stipulis acuminatis, petalis superioribus venosis, tubo nectarifero calyce parum longiore.

Stem shrubby, erect, branched; *branches* thickly clothed with soft villous hairs, as are the petioles, peduncles, and calyx. *Leaves* cordate, deeply lobed with sharp lobes, unequally but sharply toothed, thickly clothed with a hoary pubescence, strongly and numerously nerved underneath; lower ones 5 to 7-lobed; upper ones 3 to 5-lobed, more acute. *Petioles* flattened and furrowed on the upper side and convex on the lower. *Stipules* broadly lanceolate, taper-pointed, fringed. *Peduncles* 3 to 5-flowered, longer than the leaves. *Involucre* of six or seven lanceolate, keeled, taper-pointed, ciliate bractes. *Pedicles* longer than the bractes, villous. *Calyx* 5-cleft; segments lanceolate, taper-pointed, erect. *Nectariferous tube* a little longer than the calyx, flattened on each side, of a brownish purple. *Petals* 5, the two upper ones oblongly ovate, oblique at the base, of a pale lilac, with a dark velvetty spot in the centre, and from the base to the point, branch numerous purple lines in all directions; lower petals oblong, spreading, pale lilac. *Filaments* 10, united at the base, seven bearing anthers: *pollen* orange-coloured. *Style* red, very hairy on the lower part, and smooth on the upper. *Stigmas* 5, of the same colour, reflexed.

The present plant is of hybrid origin, and was raised last year, at the Nursery of Mr. Colvill, from a seed of P. *dumosum* that had been mixed with the pollen of one of the larger sorts, perhaps P. *œmulum* or *cardiifolium*. It is a very fine strong-growing sort, and its beautiful large flowers, which are produced in abundance, make it a very desirable plant. It may be considered as one of the late-flowering sorts, as it continued in flower this autumn till the beginning of December. It thrives well in a mixture of turfy loam and peat, or any other rich vegetable soil. Cuttings soon strike root, if planted in pots and placed in a sheltered situation.

204.

E. D. Smith. del. Pub by J. Ridgway 170 Piccadilly Mar. 1. 1824. J. Watts sc.

PELARGONIUM modestum.

Modest Stork's-bill.

P. *modestum*, pedunculis villosis 2-3-floris, foliis cordatis trilobis undulatis rugosis denticulatis obtusis utrinque hirsutis; lobis rotundatis divaricatis, caule erecto ramoso, calycibus reflexis, tubo nectarifero calyce parum breviore.

Stem shrubby, erect, much branched; *branches* short, spreading, thickly clothed with long villous hairs, as are the petioles, peduncles, and calyx. *Leaves* small, cordate, 3-lobed, undulate, rugose, and toothed with small pointed teeth, thickly covered with hairs on both sides: *lobes* spreading, blunt, and rounded, terminal one largest, strongly veined. *Petioles* about the length of the leaves, flattened and furrowed on the upper side, and convex on the lower, widened at the base. *Stipules* short and broad, cordate, acute, fringed. *Peduncles* short, cylindrical, 2 to 3-flowered. *Involucre* of six or seven short, cordate or broadly ovate, acute, fringed bractes, which are often toothed. *Pedicles* long and robust, unequal in length, bent upwards. *Calyx* 5-cleft; segments unequal, all reflexed, the upper one largest, ovate, the others broadly lanceolate. *Nectariferous tube* short and broad, scarcely as long as the calyx. *Petals* 5, the two upper ones roundly obovate, oblique at the base, of a pale blush-colour, marked in the centre with a large patch of pale red, at the base of which are some darker marks; lower petals oblong, obtuse, pale blush. *Filaments* 10, united at the base, seven bearing anthers. *Pollen* orange-coloured. *Germen* and *aristæ* villous. *Style* pale red, hairy at the base and smooth upwards. *Stigmas* 5, reflexed.

Our drawing of this very pretty plant was taken from a fine specimen at the Nursery of Mr. Colvill, where it was raised from a seed of P. *ornatum* mixed with the pollen of one of the larger sorts, perhaps P. *platypetalum*. It grows to the height of three feet, and is very bushy, bearing abundance of flowers all the summer. It succeeds well in a mixture of turfy loam and peat, or any other rich vegetable soil; and cuttings root freely, if planted in pots and placed on a shelf in the greenhouse.

205.

S. D. Smith del. Pub by J. Ridgway 170 Piccadilly Ap. 1. 1824. J. Watts sc.

PELARGONIUM Saundersii.

Saunders' Stork's-bill.

P. *Saundersii*, umbellis subquadrifloris, foliis basi truncatis trilobis planis glabriusculis: lobis divaricatis obtusis inæqualiter obtuse dentatis, stipulis cordatis acutis ciliatis, tubo nectarifero calyce parum breviore.

Stem shrubby, much branched; *branches* glossy, thinly clothed with short hairs. *Leaves* truncate at the base, deeply 3-lobed, flat, smooth on the upper side, and covered with a very short pubescence on the lower; nerves few, but prominent, branched: lobes divaricate, obtuse, unequally toothed with short blunt teeth. *Petiole* slender, flattened and furrowed on the upper side and convex on the lower, slightly pubescent. *Stipules* short and flat, broadly cordate, acute, entire, fringed. *Peduncles* cylindrical, generally 3 or 4-flowered, clothed with short spreading hairs. *Involucre* of six ovate, acute, fringed bractes. *Pedicles* unequal in length, longer than the bractes. *Calyx* 5-cleft; segments lanceolate, acute, fringed; upper one erect, the others reflexed. *Nectariferous tube* unequal in length, some about half the length, others scarcely shorter than the calyx. *Petals* 5, the two upper ones obovate, oblique at the base, of a rosy lilac, with a dark velvet spot in the centre, and a few short dark lines below it and branching from it: lower petals oblong, obtuse, of a lighter colour. *Filaments* 10, united at the base, seven bearing anthers. *Pollen* orange-coloured. *Style* red, hairy on the lower part and smooth upwards. *Stigmas* 5, reflexed.

The plant from which our drawing was taken was kindly sent to us from the collection of C. Hoare, Esq. We have named it in compliment to Mr. Richard Saunders, the gardener; who informs us, that he raised it from a seed of P. *Thymneæ*, that had been fertilized by the pollen of P. *dumosum;* and it is as near as possible intermediate between the two. Like its parents, it is an abundant bloomer, and continues to flower the whole of the summer. It thrives well in a mixture of turfy loam and peat, or any other rich vegetable mould; and cuttings strike root readily, if planted in pots and placed in a sheltered situation.

206.

Smith. del. Pub. by J. Ridgway 170 Piccadilly Ap. 1. 1824. Watts sc.

SEYMOURIA asarifolia.

Asarum-leaved Seymouria.

Seymouria. *Pet.* 2 basi distincta, medio abrupte reflexa. *Stam.* 5 subæqualia, longe tubulosa recta, omnia antherifera: sterilia nulla. Herbæ *acaules? radice tuberoso-rapiformi; foliis indivisis.*

S. *asarifolia*, foliis rotundato-cordatis obtusiusculis integerrimis ciliatis: super glabris nitentibus: subtus tomentoso-velutinis, umbella composita capitato-depressa, petalis lanceolato-spatulatis emarginatis.

Root tuberous, large. *Stem* none, or very short. *Leaves* roundly cordate, bluntish, entire, ciliate; of a bright shining green on the upper side, and densely tomentose underneath. *Petioles* rather broadest at the base and point, flattened on the upper side and convex on the lower, hairy. *Stipules* small, taper-pointed, joined to the base of the petioles. *Scape* leafless, branching, thickly clothed with soft villous hairs, as are the peduncles, bractes, and calyx. *Bracte* inclosing the peduncles at the base, divided into several unequal ovate and lanceolate, concave, acute segments. *Peduncles* slender, cylindrical. *Umbels* in a small depressed head, many-flowered. *Involucre* of six or seven narrow taper-pointed bractes; some lanceolate, others subulate. *Calyx* 5-cleft, segments linear, acute, all reflexed. *Nectariferous tube* about the length of the calyx, slightly nodding, hairy. *Petals* only 2, lanceolately-spatulate, notched at the point, reflexed from about the middle, of a brilliant dark purple, variegated and spotted with a blackish velvet: no rudiments of lower petals. *Filaments* 5, purple, straight, nearly equal, connected into a long tube, all bearing anthers: no rudiments of sterile ones. *Pollen* orange-coloured. *Style* very hairy, about the length of the stamens. *Stigmas* 5, at length revolute.

This very curious plant is a native of the Cape, and was received from thence, about three years since, by Mr. Colvill, at whose Nursery it first flowered in December 1822, at which time our drawing was taken; it flowered again in November and December 1823, when we made our description. We have proposed it as a distinct genus, and have named it in compliment to the Hon. Mrs. Seymour, of Woburn, Bedfordshire, a lady much attached to botanical science, and particularly partial to the Geraniaceæ; also a great admirer of neat little Alpine plants, to which the present genus bears a strong resemblance. Another species, or a very distinct variety, has also flowered at Mr. Colvill's, with smaller acute petals; but we wish to see it in flower again before we publish it. Pelargonium *dipetalum* of L'Héritier will no doubt rank as another species, and may be named *Seymouria Héritieri*.

The species of this genus require the same kind of treatment as the other tuberous-rooted species of the family; but as they flower in winter, or late in autumn, they must be kept growing at that season, watering them sparingly when dry, and letting them become dormant after flowering. They succeed well in a mixture of turfy loam, peat, and sand, an equal quantity of each; and they may be increased by the little tubers from the roots.

207.

E. D. Smith. del. Pub by J. Ridgway 170 Piccadilly Ap 1. 1824. J. Watts sc

PELARGONIUM phœniceum.

Reddish purple Stork's-bill.

P. *phœniceum*, umbellis plurifloris, foliis rotundato-reniformibus undulatis cucullatis rugosis villosis inæqualiter dentatis, stipulis cordato-ovatis acutis, calycibus villosissimis, tubo nectarifero calyce parum breviore.

Stem erect, branching; *branches* spreading, thickly clothed with long white villous hairs, as are the petioles, peduncles, and calyx. *Leaves* roundly-reniform, undulate, cucullate, rigid, rugose, thickly clothed with short villous hairs, and toothed with numerous unequal teeth. *Petioles* gradually tapering upwards, flattened and furrowed on the upper side and convex on the lower, a little widened at the base. *Stipules* cordate, or broadly ovate, acute, ciliate. *Peduncles* cylindrical, several-flowered. *Involucre* of six ovate, acute, keeled, ciliate bractes. *Pedicles* villous, about the length of the bractes. *Calyx* 5-cleft, segments broadly lanceolate, acute, thickly clothed with long villous hairs. *Nectariferous tube* scarcely as long as the calyx, flattened on each side, gibbous at the base, villous. *Petals* 5, the two upper ones broadly ovate, oblique at the base, of a dark reddish purple, with a dark velvetty spot in the centre, and below that are numerous dark branching lines; lower petals obovately-oblong, of rather a lighter colour. *Filaments* 10, united at the base, seven bearing anthers. *Style* red, very hairy. *Stigmas* 5, purple, revolute.

Our drawing of this plant was taken at the Nursery of Mr. Colvill last October. It was raised the preceding spring from a seed of P. *spectabile* δ. *recurvum*, that had been fertilized by the pollen of P. *Dennisianum*. The seed was sown in February, and the plant flowered in September; so that it was only seven months from the time the seed was sown till it flowered, and it continued in full bloom to the end of December. It is now forward in bud again, so that we may expect it will flower nearly all the year through. It appears to be of very free growth, and as hardy as any of the nearly related sorts, thriving well in a mixture of turfy loam, peat, and sand; and cuttings root readily planted in pots in the same kind of soil, and placed on a shelf in the greenhouse.

This may be considered as one of the most desirable mules that has yet been raised, both from the abundance of bloom, and its brilliancy of colour, which partakes of a mixture of scarlet and purple, and is difficult of imitation by the artist, whose colours can never equal nature. Though we have often been told that our figures are flattered, yet if any person will take the trouble of comparing them with the living plants, he will readily perceive his mistake.

208.

D. Smith del. Pub by J. Ridgway 170 Piccadilly Ap. 1, 1824. J. Watts sc.

PELARGONIUM notatum

Marked-petaled Stork's-bill.

P. *notatum*, pedunculis elongatis plurifloris, foliis cordatis trilobis concavis scabris: margine crispis denticulatis, stipulis acuminatis, petalis venosis, tubo nectarifero calyce reflexo sesquilongiori.

Rosalind Geranium. *Hoare MSS.*

Stem shrubby, slender, branching: *branches* slender, elongated, spreading, thickly clothed with short white pubescent hairs, and slightly knotted at the joints. *Leaves* cordate, acute, 3-lobed, concave, roughish, clothed on both sides with short white hairs, margins curled, and toothed with small unequal teeth. *Petioles* long and slender, flattened and furrowed on the upper side, pubescent. *Stipules* lanceolate, taper-pointed, fringed. *Peduncles* long and slender, cylindrical, pubescent. *Involucre* of six lanceolate, taper-pointed, fringed bractes. *Pedicles* long and slender, pubescent. *Calyx* 5-cleft, segments broadly lanceolate, acute, the upper one erect, the others reflexed. *Nectariferous tube* much flattened, gibbous at the base, pubescent, about half as long again as the calyx. *Petals* 5, much veined, the two upper ones obovate, oblique, of a rosy lilac, with a bright purple mark in the centre, and numerous purple lines branching in every direction; lower petals oblongly obovate, slender at the base, of a lighter colour and not so much veined. *Filaments* 10, connected at the base, seven bearing anthers. *Germen* villous. *Style* very hairy at the base, and smooth upwards. *Stigmas* 5, red, reflexed.

This neat little plant is of hybrid origin, and was

raised from seed by Sir R. C. Hoare, who sent us the plant from which our drawing was taken. What its parents were is at present unknown to us: perhaps hybrid for several generations. Being so different from all others, it is a very desirable plant; and being of small growth, it takes but little room: it is also as hardy as any of the genus, and thrives well in a mixture of turfy loam and peat, or any rich light soil. Cuttings root freely, if planted in pots, and set on a shelf in the greenhouse.

209.

E. D. Smith del. Pub by J. Ridgway 170 Piccadilly May 1. 1824. J. Watts sc.

HOAREA venosa.

Veined-petaled Hoarea.

H. *venosa*, umbella composita, foliis ternatis pinnatifidis pinnatisque canescenti-pubescentibus; foliolis oblongis ovatisque obtusis: terminali maximo, petalis superioribus spatulato-ligulatis reflexis venosis.

Root tuberous. *Stem* none. *Leaves* variable, lower ones simple, roundly ovate, others ternate, pinnatifid, or pinnate: leaflets opposite or alternate, oblong or ovate, bluntly rounded; the lowermost smallest and narrowest, terminal, one very large, rounded, all covered with a white mealy pubescence. *Petioles* slender, slightly flattened on the upper side and convex on the lower, thickly clothed with short white hairs, as are the peduncles and calyx. *Stipules* subulately-linear, joined to the base of the petioles. *Scape* leafy, producing several umbels of flowers. *Peduncles* cylindrical. *Umbels* many-flowered. *Involucre* of numerous linear taper-pointed fringed bractes. *Pedicles* very short. *Calyx* 5-cleft; upper segment lanceolate, concave, erect; the others linear, reflexed. *Nectariferous tube* about twice the length of the calyx, flattened on each side, hairy. *Petals* 5; the two upper ones spatulately ligulate, reflexed about the middle, with two long ungues, much veined with red and purple veins which branch in various directions; lower petals about half the width, of a paler colour and less veined. *Filaments* 10, united at the base, five only bearing anthers; sterile ones short, their points bent inwards. *Style* short, purple, slightly hairy at the base, and smooth upwards. *Stigmas* 5, reflexed.

This pretty and curious plant is of hybrid origin, the produce of *Dimacria pinnata* that had been fertilized by the pollen of *Hoarea reticulata:* the leaves partake chiefly of the former, and the flowers of the latter: its stamens are perfect, and it produces seeds. The same kind of treatment, as recommended for the other tuberous-rooted species, is also applicable to the present, keeping it quite dry while dormant, and it may be increased by the little tubers of its roots.

Drawn at the Nursery of Mr. Colvill last summer, where it continued to be covered with flowers, in succession, from June to October.

210.

C. D. Smith del. Pub by J. Ridgway 170 Piccadilly May 1 1824.

PELARGONIUM fuscatum.

Brown-marked Stork's-bill.

P. *fuscatum*, pedunculis plurifloris, foliis cordatis obsolete trilobis planis inæqualiter dentatis villosis, stipulis cordato ovatis subdentatis, caule villoso, tubo nectarifero calyce parum longiore.

Pelargonium fuscatum. *Colv. catal. ed. 2. p. 22. col. 3.*

Stem shrubby, erect, much branched; *branches* erect, thickly clothed with long villous hairs, as is every other part of the plant, except the corolla. *Leaves* flat, cordate, rounded, slightly 3-lobed, unequally toothed with numerous small sharp teeth, prominently and numerously veined underneath. *Petioles* flattened and furrowed on the upper side, and convex on the lower; a little widened at the base. *Stipules* short, cordate or ovate, sometimes toothed, acute, fringed. *Peduncles* cylindrical, several-flowered. *Involucre* of six or seven ovate, acute, fringed bractes. *Pedicles* unequal in length, longer than the nectariferous tube. *Calyx* 5-cleft, segments all reflexed; the upper one ovate, the others lanceolate, acute, fringed. *Nectariferous tube* much flattened and gibbous at the base; a little longer than the calyx. *Petals* 5, the two upper ones roundly ovate, of a bluish lilac, with a large dark brown mark in the centre, stained round with red, and below it are a few dark lines, that are slightly branched: lower petals oblong, of a bluish lilac. *Filaments* 10, united at the base, seven bearing anthers. *Germen* villous. *Style* very hairy about half-way up, and smooth on the upper part. *Stigmas* 5, reflexed.

The present subject is a hybrid production, and

was raised the year before last at the Nursery of Mr. Colvill, where our drawing was made last summer. It is the produce of P. *dumosum*, that had been mixed with the pollen of one of the larger sorts, perhaps P. *multinerve;* but of this we are not quite certain. It is a very ornamental plant, and an abundant bloomer like its parent, and grows to a middle size: it is also as hardy as any of the genus, and thrives well in a mixture of sandy loam and peat, or any light rich vegetable mould. Cuttings strike root freely, if planted in pots and placed in a sheltered situation.

E. D. Smith del. Pub. by J. Ridgway 170 Piccadilly May 1. 1824. J. Watts sc.

PELARGONIUM heracleifolium.

Heracleum-leaved Stork's-bill.

P. *heracleifolium*, acaule, umbellis plurifloris, foliis inferioribus oblongis integris laciniatisque superioribus pinnatifidis pinnatisque pulverulento-pubescentibus; segmentis foliolisque oblongis obtusis sinuato-lobatis inæqualiter obtuse dentatis, calycibus reflexis, tubo nectarifero calyce triplo longiori.

Pelargonium heracleifolium. *Lodd. bot. cab. t.* 437. *Colv. catal. ed.* 2. *p.* 22. *col.* 1. *DC. prodr. syst. nat.* 1. *p.* 654.

Root tuberous, very large and uneven, and clothed with a hard scaly shell, producing very few small tubers or fibres. *Stem* none, or very short. *Leaves* very variable, covered with a powdery pubescence: lower ones oblong, simple, or lacinated; upper ones ternate, pinnatifid or pinnate, strongly nerved underneath; segments or leaflets oblong, obtuse, sinuately lobed, the upper one much the largest and most divided; margins a little waved or curled, bluntly but deeply toothed with numerous unequal teeth. *Petioles* nearly round, or slightly flattened on the upper side, thickly clothed with short villous hairs. *Stipules* short, cordate, acute, membranaceous. *Peduncles* long, several-flowered, and clothed with short spreading hairs, with a few long ones intermixed. *Involucre* of 8 or 9 unequal linear, or lanceolate, pointed bractes. *Pedicles* short, scarcely as long as the bractes. *Calyx* 5-cleft, segments unequal, lanceolate, bluntish, all reflexed or revolute. *Nectariferous tube* more than three times the length of the calyx, slender at the base, and gradually widening upwards. *Petals* 5, the two upper ones rather the largest, of a dull greenish straw-colour, marked near the centre with two obscure purplish spots; lower petals rather darker, with two bright purple lines extending nearly all their length. *Filaments* 10, united at the base, seven bearing anthers; one of those is a flat spatula-shaped one, as in the other species of this section. *Germen* thickly clothed with a dense wool. *Style* greenish, very short and smooth. *Stigmas* 5, spreading.

The present curious species is a native of the Cape of Good Hope, from whence many roots of it have been introduced to different collections in this country within these four years. It is nearly related to P. *lobatum* and P. *triste;* but we think there can be no doubt of its being a genuine species. It varies considerably in the colour of its flowers, being either darker or lighter, much in the same manner as P. *lobatum.* Several other curious species belonging to this section are now in the extensive collection of Mr. Colvill, who has imported them from the Cape within those few years: many of them have flowered; and we intend soon to publish them, and not to let them die in oblivion, as many a fine plant is suffered to do in some collections, without ever being recorded, or even seen, except by the dunces who manage to destroy them.

Our drawing was taken from a fine plant, in the collection of Robert Henry Jenkinson, last summer.

212

Smith del. Pub by J. Ridgway 170 Piccadilly May 1 1824. J. Watts sc.

PELARGONIUM Stapletoni.

Miss C. Stapleton's Stork's-bill.

P. *Stapletoni*, umbellis multifloris, petalis obcordatis, foliis cordatis quinquelobis undulatis obsolete crenulatis pubescentibus, stipulis persistentibus spinescentibus rectis, caule crasso carnoso, tubo nectarifero calyce quadruplo longiore.

Stem shrubby, erect, thick and succulent, clothed with a hard glossy bark, not much branched. *Leaves* cordate, 5-lobed, very much undulate, shallowly notched, and clothed with a short hoary pubescence on both sides, points bent downwards. *Petioles* slightly flattened on the upper side, and rounded on the lower; swollen at the base, thickly clothed with white villous hairs. *Stipules* subulate, straight, persistent, hardening into a spine. *Scape* branching, thickly clothed with long villous hairs, as are the peduncles and calyx. *Peduncles* cylindrical, bent towards the point, many flowered. *Involucre* of several unequal bractes, some ovate, others lanceolate, acute, fringed. *Pedicles* very short. *Calyx* 5-cleft: upper segment oblong, obtuse, erect; the others narrower and reflexed. *Nectariferous tube* about four times the length of the calyx, very hairy. *Petals* 5, obcordate, the two uppermost largest, rose-coloured, white near the base; betwixt the two colours is a large bright purple spot, and below that are two or three light purple slightly branching specks: lower petals smaller, rose-coloured, with a bright red spot in the centre of each. *Filaments* 10, united at the base, six bearing anthers, besides a large spatulate-shaped one, as in the others of this section: this produces no anther. *Pollen* yellow. *Style* short, smooth. *Stigmas* 5, purple, reflexed.

This very handsome plant is of hybrid origin, the produce of P. *echinatum*, mixed with the pollen of P. *sæpeflorens*. We have named it, in compliment to Miss C. Stapleton, of Grey's Court, Henley on Thames, a lady much attached to the GERANIACEÆ, and to whom we feel much obliged. Like its parents, the present plant is of a succulent habit, and is as near as possible intermediate between the two; but its flowers are more beautiful than either: it is also of shorter and more upright growth. It was raised from seed, in 1822, at the Nursery of Mr. Colvill, and flowered last autumn for the first time. We expect it will remain scarce for some time, as it produces but few branches; but it will probably be more readily increased by the tubers of its roots, when it attains a proper size. An equal mixture of turfy loam, peat, and sand, is the most proper compost for it, watering it but sparingly in winter. The best time for planting the cuttings is when the plant is growing most freely; they must be planted in the same kind of soil, and placed on a shelf in the greenhouse.

We understand we are very much envied in a certain quarter for raising so many beautiful hybrid plants; and more so for publishing them: but we mind not their envy, as long as we are so ably supported by our numerous subscribers, to whom we beg our most grateful acknowledgments, and who we shall always use our utmost endeavours to please, by giving figures and descriptions of the most interesting plants.

We also have it in contemplation to publish a work on the same plan, entirely on hybrid productions of the plants of different families; so many beautiful and interesting ones, both hardy and tender, having been lately raised from seeds in different collections, particularly at the Nursery of Mr. Colvill.

213.
Smith del.
Pub by J. Ridgway 170 Piccadilly June. 1. 1824.
J. Watts sc.

PELARGONIUM mutabile.

Changeable-coloured Stork's-bill.

P. *mutabile*, caule fruticoso carnoso nodis tumidis, foliis ternatis glabris subtus pilosis; foliolis obtusis cuneatis grosse dentatis; intermedio maximo laciniato apice reflexo, stipulis longe acuminatis subpersistentibus: inferioribus cordatis; superioribus lanceolatis subulatis, umbellis multifloris, tubo nectarifero calyce triplo longiore.

Root fleshy, producing numerous tubers. *Stem* shrubby, succulent, very thick at the base, flexuose, swoln at the joints, smooth and glossy, not much branched. *Leaves* large, ternate, smooth and glossy on the upper side, and thickly clothed with short soft hairs on the lower: *leaflets* obtuse, wedge-shaped, deeply but unequally toothed, with large blunt teeth and smaller ones intermixed; lower one 2-lobed; upper one much larger, 5-lobed or laciniate, points bent downwards. *Petioles* long, nearly cylindrical, swoln at the base and thickening towards the point, thickly clothed with unequal spreading hairs. *Stipules* variable, taper-pointed, fringed, nearly persistent; lower ones broadly cordate; upper ones lanceolately subulate, terminating in long slender points. *Peduncles* axillary, or opposite to the leaf, gibbous at the base, hairy. *Umbels* many-flowered. *Involucre* of several lanceolate, acute, fringed bractes. *Pedicles* very short, or scarcely any. *Calyx* 5-cleft, segments lanceolate, obtuse. *Nectariferous tube* more than three times longer than the calyx, hairy. *Petals* 5, obovate or slightly obcordate: the two upper ones largest, green, tinged with purple; lower ones pale purple, but changing the second day to a yellowish green. *Filaments* 10, straight, united at the base, seven bearing anthers; one of those is a spatula-shaped one, with a smaller anther. *Style* short, hairy at the base. *Stigmas* 5, reflexed.

This curious plant is a hybrid production, and was raised at the nursery of Mr. Colvill, in 1822, from a seed of P. *gibbosum* that had been fertilized by the pollen of P. *particeps,* and it is as near as possible intermediate between the two: the flowers, when first expanded, are of a light purple colour, but they soon change to a yellowish green, and are fragrant in the evening. Several other curious mules from plants belonging to this section we expect to see flower this season: some between P. *gibbosum* and P. *multiradiatum;* others between the latter and P. *ardens* we are in hopes of seeing bloom before long; and also several very curious ones from P. *sanguineum,* some of which are shrubby, and others stemless; some with divided leaves, and others entire.

The present plant thrives well, and grows very strong in an equal mixture of rich turfy loam, peat, and sand. Cuttings of it strike root readily, if planted in pots and placed in the greenhouse: it may also be increased by the tubers of its roots. Drawn at the nursery of Mr. Colvill, in October last.

214

E. D. Smith. del. Pub. by J. Ridgway 170 Piccadilly June 1. 1824

PELARGONIUM armatum.

Strong-spined Stork's-bill.

P. *armatum*, umbellis multifloris paniculatis, foliis cordatis 5-7-lobis crenatis: supra glabris nitentibus; subtus tomentosis multinerviis, caule stricto crasso carnoso, stipulis subulatis persistentibus spinescentibus rectis.

Pelargonium armatum. *Nobis supra fol.* 48. *in adn. Colv. catal. ed.* 1. *p.* 21. *col.* 2. *ed.* 2. *p.* 22. *col.* 1.

Geranium echinatum; rubrum. *Andrews, c. ic.*

Root large, branching out into numerous tubers of various shapes and sizes. *Stem* shrubby, stiff, erect, very thick, and succulent, clothed with a hard brown shining bark, and thickly beset with long straight persistent stipules; *branches* short, straight, rigid. *Leaves* cordate, 5 to 7-lobed, deeply but unequally notched, of a shining green but slightly pubescent on the upper side, and densely tomentose underneath: nerves numerous, much branched. *Petioles* slightly flattened on the upper side, and rounded on the lower; swollen at the base, thickly clothed with very short spreading, unequal hairs. *Stipules* straight, subulate, persistent; when young tapering to a fine point, afterwards becoming stiff and horny, and more blunt; not recurved, as in P. *echinatum*. *Peduncles* panicled, cylindrical, thickened at the base, hairy. *Umbels* many-flowered. *Involucre* of several lanceolate, acute, fringed bractes. *Calyx* 5-cleft; segments blunt, concave; upper one erect, the others reflexed. *Nectariferous tube* very long and slender, about four times the length of the calyx. *Petals* 5, of a bright purple, with a dark spot in the centre of each: upper ones obcordate; lower ones narrower. *Filaments* 10, united at the base, six only bearing anthers: at the back is a large spatula-shaped sterile filament, as in the plants of this section. *Style* smooth, purple. *Stigmas* 5, reflexed.

This beautiful species, which there can be no doubt but it really is, was raised from seed received from the Cape, at the Nursery of Mr. Colvill, at the same time as P. *echinatum*. Although it has been in the collections about London so many years, it is still very little known, and continues scarce, chiefly owing, we believe, to the want of a figure to show it in perfection. The one published by Mr. Andrews being very poor and imperfect, we think it will now become a popular plant. It requires the same kind of management as P. *echinatum*, from which it differs in many respects, being a much stronger and upright plant, and its spines are longer and straight, not recurved, as in P. *echinatum*; its leaves are also more lobed, and the flowers of a very different colour.

Our drawing was taken from a fine plant covered with flowers in May last, in the collection of the Earl of Liverpool, at Coombe Wood. The best soil to grow it in is an equal mixture of turfy loam, peat, and sand, watering it very sparingly in winter. Cuttings root freely, if taken off when the plant is in a growing state. It may also be increased by the tubers from its roots.

215.

E. D. Smith del. Pub by J. Ridgway 170 Piccadilly June 1. 1824. J. Watts sc.

PELARGONIUM formosissimum.

Superb white Stork's-bill.

P. *formosissimum,* umbellis plurifloris, foliis ovatis acutis concavis rigidis sublobatis inæqualiter cartilagineo-dentatis basi truncatis multinerviis, bracteis ovatis pedicellis subbrevioribus, tubo nectarifero brevissimo calyce triplo breviore.

Pelargonium formosissimum. *Pers. syn.* 2. *p.* 231.

Pelargonium formosum. *Desf. arb.* 2. *p.* 459. *Horn. supp.* 75. *non Andrewsii.*

α. album. Supra fig. a.

β. lineatum. Supra fig. b.

Pelargonium superbum. *Nob. in Colv. catal. p.* 22. *col.* 1. *Supra No.* 33. *in obs.*

Geranium speciosum. *Andrews's geran.* c. *ic. non Willdenovii.*

Stem shrubby, erect, branching; *branches* short and stiff, nearly erect, thickly clothed with leaves, and covered with soft villous unequal hairs. *Leaves* ovate, acute, concave, rigid, sharply and unequally toothed with long cartilaginous teeth, slightly hairy on both sides, truncate and entire at the base, strongly nerved. *Petioles* widely flattened and furrowed on the upper side and convex on the lower, a little dilated at the base and apex; thickly clothed with soft villous unequal hairs, as are the peduncles, pedicles, and calyx. *Stipules* ovate, bluntish, keeled, fringed and sometimes toothed. *Peduncles* a little flattened, 3 to 6-flowered. *Involucre* of about six or eight ovate, keeled bractes, which are sometimes toothed and mucronate. *Pedicles* longer than the bractes or the nectariferous tube. *Calyx* 5-cleft; segments lanceolate, acute, erect. *Nectariferous tube* short, but unequal in length, sometimes wanting altogether, flattened on each side and gibbous at the base, not half the length of the calyx. *Petals* five, oblongly ovate and rounded at the points, white, or slightly tinged with pink; the two uppermost rather widest, and slightly marked at the base with reddish lines. *Filaments* 10, united at the base, seven bearing anthers. *Pollen* orange-coloured. *Germen* villous. *Style* of a light red, very hairy. *Stigmas* 5, red and revolute.

The present plant is an old inhabitant in our greenhouses, and was raised from seed received from the Cape by Mr. Colvill several years ago. It has generally passed in our collections under the name of P. *formosum*, and P. *superbum*, and we have no doubt but it is the P. *formosum* of Desfontaines, and also the P. *formosissimum* of Persoon.. It varies with flowers more or less striated, and the petals more or less spreading; the nectariferous tube is also very variable in its length, sometimes altogether wanting.

M. Decandolle, in his Prodromus, has given the above as synonyms to our P. *Bayleæ*, which is a very different plant, though we believe one of its parents was the present, as we mentioned when we published it.

ERRATA.

In our last Number, folio 210, line 1 and 3, for Pelargonium *fuscatum*, read Pelargonium *fusciflorum*, there being already a P. *fuscatum* figured by Jacquin.

216.
Smith del. Pub by J. Ridgway 170 Piccadilly June 1. 1824. S. Watts

PELARGONIUM laxiflorum.

Spreading-umbelled Stork's-bill.

P. *laxiflorum*, umbellis subquinquefloris, foliis cordatis quinquelobis undulatis inæqualiter grosseque dentatis glabriusculis carnosis rigidis, tubo nectarifero calyce duplo longiore.

Stem shrubby, not much branched, rather succulent, thickly clothed with soft villous hairs, as are the petioles, peduncles, and calyx. *Leaves* cordate, thick, and fleshy, undulate, deeply divided into three lobes: upper lobe 3-lobed, lower ones 2-lobed; deeply but unequally toothed, smoothish or thinly pubescent. *Petioles* thick, slightly flattened on the upper and convex on the lower side. *Peduncles* generally 5-flowered. *Involucre* of several ovate, acute, villous bractes. *Pedicles* about the length of the bractes. *Calyx* 5-cleft: upper segment, ovate, keeled, erect; the others broadly lanceolate, reflexed. *Nectariferous tube* about double the length of the calyx. *Petals* 5, the two upper ones roundly obovate, oblique at the base, of a bright scarlet, with a purple spot in the centre, and numerous dark lines from the base that branch in various directions; lower petals ligulate, spreading. *Filaments* 10, united at the base, seven bearing anthers. *Style* flesh-coloured, hairy at the base, and smooth upwards. *Stigmas* 5, reflexed.

This fine flowering plant is of hybrid origin, and was raised by Mr. Smith from a seed of P. *ignescens*, that had been set with the pollen of one of the large growing sorts. Our drawing was taken from a fine plant, last autumn, in the collection of the Earl of Liverpool, Coombe Wood, and we believe it is at present in no other collection: it differs from all its near relatives in its loose spreading umbels and rigid leaves. Like all the others, to which it is allied, it thrives best in a mixture of rich turfy loam, peat, and sand; and cuttings will strike root without difficulty, if planted in pots and placed on a shelf in the greenhouse.

217
Pub. by J. Ridgway 170 Piccadilly July 1. 1824

PELARGONIUM grandidentatum.

Large-toothed Stork's-bill.

P. *grandidentatum*, caule fruticoso ramoso; ramis villosis, foliis inferioribus magnis flabelliformibus inæqualiter acute dentatis multinerviis basi integerrimis: mediis sublobatis basi angustatis; superioribus oblongo-ovatis, stipulis cordato-lanceolatis carinatis acuminatis, umbellis multifloris, petalis laxis patentibus, tubo nectarifero calyce subæquali.

Stem shrubby, branching; branches slender, thickly clothed with long soft unequal villous hairs, as are the petioles, peduncles, and calyx. *Leaves* large, numerously and prominently nerved underneath, rigidly and sharply toothed, with long unequal taper-pointed teeth, entire near the base: upper side furrowed, smooth, and glossy; nerves and under side hairy: *lower ones* fan-shaped, about half as broad again as long; middle ones slightly lobed, narrowed to the base; those near the flowers oblong, ovate, or lanceolate, all sharply toothed. *Petioles* much flattened and furrowed on the upper side and convex on the lower, dilated at the base and apex. *Stipules* cordate or lanceolate, taper-pointed, keeled, entire, or sometimes toothed. *Umbels* many-flowered, panicled. *Peduncles* jointed at the base, more or less bent or crooked. *Involucre* of several large, ovate, acute, villous, imbricate bractes. *Pedicles* bent upwards. *Calyx* 5-cleft, segments long, lanceolate, taper-pointed, when in flower all reflexed. *Nectariferous tube* about the length of the calyx, flattened on each side and gibbous at the base. *Petals* 5, obovate, spreading; the two upper ones largest, of a pale blush, marked in the middle with a large dark purple patch, and from it to the base are numerous crowded lines and marks; lower petals also marked with two pale red lines. *Stamens* 10, united at the base, seven bearing anthers. *Style* red, slightly hairy at the base. *Stigmas* 5, red and revolute.

This magnificent plant is of hybrid origin, and was raised, by Mr. Smith, at the Earl of Liverpool's, Coombe Wood, from a seed of P. *involucratum maximum,* that had been fertilized with the pollen of P. *triumphans,* and it is as near as possible intermediate between the two. No plant in the whole genus with which we are acquainted, makes a more magnificent appearance than the present; as it bears an abundance of blossoms, each of which continues in flower for a considerable time: it is also as hardy as any of the common sorts, thriving well in a rich light soil, or a mixture of sandy loam and peat will suit it very well. Cuttings strike root freely, if planted in pots and placed in a sheltered situation.

218.

E. D. Smith del.
Pub by J. Ridgway 170 Piccadilly July 1 1824.
J. Watts sc.

PELARGONIUM pulverulentum.

Powdered-leaved Stork's-bill.

P. *pulverulentum*, subacaule, scapo subramoso, umbellis multifloris, foliis rotundato-cordatis sublobatis crenatis pulverulento-tomentosis carnosis, petalis superioribus paulo minoribus bimaculatis.

Pelargonium pulverulentum. *Colv. catal. ed.* 2. *p.* 22. *col.* 1.

Root tuberous, very large, and covered with a rough brown, cracked bark. *Stems* very short and rough. *Leaves* succulent, roundly cordate, obtuse, more or less lobed, unequally and bluntly notched, covered on both sides with a dense powdery pubescence, quite white when young. *Petioles* about the length of the leaves, flattened on the upper side and rounded on the lower, thickly clothed with short white hairs, as are the peduncles, calyx, and nectariferous tube. *Stipules* cordate, acute, fringed. *Scape* leafy, slightly branched. *Peduncles* long, many-flowered. *Involucre* of from six to eight broadly lanceolate taper-pointed bractes. *Pedicles* very short. *Calyx* 5-cleft, segments lanceolate, concave, all reflexed. *Nectariferous tube* more than three times longer than the calyx, flattened on each side, gradually thickening upwards. *Petals* 5, obovate, concave, the two upper ones rather smallest, yellow, with two dark spots above the middle; lower petals edged with yellow, with a dark velvetty middle. *Filaments* 10, short and straight, united at the base, one of them a very large spatulate one; as in the others of the section, this bears no anther, six of the others bearing fertile anthers. *Style* short, smooth. *Stigmas* 5, fimbriate, revolute.

This curious and pretty species is a native of the Cape, from whence Mr. Colvill received several plants of it in the year 1822. It is readily distinguished from its congeners by its powdered leaves and habit altogether. Another nearly related species is in Mr. C.'s collection, with rounder smooth leaves of a greasy appearance, but that has not yet flowered.

Like the other plants of this section, the present species thrives well in an equal mixture of loam, peat, and sand, with the pots well drained; and requires very little or no water in winter when in a dormant state. It may be increased by seeds, or by the little tubers from its root.

219.

E. D. Smith del. Pub. by J. Ridgway 170 Piccadilly July 1. 1824. S. Watts sc.

PELARGONIUM planifolium.

Flat-leaved Stork's-bill.

P. *planifolium*, caule fruticoso ramoso; ramis erectis hirsutis, foliis planis cordatis trilobis denticulatis carnosis glabriusculis, stipulis cordatis acutis subdentatis, pedunculis 3-4-floris, tubo nectarifero calyce subæquali.

Stem shrubby, erect, branching; *branches* purplish, erect, thickly clothed with short white spreading hairs, as are the petioles, peduncles, and calyx. *Leaves* flat, carnose, cordate, 3-lobed, toothed with short blunt unequal teeth, prominently nerved underneath, glossy on the upper side, but slightly hairy all over; lobes blunt. *Petioles* short, much flattened on the upper side and convex on the lower. *Stipules* cordate, taper-pointed, sometimes toothed, hairy. *Peduncles* long and slender, 3 or 4-flowered. *Involucre* of several short ovate acute bractes. *Calyx* 5-cleft; segments broadly lanceolate, acute, erect. *Nectariferous tube* about the length of the calyx, purple, flattened on both sides, gibbous at the base. *Petals* 5, obovate, the two upper ones largest, of a bright bluish lilac, with a large dark purple patch in the centre and numerous lines from the base, which branch all over the petals; lower ones narrower, of a deep blush, also marked with lines at the base. *Stamens* 10, connected at the base, seven of them bearing anthers. *Style* red, hairy all over. *Stigmas* 5, red, reflexed.

This plant is of hybrid origin, and was raised at the Nursery of Mr. Colvill, from a seed of P. *Hoareanum*, that had been fertilized by the pollen of one of the stronger growing sorts; but we cannot with any certainty refer to the species. It is free of growth, and an abundant bloomer; and, from its distinct habit and colour, it makes a pleasing variety. It succeeds well with us in a mixture of turfy loam and peat; and cuttings root without difficulty, if planted in pots in the same kind of soil, and set on a shelf in the greenhouse.

Drawn at the Nursery of Mr. Colvill in May last.

220.

220

PELARGONIUM dimacriæflorum.

Dimacria-flowered Stork's-bill.

P. *dimacriæflorum*, subacaule, foliis laciniato-pinnatifidis pinnatisque canescenti-pubescentibus; segmentis foliolisque oppositis oblongis integris bifidisve subdentatis, petalis patentissimis obovato-spathulatis subdeflexis, tubo nectarifero calyce reflexo duplo longiore.

Root tuberous. *Stem* short and succulent. *Leaves* tufted, laciniate, pinnatifid or pinnate, clothed with a short hoary pubescence; segments or leaflets opposite, oblong, obtuse, entire, bifid or 3-toothed. *Petioles* slender, slightly flattened on the upper side, thickly clothed with short white close-pressed hairs, as are the peduncles and calyx. *Stipules* lanceolate, acute, joined to the base of the petioles. *Scape* leafy, branching, bearing several umbels of flowers. *Peduncles* cylindrical, slightly bent inwards. *Umbels* many-flowered. *Involucre* of several linearly lanceolate, acute, keeled bractes. *Calyx* 5-cleft; segments lanceolate, acute, slightly keeled, reflexed. *Nectariferous tube* nearly sessile, about twice the length of the calyx. *Petals* 5, widely spreading, deflexed, of a bright orangy scarlet; upper ones obovate, connivent at the base with spreading points, more or less marked with branching brownish purple lines; lower ones broadly spatulate, distinct, dependent. *Stamens* 10, united at the base, seven bearing anthers; two lower fertile ones much longer than the others, as in Dimacria. *Style* silky, purple. *Stigmas* 5, purple, reflexed.

This pretty little plant is a hybrid production, and is intermediate between P. *fulgidum* and *Dimacria as-*

tragalifolia. The colour of the flowers is nearest the former, but their spreading mode of growth resembles the latter. It was raised from seed the year before last, in the magnificent collection of Robert Henry Jenkinson, Esq. where our drawing was made last summer; and we have seen it in the same collection this spring, covered with its elegant flowers. It grows freely, like its near relatives, in a mixture of turfy loam, peat, and sand, and the pots well drained with potsherds, keeping it dry when in a dormant state. It may be increased, though slowly, by cuttings, or by the little tubers from its roots, which must be planted with their tops above the earth, or the water is liable to injure them.

221.

E. D. Smith. del. Pub by J. Ridgway 170 Piccadilly Aug. 1. 1824. F. Watts sc.

PELARGONIUM serratifolium.

Saw-leaved Stork's-bill.

P. *serratifolium,* foliis planis profunde quinquelobis glaucescentibus serratis; lobis divaricatis cuneiformibus sublobatis mucronatis, stipulis cordato-ovatis acutis denticulatis, pedunculis 3-5-floris, petalis calyce duplo longioribus, tubo nectarifero calyce duplo longiore.

Stem shrubby, erect, branching; *branches* slender, glaucous, clothed with a minute glandular pubescence. *Leaves* flat, deeply 5-lobed, slightly glaucous, roughish, and clothed with a very short dense pubescence; lobes spreading, wedge-shaped, sometimes again lobed, sharply but not deeply serrated, points mucronate. *Petioles* slender, slightly flattened on the upper and convex on the lower, pubescent. *Stipules* cordately ovate, terminating in a short point, finely toothed. *Peduncles* 3 to 5-flowered, axillary or opposite to a leaf. *Involucre* of 6 ovate, acute, slightly toothed bractes. *Pedicles* about the length of the nectariferous tube, hairy. *Calyx* 5-cleft, bearded at the point; segments lanceolate, taper-pointed; upper one broadest, erect, of a brownish purple; the others spreading or slightly reflexed. *Nectariferous tube* thickly clothed with short spreading hairs, about the length of the petals and double the length of the calyx. *Petals* 5, spreading; upper ones obovate, of a pale blush, with a bright purple patch in the centre, and numerous purple lines betwixt it and the base that are slightly branched; lower petals narrowly obovate, of a pale blush, much veined with veins of the same colour. *Filaments* 10, united at the base, seven bearing anthers. *Pollen* orange-coloured. *Style* pale flesh-coloured, hairy at the base and smooth upwards. *Stigmas* 5, purple, reflexed.

The present subject is of hybrid origin, and was raised, in the collection of R. Henry Jenkinson, Esq. from a seed of P. *amplissimum,* most probably fertilized with the pollen of P. *electum,* or some nearly related sort. It is a very desirable plant on account of its abundance of bloom, which continues in succession all the summer: it is also more hardy than P. *grandiflorum,* to which it is also allied; and succeeds well in a common greenhouse, growing freely in a rich light soil. Cuttings strike root readily, if planted in pots and placed in a sheltered situation.

Our drawing was made from a fine plant, in the collection of R. Henry Jenkinson, Esq. last summer.

222

E. D. Smith del. Pub by J. Ridgway 170 Piccadilly Aug. 1. 1824. Watts sc.

CAMPYLIA elegans.

Elegant Campylia.

C. elegans, caule fruticoso adscendente; ramis elongatis gracilibus, foliis oblongo-ellipticis lanceolatisve undulatis argute serrato-dentatis sericeo-tomentosis, stipulis acuminatis, pedunculis 4-5-floris, petalis rotundato-obovatis.

Campylia elegans. *Colv. catal. ed.* 2. *p.* 21. *col.* 1.

Stem shrubby, flexuose, ascending, not strong enough to support its branches without assistance; *branches* long and slender, thickly clothed with short white down. *Leaves* oblongly elliptic, bluntish, undulate, deeply but unequally serrate or toothed, densely clothed on both sides with white silky down; upper ones lanceolate, acute. *Petioles* long and slender, densely pubescent, as are the peduncles and calyx. *Stipules* lanceolate, taper-pointed. *Peduncles* slender, 4 or 5-flowered. *Involucre* of 6 lanceolate, sharp-pointed bractes. *Pedicles* cylindrical, long and slender. *Calyx* 5-cleft, segments concave, acute, strongly veined; upper one ovate, the others elliptic or lanceolate. *Petals* 5, of a pale lilac, roundly obovate, the two upper ones largest, eared and spotted at the base; above that is a white mark, edged with rose. *Stamens* 10, united at the base, five bearing anthers; two upper sterile ones recurved, and thinly clothed with long white hairs. *Pollen* orange-coloured. *Germen* densely villous. *Style* short, smooth, purple. *Stigmas* 5, about the length of the style, of the same colour, reflexed.

This handsome plant is a hybrid production, and was raised from a seed, at the Nursery of Mr. Colvill, that had been procured from C. *blattaria,* mixed with the pollen of *Phymatanthus elatus.* It is as near as possible intermediate between the two; the leaves agreeing nearly with the latter, except in being a little broader and softer; the flowers partake more of the former, but are larger and more spreading. It is altogether a very handsome plant; and, like the others of the same tribe, succeeds well in a mixture of loam, peat, and sand, watering them freely when in a flourishing state, and giving them a dry airy situation in winter; as they are more liable to receive injury by being too much crowded with other plants, or by receiving too much moisture on their leaves, than by any other means. Cuttings will strike root freely, taken off before they get too ripe. They must be planted in pots in the same kind of soil, and may be placed on a shelf in the greenhouse.

PELARGONIUM recurvatum.

Recurved-petaled Stork's-bill.

P. *recurvatum*, caule fruticoso ramoso; ramis pubescentibus, foliis planis cordato-oblongis 3-5-lobis denticulatis pubescentibus, stipulis ovatis acutis, pedunculis 3-4-floris, petalis superioribus recurvis, tubo nectarifero calyce subæquali.

Stem shrubby, erect, much branched; *branches* pubescent, purplish. *Leaves* cordately oblong, bluntish, 3 or 5-lobed, distantly and unequally toothed, strongly veined underneath, pubescent on both sides, of a dark green colour: lower lobes long and spreading, rather pointed; upper ones short and bluntly rounded. *Petioles* flattened and slightly furrowed on the upper side and convex on the lower, gibbous at the base, pubescent. *Stipules* ovate, taper-pointed. *Peduncles* longer than the leaves, 3 or 4-flowered. *Involucre* of 6 short, ovate, acute bractes. *Pedicles* pubescent, longer than the nectariferous tube. *Calyx* 5-cleft; segments unequal, lanceolate, acute, spreading. *Petals* 5, the two upper ones recurved or revolute, of a rosy blush, marked in the centre with a dark velvetty spot, edged with red, from which branch several lines in various directions; lower ones obovate, pale lilac. *Stamens* 10, connected at the base, seven bearing anthers. *Style* red, very hairy. *Stigmas* 5, red, reflexed.

Our drawing of this plant was taken at the Nursery of Mr. Colvill, this summer. It is of hybrid origin, and is nearly related to P. *planifolium* and P. *penicillatum*, but is readily distinguished from its near relatives by its recurved petals. It is of tolerably strong growth, and thrives well in a mixture of turfy loam and peat, or any rich light vegetable mould, flowering all the summer: it is also as hardy as any of the genus, only requiring to be protected from the frost in winter. Cuttings of it soon strike root, if planted in pots and placed in a sheltered situation.

224

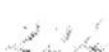

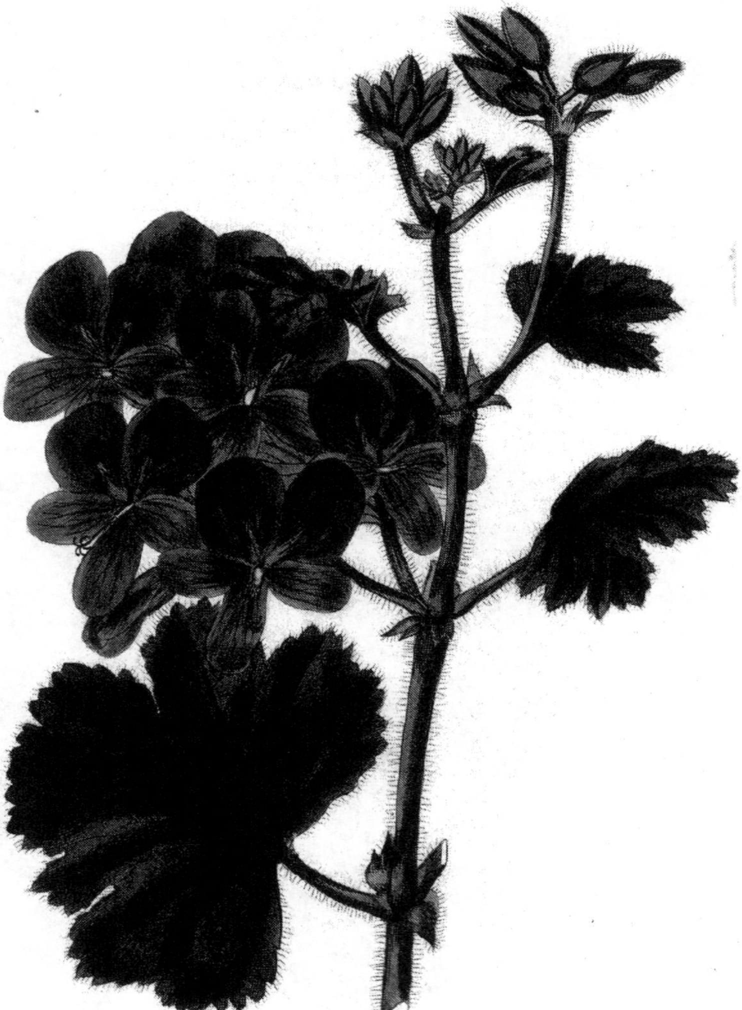

E. D. Smith del. Pub. by J. Ridgway 170 Piccadilly Aug. 1. 1824. J. Watts sc.

PELARGONIUM Palkii.

Mr. Palk's Stork's-bill.

P. *Palkii*, caule fruticoso ramoso, ramis patentibus, foliis planis cordatis trilobis dentatis: lobis distinctis patentibus rotundato-obtusis inferioribus sublobatis, stipulis cordato-ovatis ciliatis, umbellis multifloris, tubo nectarifero calyce parum longiore.

Stem shrubby, much branched; *branches* spreading, thickly clothed with long white spreading unequal hairs, as are the petioles, peduncles, bractes, and calyx. *Leaves* flat, cordate, deeply 3-lobed, toothed with large bluntly rounded teeth, clothed with short hairs on both sides, strongly nerved underneath, the nerves much branched: lobes spreading, distinct, bluntly rounded; lower ones slightly 2-lobed. *Petioles* flattened on the upper side and convex on the lower. *Stipules* cordately ovate, acute, fringed. *Peduncles* cylindrical, 4 to 8-flowered. *Involucre* of 6 or 7 bractes, some of which are ovate, others lanceolate, fringed, taper-pointed. *Pedicles* longer than the bractes, villous. *Calyx* 5-cleft; segments acute; upper one ovate, erect; the others lanceolate, reflexed. *Nectariferous tube* a little longer than the calyx, flattened on both sides, gibbous at the base. *Petals* 5, of a dark scarlet: the two upper ones broadly obovate, with an obscure spot in the centre, and from it to the base are a few dark lines that are slightly branched; lower petals oblongly ligulate, spreading. *Filaments* 10, connected at the base, seven bearing anthers, which in our specimens were all imperfect. *Style* purple, slightly hairy at the base and smooth upwards. *Stigmas* 5, purple, revolute.

This very beautiful plant is a hybrid production, and was raised at the Nursery of Mr. Colvill, from a seed of P. *Breesianum* that had been fertilized with the pollen of P. *ignescens*. Its flowers are very dark, and of a brilliant colour, which no colouring of the artist can come near to. We can scarcely imagine how so light a flower as P. *Breesianum* could produce so dark a one as the present. The same observation is applicable to P. *Kingii*, which is altogether as light, though raised from a seed of a very dark one, P. *Husseyanum*, mixed with P. *Smithii*.

The present plant, like the others to which it is related, succeeds well in a mixture of light turfy loam, peat, and sand, an equal portion of each: it will then continue to flower in succession all the summer. We have named it in compliment to the Rev. W. H. Palk, of Halldown House, near Exeter, Devon; a gentleman much attached to this family of plants, and who is in possession of a valuable collection of them.

E. D. Smith del. Pub. by J. Ridgway 170 Piccadilly Sep. 1. 1824. J. Watts sc.

PELARGONIUM Hammersleiæ.

Mrs. Hammersley's Stork's-bill.

P. *Hammersleiæ*, pedunculis paucifloris, foliis cordato-reniformibus sublobatis inæqualiter denticulatis utrinque hirsutis, petalis recurvis, tubo nectarifero calyce parum breviore.

Stem shrubby, erect, branching, clothed with a brown shining bark; *branches* slenderish, flexuose, thickly clothed with dense woolly hairs, as are the petioles, peduncles, and calyx. *Leaves* cordate or reniform, slightly lobed, unequally toothed with short teeth, thickly clothed on both sides with short hairs, underneath much veined. *Petioles* slender, a little flattened on the upper side and convex on the lower, widened at the base. *Stipules* short, cordate, acute, fringed. *Peduncles* cylindrical, 2 to 4-flowered. *Involucre* of 6 or 7 short, ovate, acute, fringed bractes, slightly keeled at the back. *Pedicles* longer than the nectariferous tube, bent upwards. *Calyx* 5-cleft, segments lanceolate, acute, fringed. *Nectariferous tube* scarcely as long as the calyx, flattened and keeled on each side. *Petals* 5, the two upper ones roundly obovate, oblique at the base, of a bright lilac, with a large dark velvetty patch in the centre, surrounded with a shade of a reddish purple, and from the base branch several purple lines; lower petals oblongly ovate, obtuse, of a pale blush, slightly tinged in the centre, and often marked with one or two linear red spots. *Filaments* 10, united at the base, seven bearing anthers. *Pollen* orange-coloured. *Germen* villous. *Style* flesh-coloured, very hairy. *Stigmas* 5, fringed and revolute.

This very handsome plant is of hybrid origin, and was raised, the year before last, at the Nursery of Mr. Colvill, from a seed of a hybrid plant allied to P. *pulcherrimum*, that had been fertilized with the pollen of P. *Hoareanum*. The present plant is as near as possible intermediate between the two. We have named it, in compliment to Mrs. Charles Hammersley, of Dulwich Hill, a lady much attached to the cultivation of handsome plants, and who possesses a select collection of them.

This plant, like the others to which it is related, is a free grower and an abundant bloomer, and is as hardy as any of the genus. It succeeds well in a mixture of light sandy loam and peat or decayed leaves, or any light rich vegetable soil. Cuttings of it soon strike root, if planted in pots, and set on a shelf in the greenhouse.

Our drawing was taken, at the Nursery of Mr. Colvill, last summer.

220.
a
b
E.D. Smith. del.
Pub. by J. Ridgway 170 Piccadilly Sep 1. 1824.
J. Watts sc.

CICONIUM Fothergillii.

Fothergill's Ciconium.

C. *Fothergillii*, caule suberecto ramoso, foliis reniformibus quinquelobis crenatis zonatis, stipulis cordato-oblongis acutis ciliatis, pedunculis longissimis, umbellis multifloris, petalis obovatis venosis, tubo nectarifero calyce triplo longiore.

Ciconium Fothergillii. *Colv. catal. ed.* 2. *p.* 21. *col.* 1.

Pelargonium Fothergillii. *Colv. catal. ed.* 1. *p.* 22. *col.* 3.

Geranium Fothergillium. *Andrews's geran. c. ic.*

α. coccineum, petalis coccineis, fig. a.

β. purpureum, petalis purpureis, fig. b.

Stem shrubby, erect, branching; *branches* long, simple, thickly clothed with short white reflexed hairs, and soft down intermixed. *Leaves* rather succulent, kidney-shaped, 5-lobed, crenated with broad shallow notches, downy on both sides, and marked with a more or less faint zone or circle. *Petioles* slightly flattened on the upper side and convex on the lower, a little swollen at the base and point, thickly clothed with short white spreading hairs. *Stipules* cordately oblong or ovate, acute, fringed, their sides generally reflexed. *Peduncle* solitary, very long, opposite to the leaf, swollen at the base, thickly clothed with short white hairs that are tipped with a resinous gland. *Involucre* of numerous ovate, or broadly lanceolate, acute, undulate, fringed bractes. *Calyx* 5-cleft; segments lanceolate, acute, spreading, thickly covered with long soft hairs. *Nectariferous tube* nearly sessile, of a brown colour, about three times the length of the calyx. *Pe-*

tals 5, obovate, much veined, their points crenulate, of a bright orangey scarlet, in variety β. inclining to purple; the three lower ones about half as large again as the upper ones. *Stamens* 10, united at the base, seven bearing anthers: *filaments* short and straight; the two upper ones very short. *Germen* villous. *Style* short, quite smooth and glossy, flesh-coloured. *Stigmas* 5, reflexed.

The present handsome subject is an old inhabitant of our greenhouses; and we suspect it is an original species, as we know of none that could have produced it by muling. It is known in collections by the name of the *Nosegay Geranium,* and also by the name that we have adopted. We do not find it recorded in the valuable Prodromus of M. Decandolle, or in any modern publication, except Mr. Andrews's Geraniums: perhaps it has been confused, with several others, under C. *zonale,* from which it differs as much as any species of one section need differ from another; and it is nearer related to P. *Bentinckianum* and P. *bracteosum* of M. Decandolle than it is to C. *zonale.* The latter plants belong also to Ciconium. Perhaps P. *bracteosum* is scarcely different from *Geranium crenatum* of Andrews; and we think it not possible to be a hybrid production between P. *fulgidum* and *hybridum.*

This plant succeeds well in a rich light soil, and continues to flower nearly all the summer. Its amazing umbels of flowers exceeds all others of the family with which we are acquainted; and none, in our opinion, can surpass the scarlet variety for brilliancy of colour. Cuttings root freely, planted in pots or under hand-glasses.

Drawn, at the Nursery of Mr. Colvill, last summer.

227.

E. D. Smith del.   Pub by J. Ridgway 177 Piccadilly Sept 1 1824.   J. Watts sc.

PELARGONIUM Brightianum.

Miss Bright's Stork's-bill.

P. *Brightianum*, caule erecto ramoso, foliis profunde trilobis serrato-dentatis pubescentibus: lobis divaricatis sublobatis, stipulis ovato-lanceolatis acutis ciliatis, umbellis sub-4-floris, petalis undulatis imbricatis, tubo nectarifero calyce villoso duplo breviore.

Stem shrubby, much branched; *branches* spreading, thickly clothed with long spreading villous hairs, as are the petioles, peduncles, and calyx. *Leaves* flat, deeply 3-lobed, pubescent, of a pale green colour; lobes obovate or cuneate, serrately dentate, sometimes again lobed. *Petioles* flattened and furrowed on the upper side and convex on the lower. *Stipules* ovately lanceolate, acute, fringed. *Peduncles* generally 4-flowered. *Involucre* of 6 ovately lanceolate, acute, villous bractes, which are longer than the pedicles. *Pedicles* short, bent upwards. *Calyx* 5-cleft; segments lanceolate, taper-pointed, very villous, upper one largest, erect, the others reflexed. *Nectariferous tube* about half the length of the calyx. *Petals* 5, imbricate, very much undulate; two upper ones very broad, roundly obovate, white with a bright purple spot in the centre, below which are numerous purple stripes; lower petals narrowly obovate, white. *Filaments* 10, united at the base, seven bearing anthers. *Pollen* orange-coloured. *Style* pale red, hairy at the base and smooth upwards. *Stigmas* 5, of the same colour, with revolute points.

This pretty plant is a hybrid production, and was raised, last year, at the Nursery of Mr. Colvill, from a seed of P. *concinnum*, that had been fertilized by one of the white-flowered sorts, perhaps P. *candidum* or P. *Boyleæ*. We have named it in compliment to Miss Bright, of Hamgreen, near Bristol, an admirer of handsome plants, and an encourager of botanical science.

Like the other plants to which the present is related, it succeeds well in a mixture of sandy loam and peat, or any rich light vegetable soil; flowering abundantly all the summer and till late in autumn: it is also as hardy as its near relatives, only wanting protection from frost in winter. Cuttings strike root freely, if planted in pots and set on a shelf in the greenhouse.

223.

E. D. Smith del. *Pub. by J. Ridgway 170 Piccadilly Sept. 1. 1824.* *J. Watts sc.*

GERANIUM Vlassovianum.

Vlassof's Crane's-bill.

G. *Vlassovianum*, caule tereti, foliis 5-lobis; lobis ovali-acuminatis inciso-dentatis, stipulis cujusque folii in unicam apice bifidam connatis, petalis obovatis integris. *DC. in mem. soc. gen.* 1. *p.* 441. *Prodr. reg. veg.* 1. *p.* 641.

Geranium Wlassovianum. *Link enum. v.* 2. *Colv. catal. ed.* 2. *p.* 21. *col.* 3.

A hardy herbaceous *perennial.—Stem* erect or ascending, cylindrical, hairy. *Leaves* 5-lobed; *lobes* oval, acuminate, sharply cut or deeply toothed. *Stipules* linearly-lanceolate, acute, sometimes connected at the base, and terminating in two points, but generally distinct. *Peduncles* 2-flowered, long and slender, thickly clothed with procumbent, close-pressed hairs, as are the petioles, pedicles, and calyx. *Involucre* of four subulate keeled bractes. *Pedicles* long and slender, erect when in flower, but elbowed when in fruit. *Calyx* of five sepals, which are broadly lanceolate, strongly nerved, and terminated with a sharp innocuous mucro. *Petals* 5, obovate, entire, bearded at the base, about half as long again as the calyx, of a pale bluish blush, with five strong purple nerves from the base that are slightly branched. *Filaments* 10, smooth, united at the base, all bearing perfect anthers. *Style* pale, hairy. *Stigmas* 5, revolute. *Capsules* 5, inflated, very hairy.

This pretty species is a native of Siberia, and was introduced to this country in 1821, when it was raised from seed in several collections. It is quite hardy, thriving well in the open borders, and prefers a rich light soil, growing to the height of a foot or eighteen inches, and continues to flower for a considerable time. It may be increased by dividing at the root, or by seeds, which ripen plentifully.

The plant from which our drawing and description were taken, was kindly communicated to us by Mr. William Anderson, the worthy curator of the Apothecaries' Company's garden, at Chelsea, last summer. The stipules are not all connected at the base, as described by M. Decandolle; we have more frequently found them distinct; which is also the case with G. *Wallichianum*, which also appears to be quite hardy, as we have had it and the G. *pilosum*, from New Zealand, both planted out in the open ground, where it survived well all last winter, and flowered this summer much finer than in pots. When we published the latter species, we were not certain whether it was a perennial or annual plant; we now have ascertained it to be strictly perennial, with a large fleshy root.

C. D. Smith. del. Pub by J. Ridgway 170 Piccadilly Jul. 1824.

PELARGONIUM Allenii.

Mr. Allen's Stork's-bill.

P. *Allenii*, caule fruticoso ramoso diffuso, foliis cordatis profunde trilobis cartilagineo-dentatis acutis utrinque hirsutis: lobo intermedio subtrilobo, stipulis lato-cordatis acutis villosis, pedunculis multifloris, calycibus reflexis, tubo nectarifero calyce subæquali.

Stem shrubby, much branched; *branches* spreading, thickly clothed with long spreading white hairs, and shorter villous ones intermixed. *Leaves* cordate, about as broad as long, deeply 3-lobed, acute, unequally toothed with long sharp cartilaginous teeth, hairy on both sides, strongly nerved underneath: upper lobe largest, generally 3-lobed; side ones mostly 2-lobed, sinuses acute. *Petioles* flattened and furrowed on the upper side, and convex on the lower, thickly clothed with spreading villous hairs, as are the peduncles, bractes, and calyx. *Stipules* broadly cordate, acute, sometimes toothed, villous. *Peduncles* cylindrical, from 5 to 8-flowered. *Involucre* of from 6 to 8, ovate, acute bractes. *Pedicles* unequal in length, longer than the bractes. *Calyx* 5-clefted; segments lanceolate, acute, densely villous, the upper one broadest, erect, the others reflexed. *Nectariferous tube* about the length of the calyx, much flattened on each side, and gibbous at the base; scarcely as long as the pedicles. *Petals* 5, of a dark scarlet, tinged with purple; the two upper ones obovate, marked in the centre with an obscure spot; between it and the base are numerous dark lines, branching in all directions; lower petals obovately oblong, of rather a lighter colour. *Filaments* 10, united at the base, seven bearing anthers, which are generally sterile. *Style* pale red, very hairy. *Stigmas* 5, purple, reflexed.

Our drawing of this beautiful plant was taken at the Nursery of Messrs. Allen and Co. in the King's Road, where it was raised from seed; it is a hybrid production, and from its habit we should suppose one of its parents to be P. *concolor;* perhaps the other might be P. *Daveyanum,* or some nearly related sort. We have named it in compliment to Mr. Allen, at whose Nursery several other handsome hybrid sorts have been raised. In habit, the present differs widely from most others, being a very branching sort, and its flowers are produced in a kind of panicle, which continues to bloom, in succession, all the summer; this makes it a very desirable acquisition. It requires precisely the same method of treatment as its parents, growing freely in a light sandy soil, and requiring but little water. Cuttings of it strike root readily, planted in pots and placed on a shelf in the greenhouse.

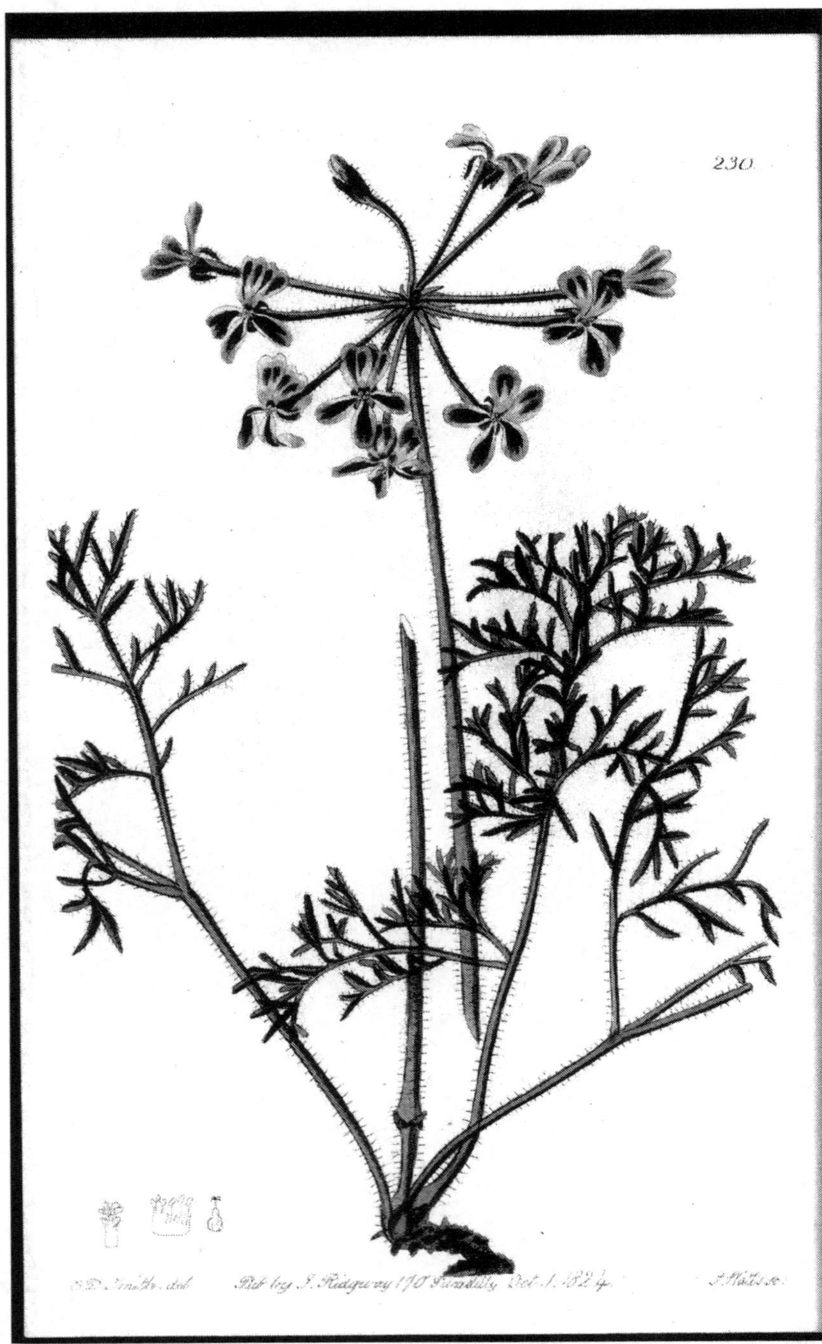
230.
E.D. Smith del.
Pub by J. Ridgway 170 Piccadilly Oct. 1. 1824.
J. Watts sc.

PELARGONIUM millefoliatum.

Milfoil-leaved Stork's-bill.

P. *millefoliatum*, subacaule, foliis decompositis glabris: foliolis laciniatis; segmentis canaliculatis linearibus, umbellis multifloris, calycibus reflexis, tubo nectarifero subsessili calyce quintuplo longiore.

Pelargonium millefoliatum. *Colv. catal. ed.* 2. *p.* 22. *col.* 1.

Root tuberous, branching out into other smaller tubers of different shapes and sizes. *Stem* none, or very short. *Leaves* decompound, smooth, and of a dark green shining colour; leaflets slightly decurrent, and much divided; segments channelled, linear, with rather a bluntish termination. *Petioles* long and slender, nearly cylindrical, smooth, except a few hairs scattered here and there. *Stipules* cordate, acute, joined to the swollen base of the petioles. *Peduncle* simple, long and slender, thickly clothed with unequal spreading hairs. *Umbel* many-flowered. *Involucre* of numerous lanceolate fringed bractes. *Calyx* 5-cleft; segments oblong, obtuse, ciliate, all reflexed. *Nectariferous tube* about five times as long as the calyx, flattened, and furrowed on each side. *Petals* 5, obovate, the two uppermost widest, emarginate, of a dingy brown colour, marked irregularly through the centre with a darker colour. *Filaments* 10, short and erect, united at the base, seven bearing anthers, one of the anthers about half the size of the others, on a flat spatula-shaped filament. *Pollen* pale yellow. *Style* very short, hairy. *Stigmas* 5, reflexed.

The present very distinct species is a native of the Cape, from whence many plants of it have been received, within these few years, by different collectors. We first observed it, about five years since, at the Nursery of Messrs. Loddiges, at Hackney, where it was known by the name of P. *oxalidifolium;* since that time, we have seen it in various collections, but we believe it has never been before published. It belongs to the same tribe as P. *triste,* P. *lobatum,* and many others; and, like them, expands its flowers in the evening, which are then very agreeably scented. It requires the same kind of treatment as the other tuberous-rooted species: a mixture of light turfy loam, peat, and sand, is the most proper soil for it; keeping it quite dry when in a dormant state, and fresh potting it as soon as it begins to grow; it will then flower profusely. The best method of increasing it, is by the tubers of its root, or by seeds, which ripen plentifully if some pollen be attached to the stigmas when in bloom.

Our drawing was taken at the Nursery of Mr. Colvill, last autumn; at which time it was in full flower, and may be considered as an autumn flowering species.

231.

E. D. Smith. del.
Pub by J. Ridgway 170 Piccadilly Oct. 1. 1824.
J. Watts sc.

PELARGONIUM ardescens.

Burnished Stork's-bill.

P. *ardescens,* caule fruticoso ramoso; ramis erectis, foliis cordatis acutis acute et profunde lobatis inciso-dentatis canescentibus, umbellis plurifloris paniculatis, tubo nectarifero calyce subæquali aut paulo longiore.

Pelargonium ardescens. *Colv. catal. ed.* 2. *p.* 22. *col.* 2.

Stem shrubby, rather succulent, erect, branching; *branches* erect, slightly flexuose, thickly clothed with short white hairs, and a few longer ones intermixed, as are the petioles, peduncles, and calyx. *Leaves* concave, cordate, acute, trifid, acutely lobed, sharply and deeply cut and toothed, canescently pubescent; lobes spreading. *Petioles* flattened on the upper side and convex on the lower, dilated at the base. *Stipules* lanceolate, taper-pointed, broad at the base. *Flower-stalk* paniculate. *Peduncle* cylindrical, several-flowered. *Involucre* of 6-lanceolate, acute, keeled bractes. *Calyx* 5-cleft; segments keeled, acute, the upper one ovate, the others lanceolate. *Nectariferous tube* about the length, or a little longer, than the calyx, much flattened on both sides and gibbous at the base. *Petals* 5, of a bright scarlet, clouded with a dark shining crimson; upper ones roundly obovate, oblique at the base, and marked with numerous branching dark stripes. lower petals narrowly obovate, also lined near the base. *Filaments* 10, united at the base, seven bearing anthers, which are always sterile. *Style* pale coloured, slightly hairy at the base, and smooth upwards. *Stigmas* 5, purple, reflexed.

This brilliant flowered plant is of hybrid origin, and was raised in the superb collection of Robert Henry Jenkinson, Esq. from a seed of P. *fulgidum*, that had been fertilized by some other sort, which from its habit we should suspect to have been one related to P. *maculatum*; as the present plant much resembles that tribe in its mode of growth; and from the size of its leaves it must have been one of the large-leaved sorts. Its flowers are not so large as some others of the scarlet flowering sorts; but their brilliance and abundance make good that deficiency. It thrives best in a light sandy soil, like those to which it is nearest related; and great care must be taken not to over water it, as its leaves are very apt to get cankered and turn brown, if it chances to obtain too much moisture. Cuttings of it strike root freely, if planted in pots and placed on a shelf in the greenhouse.

232.
E. D. Smith. del.
Pub. by J. Ridgway 170 Piccadilly Oct. 1. 1824.
J. Watts. sc.

PELARGONIUM schizopetalum.

Divided-petaled Stork's-bill.

P. *schizopetalum,* caule suffruticoso carnoso squamoso, foliis ternatis trifidisve oblongo-ovalibus obtusis undulatis utrinque hirsutis apice revolutis: foliolis lateralibus bilobis inciso-dentatis; intermedio maximo multilobato obtuse dentato, umbellis plurifloris longe pedunculatis, petalis subæqualibus bipartitis; segmentis multifido-laciniatis, tubo nectarifero calyce triplo longiore.

Root tuberous, branching in various directions. *Stem* short, suffruticose, rather succulent, scaly, somewhat branched; *branches* short, more or less spreading. *Leaves* about 6 inches long to 2 broad, ternate or deeply trifid, obtuse, oblongly oval, undulate, hairy on both sides, unequally toothed with blunt rounded teeth, fringed, the points revolute or much recurved, of a dark green colour; *terminal leaflet* very large, 11 to 13-lobed, the lobes overlapping each other, more or less incised, and bluntly toothed; *side leaflets* much smaller, cuneate, oblique at the base, deeply 2-lobed, incised, and bluntly toothed. *Petioles* flattened and channelled on the upper side, and rounded on the lower, widened at the base, thickly clothed with a dense pubescence and long spreading hairs intermixed. *Stipules* lanceolate, taper-pointed, fringed, and joined to the base of the petioles. *Peduncles* simple, very long and stout, densely hairy at the base, but less so upwards. *Umbel* several-flowered, spreading. *Involucre* of several narrowly lanceolate, acute, fringed bractes, all connected at the base, *Pedicles* shorter than the bractes. *Calyx* 5-cleft; segments uneqnal, linearly lanceolate, keeled, all reflexed, the upper one largest and bluntest. *Nectariferous tube* large, slightly angular, thickly clothed with short hairs, about three times longer than the calyx. *Petals* 5, nearly equal, 2-parted, the divisions multifidly laciniate, or divided into numerous branching linear sharp-pointed segments; two upper ones of a pale yellow, lower ones of a brownish purple. *Stamens* 10, connected at the base, seven bearing anthers; *filaments* smooth, ascending; *anthers* incumbent, purple; *pollen* orange-coloured. *Style* pale, hairy on the lower part, and smooth upwards. *Stigmas* 5, flesh-coloured, spreading.

Several plants of this most curious species were received by Mr. Colvill, from the Cape, in 1821; some of them flowered last summer, when our drawing was taken. Its divided petals seem to be quite an anomaly in the family. Its nearest relatives are P. *elegans* and P. *ovale*, with which it agrees in the number and direction of its stamens, and with whom we should place it in a natural arrangement; on the other hand, it agrees with the tribe to which P. *triste* and P. *lobatum* belongs in its colour and expansion in the evening, but differs entirely in its scent, which is rather unpleasant than otherwise, and is not very unlike to the scent of some species of Ambrosia.

Like the other tuberous-rooted species, it succeeds well in a mixture of light turfy loam, peat, and sand; requiring but little water when in a dormant state. It may be increased, but slowly, by the tubers from its roots.

233.

Pub. by J. Ridgway 170 Piccadilly Nov. 1. 1824.

J. Watts sc.

PELARGONIUM anthriscifolium.

Anthriscus-leaved Stork's-bill.

P. *anthriscifolium*, caule suberecto carnoso squamoso, foliis pinnatis utrinque hirsutis; foliolis pinnatifidis incisisve; segmentis lanceolatis obtusiusculis, pedunculis plurifloris, tubo nectarifero calyce duplo longiore.

Stem nearly erect, shrubby, succulent, clothed with a brown scaly bark. *Leaves* smallish, pinnate, hairy on both sides; leaflets wedge-shaped, pinnatifid or deeply incised; segments lanceolate, bluntish. *Petioles* short, hairy, flattened on the upper side and convex on the lower, widened at the base. *Stipules* lanceolate, acute, joined to the base of the petioles, and partly remaining persistent. *Scape* leafy, branching, thickly covered with hairs, as are the peduncles, calyx, and nectariferous tube. *Peduncles* cylindrical, bent upwards. *Umbels* several-flowered. *Involucre* of several lanceolate, acute, hairy bractes. *Pedicles* short, some about the length, and others a little longer than the bractes. *Calyx* 5-cleft; segments lanceolate, acute, the upper one largest, erect, the others spreading or slightly reflexed. *Nectariferous tube* more than double the length of the calyx, gradually widening upwards, and gibbous at the base. *Petals* 5, of a bright scarlet tinged with dark brown, the two upper ones broadest, obovately cuneate; lower ones ligulate. *Filaments* 10, united at the base, seven bearing anthers. *Style* short, pale flesh-coloured, densely hairy. *Stigmas* 5, purple, reflexed.

This very singular and handsome plant is of hybrid origin, and is the produce of P. *hirtum* that had been fertilized with the pollen of P. *fulgidum;* and it is as near as possible intermediate between the two. It was raised from seed, last year, at the Nursery of Mr. Colvill, where our drawing was made in August last. It appears to be of as free growth, and as easily managed, as its relatives, succeeding well in a mixture of loam, peat, and sand; but, being of a succulent nature, it requires but little water, and the pots to be well drained with potsherds broken small, as the roots are very fond of running amongst them: it also requires a dry airy situation. Cuttings of it will strike root freely, if taken off when the plant is in a free-growing state; those must be planted in pots in the same kind of soil, and should then be placed in a warm part of the greenhouse, watering them very sparingly at first, or they will be liable to rot.

234.

E. D. Smith. del. Pub by J. Ridgway 170 Piccadilly Nov. 1. 1824. J. Watts. sc.

PELARGONIUM Mattocksianum.

Mrs. Sweet's Stork's-bill.

P. *Mattocksianum* caule fruticoso ramoso, ramis erecto-patentibus, foliis profunde trilobis utrinque hirsutis; lobis acutis acute serrato-dentatis, pedunculis trifloris, petalis superioribus rotundatis inferioribus obovato-oblongis, tubo nectarifero calyce sesquilongiore.

Stem shrubby, dwarf and bushy; *branches* erect or slightly spreading, thickly clothed with long spreading villous hairs, as are the petioles, peduncles, and calyx. *Leaves* between cordate and cuneate, deeply 3-lobed, slightly concave, numerously and prominently nerved underneath, hairy on both sides; lobes straight, acute, sharply sawed or toothed, the teeth unequal in length. *Petioles* slender, flattened and channelled on the upper side, and convex on the lower, a little widened at the base. *Stipules* cordate, taper-pointed, ciliate. *Peduncles* long and slender, thickened at the base, 3-flowered. *Involucre* of 6 or 7 broadly ovate taper-pointed fringed bractes. *Pedicles* more than double the length of the bractes. *Calyx* 5-cleft; laciniæ lanceolate, acute, the upper one largest, erect; the others reflexed or revolute. *Nectariferous tube* half as long again as the calyx, broadly flattened on each side and gibbous at the base. *Petals* 5, of a pure white, the two upper ones very large, nearly round, imbricate, and marked in the centre with a large dark purple spot on a red ground, below which are a few purple lines that are slightly branched; lower petals obovately oblong, spreading. *Filaments* 10, connected at the base, seven bearing anthers; *pollen* orange-coloured. *Style* pale-coloured, slightly hairy at the base and smooth upwards. *Stigmas* 5, reflexed.

This plant is also of hybrid origin, and was raised last year at the Nursery of Mr. Colvill, from a seed of P. *compar*, that had been fertilized with the pollen of P. *obscurum*, or some one nearly related. It is a very pretty growing bushy plant; but is rather more tender than its relatives, being very apt to rot off at the root, if it happens to get too much moisture: it will not, therefore, bear exposure out of doors so well as most others, particularly if the season prove wet like the present; but will succeed better in a good airy part of a greenhouse. It grows freely in a rich light soil; or a mixture of loam, peat, and sand, suits it very well. Cuttings, taken off in the young wood, root freely, but they must also be watered sparingly, or they will rot off. Our drawing was taken at Mr. Colvill's Nursery this summer.

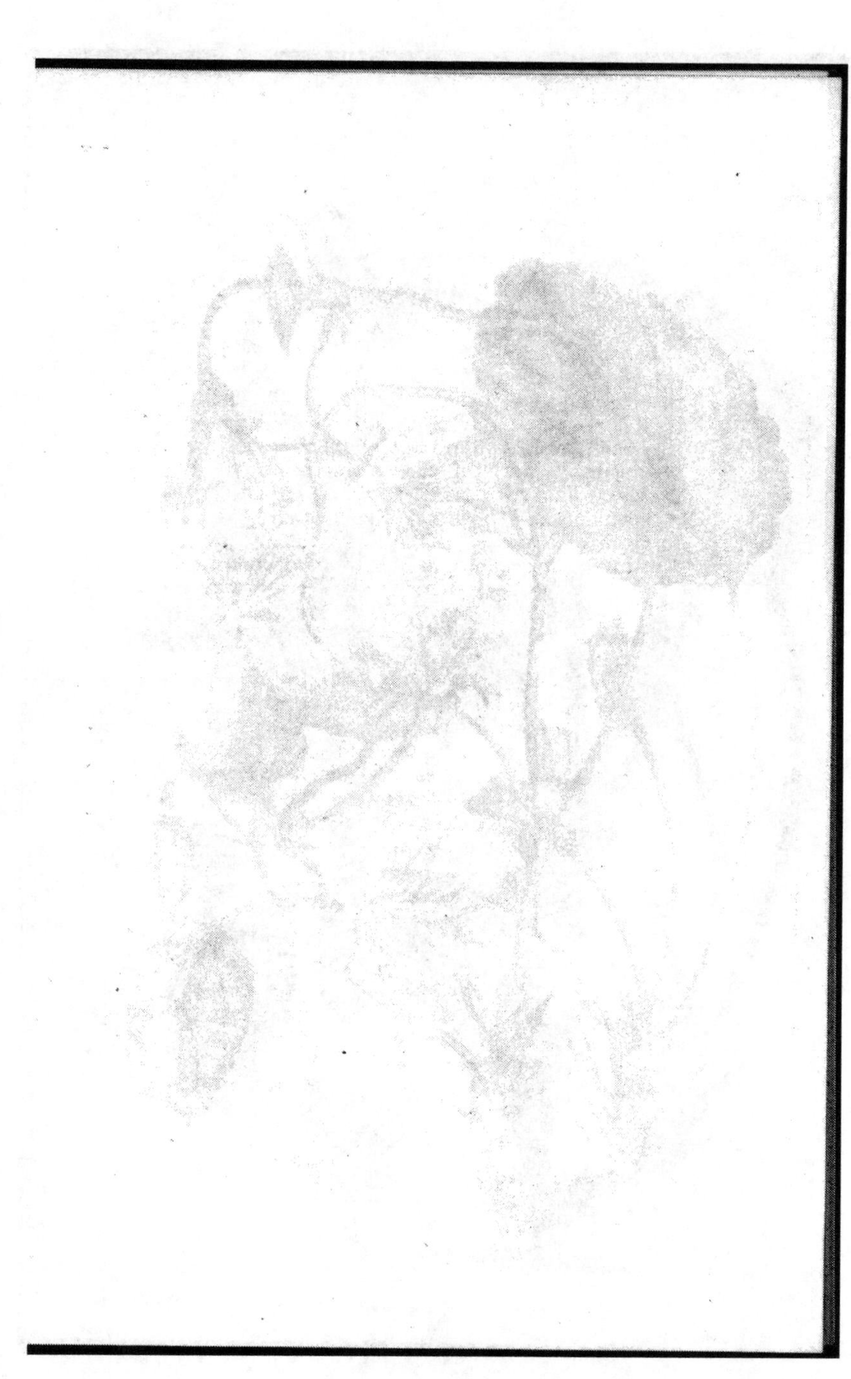

235.

E. D. Smith del. Pub by J. Ridgway 170 Piccadilly Nov. 1. 1824. S. Watts sc.

PELARGONIUM ovale.

Oval-leaved Stork's-bill.

P. *ovale*, caule suffruticoso tortuoso debili prostrato; ramis petiolis pedunculisque molliter hispidis; foliis ovalibus acutis dentatis canescentibus, umbellis sub-5-floris longe pedunculatis, tubo nectarifero calyce breviore. *DC. prod.* 1. *p.* 666.

Pelargonium ovale. *L'Hérit. ger. t.* 28. *Willden. sp. pl.* 3. *p.* 653. *Pers. syn.* 2. *p.* 228. *Hort. Kew. ed.* 2. *v.* 4. *p.* 166.

Stem suffruticose, weak and trailing, more or less twisted, clothed with brown persistent stipules; *branches* ascending, thickly covered with long soft villous hairs, as are the petioles, peduncles, and calyx. *Leaves* oval, acute, sharply and deeply toothed, strongly veined underneath, densely clothed on both sides with a soft canescent pubescence. *Petioles* long and slender, flattened and furrowed on the upper side and convex on the lower, swollen at the base. *Stipules* broadly lanceolate, taper-pointed, brown and scariose, fringed. *Peduncles* very long, much twisted, 4 or 5-flowered. *Involucre* of 6 or 7 linear, acute, villous bractes. *Pedicles* long and slender, unequal in length. *Calyx* 5-cleft, segments lanceolate, acute, all reflexed. *Nectariferous tube* about half the length of the calyx, flattened on each side, villous. *Petals* 5, narrowly obovate or oblong, the two upper ones rather the shortest, slightly retuse, one of them auriculate on one side at the base of the unguis, the ear turned back, of a pinky lilac, slightly streaked at the bottom; lower ones of rather a lighter colour. *Filaments* 10, united at the base, glandularly hairy, seven bearing anthers. *Style* very hairy. *Stigmas* 5, purple, reflexed or revolute.

This curious and very distinct species is an old inhabitant of our gardens, though now very rarely to be met with. It belongs, with P. *elegans* and P. *schizopetalum*, to our section CALLIOPSIS, the PLATYPETALA of Decandolle. Being so very different from all others, and likewise a pretty flowering species, makes it a desirable plant; and we are rather surprised that it should have been so neglected as to occasion its present scarcity. It requires precisely the same kind of treatment as the others of this section, succeeding well in a mixture of peat, loam, and sand, with the pots well drained with potsherds. Cuttings strike root without difficulty, if planted in pots in the same kind of soil, and placed on a shelf in the greenhouse.

The plant from which our drawing was taken, was kindly sent to us by the Rev. Thomas Hulse, from his collection at Englefield, in Berkshire; to whom we are also obliged for some curious hybrid varieties raised by him from seeds.

236

E. D. Smith del. Pub. by J. Ridgway 170 Piccadilly Nov. 1. 1824. J. Watts sc.

PELARGONIUM latilobum.

Broad-lobed Stork's-bill.

P. *latilobum*, foliis planis basi dilatatis 5-7-lobis obtuse dentatis molliter pubescentibus; lobis profundis rotundatis subimbricatis, stipulis oblongis acutis subdentatis, umbellis plurifloris subpaniculatis, calycibus reflexis, tubo nectarifero calyce subæquali.

Stem shrubby, erect, much branched. *Leaves* large, very broad at the base: *lower ones* deeply 7 or 9-lobed, unequally toothed with largish blunt teeth, covered on both sides with a soft pubescence; lobes broad and rounded, frequently overlapping each other; nerves numerous underneath, large and prominent, branching in all directions: *upper leaves* smaller, 5-lobed, more sharply toothed, base truncate. *Petioles* flattened and furrowed on the upper side and convex on the lower, widened upwards, where it branches off into nerves, clothed with unequal spreading hairs and short down intermixed. *Stipules* oblong or broadly lanceolate, taper-pointed, sometimes toothed, fringed, very hairy. *Umbels* several-flowered, in a kind of panicle. *Peduncles* cylindrical, thickly clothed with unequal spreading hairs, as are the bractes, calyx, and nectariferous tube. *Involucre* of 6 ovate, bluntish, mucronate, fringed bractes. *Pedicles* shorter than the bractes. *Calyx* 5-cleft, upper segment erect, oblong, acute; the others lanceolate, reflexed. *Nectariferous tube* about the length of the calyx, flattened on both sides, gibbous at the base. *Petals* 5, the two upper ones obovate, of a bright orangey scarlet, with a small dark mark in the centre, and numerous purple lines from the base, which branch in various directions; lower petals narrower, oblong.

Filaments 10, united at the base, seven bearing anthers. *Style* pale purple, slightly hairy at the base and smooth upwards. *Stigmas* 5, purple, reflexed.

This grand plant is a hybrid production, and was raised, last year, from seed, by Mr. Smith, at the Earl of Liverpool's, Coombe Wood. We should suppose one of its parents to be P. *oblatum* or P. *eximium*, and the other P. *ignescens*. It is the strongest grower of the scarlet sorts that we have yet seen. The plant from which our drawing was taken, being about three feet high, and very strong and bushy, with an amazing panicle of flowers on the centre shoot, which gave it a very grand appearance. It requires the same kind of treatment as others of the free-growing sorts; any light rich mould, or a mixture of turfy loam, peat, and sand, will suit it very well. Cuttings strike root readily, planted in pots and placed on a shelf in the greenhouse.

237.

E. D. Smith del. Pub by J. Ridgway 170 Piccadilly Dec. 1. 1824. J. Watts sc.

PELARGONIUM concavum.

Concave-petaled Stork's-bill.

P. *concavum*, scapo subramoso; foliis ternatis pinnatifidis laciniatisque utrinque pilosis; segmentis foliolisque obtusis inæqualiter inciso-dentatis, umbellis multifloris, petalis concavis inferioribus subconniventibus, calycibus reflexis, tubo nectarifero calyce triplo longiore.

Root tuberous. *Stem* none, or very short. *Leaves* very variable; lower ones ternate, intermediate ones laciniate, upper ones pinnatifid, thickly covered on both sides with short white hairs: segments on the lower leaves rounded, bluntly toothed with unequal teeth; intermediate ones more deeply and sharply toothed; upper ones incised or deeply cut, and unequally toothed. *Petioles* seldom the length of the leaves, flattened and slightly furrowed on the upper side and convex on the lower, densely clothed with white spreading unequal hairs. *Stipules* lanceolate, taper-pointed, joined to the base of the petioles. *Scape* long and slender, not much branched, producing a few small leaves at the base of the peduncles. *Peduncles* long, unequally bent, thickly clothed with white spreading unequal hairs. *Involucre* of about 9 or 10 linearly lanceolate, taper-pointed, concave bractes, very hairy at the back. *Pedicles* unequal in length, seldom longer than the bractes. *Calyx* 5-cleft, segments lanceolate, acute, all reflexed, and clothed with short white hairs. *Nectariferous tube* about three times longer than the calyx, flattened on each side, a little gibbous at the base, gradually widening upwards, also clothed with short hairs. *Petals* 5, of a bright salmon colour; the two upper ones spatulate, reflexed about the middle, with a forked white mark near the base, from which branch numerous short purple lines; lower ones ligulate, concave, more or less connivent. *Filaments* 10, connected at the base, seven bearing anthers, which were all perfect. *Pollen* bright yellow. *Style* very hairy at the base, and smooth on the upper part. *Stigmas* 5, reflexed.

This pretty plant is of hybrid origin, and was raised at the Nursery of Mr. Colvill, in 1822, from a seed of P. *fulgidum*, that had been fertilized with the pollen of *Hoarea corydaliflora*. It is of free growth, and easily managed, if treated in the same manner as is already stated for the treatment of the tuberous-rooted sorts; planting it in an equal mixture of light loam, peat, and sand, and giving it scarcely any water when in a dormant state. It begins to flower very early in spring, and continues to bloom all the summer and till late in autumn. It may be propagated by the little tubers from the roots, or from seeds, if the flowers are fertilized by their own pollen.

238.

E. D. Smith del. Pub. by J. Ridgway 170 Piccadilly Dec. 1. 1824. J. Watts sc.

PELARGONIUM electum.

Elected Stork's-bill.

P. *electum*, caule fruticoso ramosissimo; ramis gracilibus flexuosis, foliis cordatis profunde trilobis glabris serrato-dentatis: lobis cuneatis divaricato-patentibus; intermedio trilobo, stipulis cordatis acutis, pedunculis subtrifloris, tubo nectarifero scaberrimo calyce duplo longiore.

Pelargonium electum. *Colv. catal. p.* 22. *col.* 1; *edit.* 2. *p.* 23. *col.* 1.

Geranium grandiflorum; *var.* parvifoliata. *Andrews's geran. c. ic.*

Stem shrubby, very much branched; *branches* slender, flexuose, spreading in all directions, and thinly covered with small gland-like transparent hairs. *Leaves* cordate, deeply 3-lobed, sharply toothed with small unequal teeth, green and glossy, margins fringed with short hairs: *lobes* widely spreading, wedge-shaped, acute; the upper one 3-lobed, side ones 2-lobed. *Petioles* long and slender, slightly flattened on the upper side and rounded on the lower, slightly clothed with short hairs, as are the peduncles, bractes, and nectariferous tube. *Stipules* short, cordate, acute. *Peduncles* cylindrical, generally 3-flowered, swollen and jointed at the base. *Involucre* of 4 short, narrowly ovate, acute, keeled bractes. *Pedicles* longer than the bractes. *Calyx* 5-cleft, segments lanceolate, acute, very hairy; the upper one broadest, erect; the others reflexed. *Nectariferous tube* about double the length of the calyx, flattened and furrowed on each side, very scabrous. *Petals* 5, the two upper ones obovate, more than double the length of the calyx, white sometimes tinged with blush, with two small bright purple spots in the centre, that join two purple lines from the base, which branch in various directions; lower petals spatulately linear, white. *Filaments* 10, united at the base, seven bearing anthers: *pollen* orange-coloured. *Style* pale, hairy at the base, and smooth upwards. *Stigmas* 5, reflexed.

The present plant is an old inhabitant of our gardens; but is now become rather scarce, having been neglected for the sake of novelty. It is, we suspect, of hybrid origin, and was raised from seed, many years back, at the Nursery of Mr. Colvill. We believe one of its parents to be P. *grandiflorum* or P. *amplissimum*, and the other might be P. *hermannifolium*, or one of the small-leaved species. It is more hardy and easier managed than P. *grandiflorum*, thriving well in a mixture of light sandy loam and peat, or any light rich earth; and cuttings of it strike root readily, if planted in pots and placed on a shelf in the greenhouse.

239.
E. D. Smith. del.
Pub by J. Ridgway 170 Piccadilly Dec 1. 1824.
T. Watts sc.

PELARGONIUM vespertinum.

Evening-scented Stork's-bill.

P. *vespertinum*, caule fruticoso carnoso nodoso flexuoso: nodis tumidis, foliis ternatis subglaucis pubescentibus: foliolis cuneatis inciso-dentatis barbatis; intermedio petiolato 5-7-lobato, umbellis multifloris, petalis obovatis, tubo nectarifero calyce quintuplo longiore.

Stem shrubby, very thick and succulent, slender in places, flexuose, swollen at the joints, the young shoots thickly clothed with long spreading soft villous hairs. *Leaves* ternate, slightly glaucous, clothed on both sides with a short pubescence, margins curved inwards: *leaflets* wedge-shaped, incised, or toothed with blunt rounded unequal bearded teeth; middle one petiolate, deeply divided into 5 or 7 lobes, sinuses rounded; lower ones smaller, deeply 2-lobed. *Petioles* slightly flattened on the upper side and rounded on the lower, thinly clothed with long spreading hairs. *Stipules* lanceolate, taper-pointed, hairy, and ciliate. *Peduncles* thick, cylindrical, from 12 to 25-flowered. *Involucre* of numerous lanceolate acute bractes, all joined into one at the base and bearded at the points. *Pedicles* very short, scarcely any. *Flowers* very fragrant in the evening, but without scent during the day. *Calyx* 5-cleft, villous, segments lanceolate, bluntish, all reflexed or revolute. *Nectariferous tube* 5 or 6 times longer than the calyx, flattened on each side, gradually tapering downwards, very hairy. *Petals* 5, obovate, the two upper ones nearly obcordate, of a bright pink, lighter towards the base, where they are marked with a few small linear spots; lower petals darker, altogether bright pink. *Filaments* 10, straight, joined at the base, seven bearing perfect anthers, one of them a very small one on a large spatulate filament, as in several plants of this section: *pollen* pale yellow. *Germen* densely villous. *Style* short, pale, quite smooth. *Stigmas* 5, spreading.

This very handsome plant is a hybrid production, and was raised, in 1822, at the Nursery of Mr. Colvill, from a seed of P. *gibbosum*, that had been set with the pollen of P. *sæpeflorens*. It is of much stronger growth than either of its parents; and, being so very succulent, care must be taken not to overwater it. Its time of flowering is late in summer and autumn, after many of the other sorts are overblown; this makes it the more desirable, as it continues in flower a considerable time: it is also very sweet-scented in the evening, but without scent during the day. It requires precisely the same kind of treatment as the other succulent kinds. An equal mixture of turfy loam, peat, and sand, will suit it very well, watering it sparingly, particularly in winter: the pots must also be well drained with small potsherds, that the moisture may pass off readily. It is easily increased by cuttings, or from tubers of the root.

Drawn at the Nursery of Mr. Colvill, in September last.

240.
Pub by J. Ridgway 170 Piccadilly Dec 1.1824.

PELARGONIUM Bakerianum.

Mrs. Jenkinson's Stork's-bill.

P. *Bakerianum*, foliis cordatis trilobis undulatis inæqualiter dentatis utrinque hirsutis, stipulis ovato-lanceolatis acutis, umbellis multifloris, petalis subreflexis, tubo nectarifero calyce villoso subæquali.

Stem shrubby, branching; *branches* spreading, thickly clothed with long spreading hairs and shorter ones intermixed, as are the petioles, peduncles, and calyx. *Leaves* cordate, deeply 3-lobed, undulate, strongly nerved underneath, rigidly toothed with unequal sharp-pointed teeth, clothed on both sides with short soft hairs, teeth curved inwards: lobes broad and blunt; lower ones slightly 2-lobed, upper one more or less 3-lobed. *Petioles* short and stout, broadly flattened and furrowed on the upper side and convex on the lower, widened at the base and point. *Stipules* ovate or lanceolate, acute, ciliate, margins reflexed. *Umbels* many-flowered. *Peduncles* cylindrical, thickened and transparent at the base. *Involucre* of 6 lanceolate acute keeled bractes, all connected at the base. *Petioles* about the length of the bractes, villous. *Calyx* 5-cleft: segments lanceolate, acute; the upper one largest, erect, the others reflexed. *Nectariferous tube* about the length of the calyx, broadly flattened on both sides and gibbous at the base. *Petals* 5, slightly reflexed, the two upper ones roundly obovate, oblique at the base, flame-coloured, with a more or less purple spot in the centre, between which and the base branch several purple stripes; lower petals oblong or broadly ligulate, of rather a lighter colour. *Stamens* 10, united at the base, seven bearing anthers. *Pollen* orange-coloured. *Style* pale, hairy at the base and smooth upwards. *Stigmas* 5, purple, reflexed.

This splendid plant is of hybrid origin, and was raised from seed in the superb collection of Robert Henry Jenkinson, Esq. We suppose one of its parents to be P. *ignescens*, and the other P. *rubescens*, but cannot speak with certainty. We have named it in compliment to Mrs. Jenkinson, a great admirer of handsome plants, and an encourager of botanical science.

The delicate colour of the flowers of the present plant, rank it amongst one of the finest of the tribe: those are produced in abundance all the summer. It requires the same kind of treatment as its near relatives, growing freely in a mixture of turfy loam, peat, and sand, or any other light soil. Cuttings of it strike 1oot readily, if planted in pots and placed on a shelf in the greenhouse.

E. D. Smith del
Pub by J. Ridgway 170 Piccadilly Jan. 1. 1825.
J. Watts sc

PELARGONIUM jonquillinum.

Jonquil-scented Stork's-bill.

P. *jonquillinum*, caule suffruticoso erecto crasso carnoso squamoso, foliis cordatis 7-9-lobatis ternatisque canescenti-pubescentibus; segmentis foliolisque sinuato-dentatis; stipulis cordatis acuminatis, umbellis multifloris, tubo nectarifero calyce reflexo quadruplo longiore.

Root tuberous, much branched. *Stem* erect, short, and thick, succulent, scaly from the persistent stipules. *Leaves* cordate, clothed on both sides with a short white pubescence, some deeply, others shallowly 7 to 9-lobed, others ternate or pinnatifid, more or less undulate; leaflets or segments sinuate, or toothed with blunt rounded teeth. *Petioles* long and pendulous, flattened but not furrowed on the upper side, rounded on the lower, very thick at the base, densely clothed with unequal spreading white hairs, as are the peduncles, calyx, and nectariferous tube. *Stipules* cordate, taper-pointed, remaining a long time on the stem. *Scape* branching, without leaves. *Peduncles* stout, cylindrical. *Umbels* from 10 to 20-flowered. *Involucre* of numerous lanceolate, acute, fringed bractes. *Pedicles* very short. *Calyx* 5-cleft; segments unequal, obtuse, all reflexed, upper and lower ones oblong-oval, side ones oblong-lanceolate. *Nectariferous tube* about four times the length of the reflexed calyx, flattened and keeled on each side, slightly gibbous at the base. *Petals* 5, obovate, distinct, spreading, the two upper ones rather the largest, all of a diluted purple with two obscure darker spots in the centre, and light at the base. *Filaments* 10, united at the base, one of them a broad spatula-shaped one, terminated in a sharp point and bearing no anthers; six bearing anthers, which in our specimen were all without pollen. *Style* short and pale, not hairy. *Stigmas* 5, red, reflexed.

This very handsome and curious plant is of hybrid origin, and was raised at the Nursery of Mr. Colvill, in 1822, from a seed of P. *ardens* that had been fertilized by the pollen of P. *cortusæfolium*. It has precisely the stem of the latter, and the colour of the leaves are exactly the same; but those are more divided, and have the same sort of spreading footstalks as P. *ardens*. The colour of the flowers is quite distinct from both, but partakes in an equal degree of each. Its scent is exquisite in the morning and evening, nearly resembling that of the Jonquil. It is of very free growth, and requires the same kind of treatment as the succulent and tuberous-rooted sorts; thriving well in a mixture of turfy loam, peat, and sand, watering it but sparingly in winter. The only way of propagating it, is by the tubers of its roots, as it produces scarcely any branches.

If the present plant had been received from the Cape, as well as numerous other mules that have been of late years obtained from seed, no person would have had the least doubt of its being an original species; and it is our decided opinion, that numerous plants, recorded as real species, are of hybrid origin. We cannot possibly conceive how it can be otherwise in the tropical countries, where the insects and humming-birds are continually flitting from flower to flower, and fertilizing one with the pollen of another; and we see nothing confusing in all this, as the seed from a mule plant, if fertilized by its own pollen, will produce its offspring as true as any species whatever. This we have experienced in numerous trials of our own, and have not seen the least inclination to vary; and as for hybrid plants only continuing for three or four generations, as some people suppose who have never made the experiment, we can confidently assert to the contrary, and believe that they may be muled backward and forward to any extent; and very often, if a hybrid plant is obtained from two very distant species, its anthers will be sterile, yet it will generally produce perfect seed if fertilized by some other species.

E. D. Smith del. Pub by J. Ridgway 170 Piccadilly Jan. 1. 1825. J. Watts sc.

PELARGONIUM aceroides.

Maple-like Stork's-bill.

P. *aceroides*, caule fruticoso ramoso; ramis patentibus, foliis rigidis cordatis 5-7-lobis acutis cartilagineo-dentatis undulatis pubescentibus subtus multinerviis, stipulis cordato-lanceolatis acuminatis subdentatis, pedunculis plurifloris, petalis venosissimis, tubo nectarifero calyce acuminato subæquali.

Stem shrubby, much branched; *branches* short, spreading, thickly clothed with long spreading villous hairs, as are the petioles, stipules, peduncles, and calyx. *Leaves* rigid, cordate, 5 or 7-lobed, acute, sharply toothed with brown cartilaginous teeth, pubescent on both sides, underneath prominently nerved, the nerves branching in all directions, margins undulate. *Petioles* short, broadly flattened and furrowed on the upper side and convex on the lower, broadest at the base. *Stipules* cordately lanceolate, taper-pointed, often toothed. *Peduncles* cylindrical, several-flowered. *Involucre* of about six ovate, taper-pointed, keeled bractes. *Pedicles* longer than the bractes, villous. *Calyx* 5-cleft; segments long, lanceolate, taper-pointed, of a brownish purple; upper one erect, the others spreading. *Nectariferous tube* about the length of the calyx, of the same colour. *Petals* 5, the two upper ones roundly obovate, oblique at the base, of a blush-colour; with a faint purple spot in the centre; between it and the base are numerous reddish purple lines which branch all over the petals: lower ones oval, of a lighter colour, also slightly marked with reddish veins. *Filaments* 10, connected at the base, seven bearing anthers. *Style* purple, quite smooth. *Stigmas* 5, purple, reflexed.

Our drawing was taken from a fine plant in the collection of Robert Henry Jenkinson, Esq. last spring. It is of hybrid origin: and we believe one of its parents to be P. *floridum*, and the other P. *lineatum*, or perhaps P. *striatum*. It is a very desirable plant, being as hardy as any of the tribe, and a free bloomer, growing readily in a mixture of sandy loam and peat, or any rich light soil. Cuttings of it strike root readily, if planted in pots and placed in a sheltered situation.

243.

E. D. Smith del. Pub by J. Ridgway 170 Piccadilly Jan. 1. 1825.

PELARGONIUM torrefactum.

Burnt-petaled Stork's-bill.

P. *torrefactum*, caule fruticoso subcarnoso, foliis cordatis obtusis 5-7-lobatis dentatis canescenti-pubescentibus, stipulis cordato-ovatis acutis ciliatis subdentatis, umbellis multifloris paniculatis, tubo nectarifero calyce subæquali.

Stem shrubby, somewhat succulent, branching; *branches* spreading, flexuose, clothed with long spreading white hairs, and smaller ones intermixed. *Leaves* cordate, concave, 5 or 7-lobed, obtuse, toothed with large rounded unequal teeth, thickly clothed with a dense canescent pubescence; underneath strongly nerved, the nerves clothed with long white hairs. *Petioles* stout, flattened and slightly furrowed on the upper side, convex on the lower, widened at the base, thickly clothed with long spreading hairs, as are the peduncles, bractes, and calyx. *Stipules* cordately ovate, acute, ciliate, sometimes toothed. *Peduncles* panicled, cylindrical. *Umbels* many-flowered. *Involucre* of six broad lanceolate acute bractes. *Pedicles* about the length, or a little longer than the bractes. *Calyx* 5-cleft; upper segment erect, oblongly lanceolate, bluntish, keeled; the others narrower, lanceolate, acute, spreading. *Nectariferous tube* about the length of the calyx, flattened on each side and gibbous at the base, villous. *Petals* 5, spreading; the two upper ones obovate, scarlet, tinged with a dark brown, having the appearance of being scorched; from the base is a forked white mark, and from it branch numerous dark lines, which spread all over the petals: lower petals ligulate, of a lighter colour, also tinged, and from the base are two dark veins. *Filaments* 10, connected at the base, seven bearing anthers, which are always sterile. *Style* purple, slightly hairy at the base and smooth upwards. *Stigmas* 5, purple, reflexed.

This very fine strong-growing plant is of hybrid origin, and was raised, in 1822, at the Nursery of Mr. Colvill, from a seed of P. *fulgidum* that had been fertilized by P. *Husseyanum*. It is as near as possible intermediate, possessing the strong growth and large leaves of the latter parent, with the succulent substance of the former; and its flowers in size and colour partake of both. It certainly makes a very pleasing variety, as it is so distinct from most others; and its fine dark flowers, mixed with scarlet, gives it a brilliant appearance: those are produced in abundance all the summer and till late in autumn. The best soil for it is a mixture of turfy loam, peat, and sand; and being of a succulent habit, it requires but little water in winter. Cuttings root freely, planted in pots in the same sort of soil, and placed on a shelf in the greenhouse.

Pub by J. Ridgway 170 Piccadilly Jan. 1. 1824.
J. Watts sc.

GERANIUM anemonefolium.

Anemone-leaved Crane's-bill.

G. *anemonefolium*, caule fruticoso erecto, foliis glabris: inferioribus palmato-5-sectis; superioribus 3-sectis: segmentis bipinnatifido-laciniatis dentatis, pedunculis fasciculatis bifloris glabris.

Geranium anemonefolium. *DC. prodr.* 1. *p.* 640. *Willden. sp. pl.* 3. *p.* 698. *Pers. syn.* 2. *p.* 234. *L'Hérit. ger. t.* 36. *Botan. magaz.* 206. *Andrews's geran. f.* 1.

Geranium palmatum. *Cav. diss.* 4. *t.* 84. *f.* 2.

Stem shrubby, erect, simple, sometimes attaining the height of three or four feet; very rugged, occasioned by the persistent stipules. *Leaves* smooth and glossy: lower ones palmately 5-parted; those on the flower-stalks 3-parted: *segments* bipinnatifid or deeply laciniated, acute, mucronate, sharply toothed. *Petioles* long, bent towards the leaf, nearly cylindrical, slightly sulcate with several very shallow furrows, purple and much swollen at the base, and green upwards, smooth and glossy. *Stipules* large, ovate, bluntish, their margins membranaceous, of a pale purple, persistent. *Flower-stems* dichotomous, quite smooth and glossy, as are the peduncles and calyx. *Peduncles* several, fasciculate, 2-flowered. *Involucre* of four very small bractes, the two lower ones ovate, concave, bluntish, double the size of the upper ones. *Pedicles* erect, about twice the length of the calyx. *Calyx* of five sepals, which are broadly lanceolate, mucronate, deeply furrowed, with membranaceous margins. *Petals* 5, roundly obovate, of a light purple, darker at the base, about twice the length of the sepals. *Stamens* 10, all fertile. *Germen* smooth. *Style* red, glandularly hairy near the base, and smooth upwards. *Stigmas* 5, reflexed or revolute.

This curious plant is a native of Madeira, and an old inhabitant of our gardens. It may be considered a very hardy greenhouse plant, as in mild winters it will survive all the year in the open air; and I am informed that it is cultivated in the open ground at the Isle of Wight, and in some parts of Devonshire. It makes a singular and pleasing variety, by its large rugged stem, crowned with a tuft of large spreading leaves and numerous flowers, which are produced in succession nearly all the summer. It succeeds well in any rich light soil, or a mixture of loam and peat will suit it very well: and it is readily increased by seeds, which ripen in abundance.

245.

E. D. Smith. del.   Pub. by J. Ridgway. 170 Piccadilly Feb. 1. 1825.   J. Watts. sc.

GERANIUM multifidum.

Multifid-leaved Crane's-bill.

G. *multifidum*, caule ramoso diffuso; ramis gracilibus, pubescentibus, foliis subtus albo-sericeis quinatis 5-partitisve; foliolis segmentisque tripartitis multifidis linearibus, pedunculis elongatis 1-2-floris, sepalis sericeis trinerviis, petalis emarginatis calyce sesquilongioribus.

Root perennial. *Stems* several from the same root; slender, spreading, prostrate if not supported, dichotomously branching, pubescent, about a foot in length. *Leaves* of a glossy green on the upper side, and of a silky white on the lower, quinate or 5-parted; leaflets or segments deeply 3-parted; divisions multifid, linear, blunt on the lower leaves, and acute on the upper ones. *Petioles* long and slender, bent towards the leaf, nearly cylindrical, a little thickened at the base, pubescent. *Stipules* deeply divided into three or four taper-pointed subulate divisions. *Peduncles* axillary, long and slender, 1 or 2-flowered. *Involucre* of two to five subulate acute bractes. *Pedicles* long and slender. *Sepals* 5, oblong, lanceolate, sericeous, strongly 3-nerved, mucronate; margins membranaceous. *Petals* 5, bearded at the base, of a rosy purple, obcordate, emarginate, strongly veined, about half as long again as the calyx. *Stamens* 10, slightly connected at the base, all producing fertile anthers. *Filaments* a little dilated at the base, slightly fringed. *Style* very short. *Stigmas* 5, very long, purple, reflexed.

We first observed this curious species of Geranium, in the summer of 1819, in the garden of Mr. Burchell, at Fulham; where we saw several plants of it in bloom. It is a native of the Cape of Good Hope, and was raised from seed, brought from that country, by Mr. W. J. Burchell; and from a plant given by him to Robert Henry Jenkinson, Esq. our drawing and description were taken last summer. It is a hardy greenhouse plant, and will probably endure the winter in a common frame; so that it does not get too much moisture. It thrives well in a mixture of sandy loam and peat, and may be increased by cuttings, taken off while the shoots are young; or from seeds, which ripen plentifully, if some pollen be attached to the stigmas when in full bloom.

246.
E. D. Smith del.
Pub by J. Ridgway 170 Piccadilly Feb. 1. 1825.

PELARGONIUM sphondyliifolium.

Swine's Parsnep-leaved Stork's-bill.

P. *sphondyliifolium*, caule suffruticoso carnoso subdecumbente, foliis ternatis pinnatifidisque utrinque pilosis apice recurvis; foliolis segmentisque laciniatis obtuse dentatis, umbellis multifloris, tubo nectarifero calyce reflexo quintuplo longiore.

Root tuberous, branching into numerous tubers of various shapes and sizes. *Stem* short, suffruticose, succulent, unequal in size, rather decumbent, clothed with subpersistent stipules; *branches* short and thick. *Leaves* large and spreading, very hairy on both sides, ternate; lower leaflets 2-parted, intermediate one pinnatifid, the points reflexed; *segments* distant from each other, deeply divided, sometimes nearly pinnatifid, bluntly toothed, sinuses rounded. *Petioles* long, slightly flattened on the upper side and rounded on the lower, much swollen at the base, clothed with long spreading hairs and short villous ones intermixed. *Stipules* short, broadly cordate, acute, joined to the base of the petioles. *Scape* branching, leafy at the base of the peduncles. *Peduncles* very long, cylindrical, thickly covered with long spreading villous hairs. *Umbels* many-flowered. *Involucre* of numerous broadly lanceolate acute bractes. *Pedicles* about the length of the bractes. *Calyx* 5-cleft; segments short, unequal, bluntish, all reflexed, and clothed with short hairs; the upper one ovate, the others lanceolate. *Nectariferous tube* long and slender, a little flattened on each side, clothed with short hairs, more than five times the length of the calyx. *Petals* 5, obovate, equal or nearly so, of a brilliant dark velvet, scarlet at the base, the upper ones slightly lined at the bottom. *Filaments* 10, united at the base, six bearing perfect anthers; the seventh a broad spatulate one, also bearing a small anther; sterile ones short and bluntish. *Style* short, pale flesh colour, slightly hairy at the base and smooth upwards. *Stigmas* 5, reflexed.

This curious plant is of hybrid origin, and was raised in 1823, at the Nursery of Mr. Colvill, from a seed of P. *ardens*, that had been fertilized with the pollen of P. *multiradiatum*; it is as near as possible intermediate between the two, both in its habit, leaves, and colour of the flowers. It requires precisely the same sort of treatment as P. *ardens*, succeeding well in a mixture of turfy loam, peat, and sand; or any other light sandy soil. The best method of propagating it is by the tubers of its roots.

247.

Pub. by J. Ridgway 170 Piccadilly Feb. 1. 1825.

PELARGONIUM dissectum.

Dissected-leaved Stork's-bill.

P. *dissectum*, caule fruticoso ramoso diffuso, foliis cordatis 5-7-partitis canescenti-pubescentibus; segmentis flabelliformibus imbricatis inciso-dentatis obtusis, umbellis multifloris paniculatis, petalis subæqualibus, tubo nectarifero calyce subæquali aut paulo breviore.

Pelargonium dissectum. *Colv. catal. ed.* 2. *p.* 23. *col.* 3.

Stem shrubby, much branched; *branches* spreading in various directions, rather succulent, thickly clothed with short white unequal hairs. *Leaves* cordate, 5 or 7-parted, covered on both sides with a canescent pubescence, more or less undulate; segments fan-shaped, overlapping each other, more or less deeply cut and toothed, segments and teeth bluntish. *Petioles* long and slender, slightly flattened on the upper side and convex on the lower, much dilated at the base, thickly clothed with short hairs, as are the peduncles and calyx. *Stipules* lanceolate, taper-pointed, joined to the base of the petioles. *Peduncles* panicled, cylindrical. *Umbels* many-flowered in a close head. *Involucre* of numerous broadly lanceolate, acute, keeled bractes. *Pedicles* unequal in length, some not so long, others double the length of the bractes. *Calyx* 5-cleft, segments lanceolate, acute, margins membranaceous, fringed, the upper one erect, the others reflexed. *Petals* 5, nearly equal in size, spatulately ligulate, of a pale blush; the two upper ones slightly emarginate, with a dark forked spot in the centre, and several short purple lines from it to the base, that are more or less branched. *Filaments* 10, united at the base, seven bearing anthers. *Style* short, purple, slightly hairy at the base, and smooth upwards. *Stigmas* 5, purple, reflexed.

This very distinct and truly curious plant is a hybrid production, the produce of P. *australe, t.* 68, that had been fertilized by the pollen of P. *incisum* or P. *canescens,* and partakes, in an equal degree, of both. In this plant we have the New Holland and Cape species intermixed; the only instance of the kind that we are at present acquainted with. Although an hybrid from two such distinct species, it is of as free growth as either of them, and forms a larger and stronger bush; thriving well in a mixture of turfy loam, peat, and sand, or any other light rich soil. Cuttings of it strike root freely, planted in pots and placed on a shelf in the greenhouse.

Our drawing was taken from a plant in the superb collection of Robert Henry Jenkinson, Esq.; where it was raised from seed that had been produced from his plants.

248.

E. D. Smith del. Pub. by J. Ridgway 170 Piccadilly Feb. 1. 1825. S. Watts sc.

PELARGONIUM Kingii.

Mr. King's Stork's-bill.

P. *Kingii*, caule fruticoso ramoso, ramis patentibus villosis; foliis cordatis trifidis villosis: segmentis cuneatis subtrilobis, inæqualiter grosseque dentatis, stipulis ovato-lanceolatis acutis subdentatis, pedunculis 3-4-floris, petalis rotundato-obovatis, tubo nectarifero calyce subæquali.

Pelargonium Kingii. *Colv. catal. ed.* 2. *p.* 22. *col.* 2.

Stem shrubby, much branched; *branches* spreading, thickly clothed with long spreading villous hairs, and shorter ones intermixed; as is every other part of the plant, except the corolla. *Leaves* cordate, trifid, hollow in the centre, margins slightly undulate; *segments* cuneate, more or less imbricate, generally 2 or 3-lobed, deeply but unequally toothed. *Petioles* flattened on the upper side, and convex on the lower, widened at the base. *Stipules* ovately-lanceolate, acute, often toothed, ciliate. *Peduncles* 3 or 4-flowered, longer than the leaves, cylindrical. *Involucre* of six lanceolate, acute, fringed bractes. *Pedicles* longer than the bractes, about the length of the nectariferous tube. *Calyx* 5-cleft, laciniæ lanceolate, acute, the upper one broadest, erect; points of the others reflexed. *Nectariferous tube* about the length of the calyx, much flattened on each side, and gibbous at the base. *Petals* 5, roundly obovate, imbricate, of a light scarlet, or deep salmon colour, edged with purple; the two upper ones about half as large again as the lower ones, with, or sometimes without an obscure brown spot in the centre, below which are two forked dark purple lines from the base, that are more or less branched. *Stamens* 10, united at the base; seven bearing anthers, which are generally imperfect. *Style* pale flesh-colour, hairy about half way up, the upper part smooth. *Stigmas* 5, purple, reflexed or revolute.

Our drawing of this beautiful plant was made last September, at the Nursery of Mr. Colvill, where it was raised from seed, the produce of P. *Husseyanum*, that had been mixed with the pollen of P. *rubescens;* it is very little like either of its parents, yet its similarity to P. *Wellsianum*, its cousin, is readily perceptible. It is of free growth, and continues in flower nearly all the year; but the autumn flowers are the finest, and of a much richer colour than the spring ones. A plant of it was in full bloom, at the Nursery of Mr. Colvill, this winter, a little before Christmas, and the flowers were at that season very brilliant. Like its nearest relatives, it succeeds best in a mixture of light turfy loam, peat, and sand, and cuttings soon strike root, when planted in pots and placed on a shelf in the greenhouse.

We have named the present subject in compliment to John King, Esq. of South Brent, Devon; a gentleman much attached to the family of Geraniaceæ, and who possesses a superb collection of them.

249

E. D. Smith del. Pub by J. Ridgway 170 Piccadilly March 1.1825. J. Watts sc.

PELARGONIUM incurvum.

Incurved-petaled Stork's-bill.

P. *incurvum*, caule fruticoso ramoso, ramis gracilibus flexuosis, foliis tripartitis dentatis pubescentibus: segmentis lateralibus bilobis: intermedio 3-5-lobato, stipulis cordato-ovatis acutis, pedunculis subpaniculatis 3-5-floris, petalis superis margine incurvis, tubo nectarifero calyce subduplo longiore.

Pelargonium incurvum. *Swt. hort. brit. inedit.*

Stem shrubby, hard and woody, brown-barked, much branched; *branches* numerous, spreading, flexuose, slender, thickly clothed with unequal spreading villous hairs, as are the petioles, peduncles, and calyx. *Leaves* 3-parted, bluntly toothed, attenuated down the footstalk, pubescent on both sides. *Petioles* flattened on the upper side and convex on the lower, a little swollen at the base. *Stipules* cordately ovate, acute, entire, villous. *Peduncles* in a kind of panicle, long and slender, 3 to 5 flowered. *Involucre* of 6 or 7 lanceolate, bluntish bractes. *Pedicles* slender, longer than the bractes, bent towards the flowers. *Calyx* 5-cleft; segments lanceolate, acute, the upper one broadest, erect, the others reflexed. *Nectariferous tube* unequal in length, sometimes double the length, at other times scarcely longer than the calyx, flattened and keeled on both sides, gibbous at the base. *Petals* 5, the two upper ones obovate, connivent at the base, their margins bent inwards, of an orangy scarlet, marked with purple branched lines from the base, and an obscure mark in the centre; three lower ones ligulate, spreading, of rather a lighter colour. *Filaments*

10, united at the base, seven bearing anthers, which are mostly sterile. *Style* purple, very hairy. *Stigmas* 5, purple, reflexed or revolute.

This handsome and very distinct plant is of hybrid origin, and was raised from seed, at the Nursery of Mr. Colvill, in 1821. The parent plant was P. *fulgidum*, that had been fertilized by one of the small-leaved sorts, perhaps P. *melissinum*. Being of small growth, and an abundant flowerer, makes it very desirable. Its flowers are also of a very brilliant colour; and it continues to flower all the summer, and till late in autumn. Like P. *ignescens*, it succeeds best in an equal portion of light turfy loam, peat, and sand; and cuttings strike root freely, if planted in pots in the same sort of soil, and placed on a shelf in the green-house.

250
Pub. by J. Ridgway 170 Piccadilly March 1.1825.

PELARGONIUM pedicellatum.

Long-pedicled Stork's-bill.

P. *pedicellatum*, subacaule, foliis glabris ciliatis carnosis 5-7-lobatis dentatis apice reflexis, stipulis cordatis acutis, umbellis multifloris, floribus longe pedicellatis, calycibus reflexis, petalis subæqualibus, tubo nectarifero calyce quintuplo longiore.

Pelargonium pedicellatum. *Swt. hort. brit. ined.*

Root tuberous, large, and clothed with a hard brown bark. *Stem* very short and rugged. *Leaves* smooth, thick, and succulent, of rather a greasy nature, fringed, 5 or 7-lobed, and toothed with small sharp teeth, strongly nerved underneath: lobes broadly wedge-shaped, bent back at the point and margins. *Petioles* long, slightly flattened on the upper side, and rounded on the lower, thickened at the base, glossy, but clothed with long spreading white hairs. *Stipules* short, broadly cordate, acute. *Scape* producing no leaves, thickly clothed with unequal spreading white hairs. *Umbels* many-flowered. *Involucre* of numerous small unequal bractes, some of them cordate, others ovate or lanceolate, acute. *Pedicles* very long and slender, some of them more than 2½ inches in length, clothed with long spreading hairs and short down intermixed. *Calyx* 5-cleft, segments lanceolate, acute, all reflexed. *Nectariferous tube* about five times as long as the calyx, and about half the length of the pedicles, pubescent. *Petals* 5, obovate, nearly equal in size; two upper ones pale greenish yellow, marked with a bifid purple spot; lower ones dark purple, edged with pale yellow. *Filaments* 10, short and straight, united at the base, one of them a very broad spatulate one, which produces no anther, six bearing anthers. *Pollen* golden yellow. *Style* short, green and smooth. *Stigmas* 5, green, reflexed.

This very distinct and curious plant was received, by Mr. Colvill, from the Cape, in 1822; but it did not produce its flowers till last summer, at which time our drawing was taken. It belongs to the same section as P. *triste*, P. *pulverulentum*, &c. but is readily distinguished from all its nearest allies, by the long pedicles to its flowers, and its smooth greasy leaves. It requires the same kind of treatment as the other plants in the same section: an equal mixture of light turfy loam, peat, and sand, is the best soil for it, keeping it quite dry when in a dormant state, and shifting it into fresh soil in spring. The best method of increasing it is by the little tubers of its roots: those must be planted with their tops above the surface of the mould, or they will be apt to rot.

251.

E. D. Smith del. Pub. by J. Ridgway 169 Piccadilly March 1, 1825. J. Watts sc.

PELARGONIUM campyliæflorum.

Campylia-flowered Stork's-bill.

P. *campyliæflorum*, caule fruticoso flexuoso subdecumbente, foliis rotundato-cordatis reniformibusve crenatis molliter tomentosis, stipulis cordatis acutis carinatis, umbellis plurifloris, petalis superis suborbiculatis, tubo nectarifero calyce paulo longiore.

Pelargonium campyliæflorum. *Swt. hort. brit. inedit.*

Stem shrubby, branching, a little flexuose, subdecumbent, thickly clothed with a dense woolly down. *Leaves* about as broad as long, roundly cordate, crenate with numerous blunt shallow notches, densely clothed on both sides with a short soft velvetty tomentum. *Petioles* slightly flattened on the upper side and rounded on the lower, thickened at the base, densely clothed with short spreading villous hairs, as are the peduncles, calyx, and nectariferous tube. *Stipules* cordate, taper-pointed, keeled, subpersistent. *Peduncles* cylindrical, several-flowered. *Involucre* of from 6 to 8 broadly ovate bluntish bractes. *Pedicles* unequal in length, some double the length of the others. *Calyx* 5-cleft, segments roundly ovate, concave, blunt, strongly nerved. *Nectariferous tube* a little longer than the calyx, much flattened on each side, and thickened at the base. *Petals* 5, the two upper ones nearly orbicular, of a pale blush, changing to white as they fade, marked near the centre with two or three small red spots, below which is a dark purple mark on each side, a little branched; lower petals obovate, marked near the base with two faint red lines. *Filaments* 10, united at the base, one of them a broad spatulate one, which ranks the present plant in the section *Monospatalla:* this and six others produce anthers, but they are always imperfect in the specimens that we have examined. *Style* short, pale red, hairy at the base and smooth upwards. *Stigmas* 5, purple, reflexed.

The present subject is a very singular hybrid production, and was raised in the select and curious collection of Robert Henry Jenkinson, Esq. from a seed of P. *particeps,* that had been fertilized by the pollen of *Campylia cana.* It is the first hybrid that has come under our notice, intermediate between Campylia and Pelargonium; and, although its origin is between two such very different parents, it is of as free growth as any plant belonging to the family. It is as near as possible intermediate between the two. The habit of the plant and form of the leaves are of P. *particeps,* likewise the number and form of the stamens; but the stipules and form as well as the colour of the flower, are of *Campylia cana.*

It requires precisely the same kind of soil as recommended for both its parents, a mixture of turfy loam, peat, and sand, and a pretty good supply of water, keeping it as much as possible from its leaves. Cuttings strike root freely, planted in pots and placed on a shelf in the greenhouse.

252.

Smith. del. Pub by J. Ridgway 170 Piccadilly March 1. 1825.

PELARGONIUM rotundilobum.

Round-lobed Stork's-bill.

P. *rotundilobum*, foliis planis cordatis profunde quinquelobis obsolete dentatis mollibus: lobis divaricatis rotundato-obtusis, stipulis lato-cordatis acutis margine reflexis, umbellis subsexfloris, tubo nectarifero calyce reflexo subæquali.

Pelargonium rotundilobum. *Swt. hort. brit. inedit.*

Stem shrubby, branching; *branches* spreading, thickly clothed with spreading villous hairs and soft down intermixed. *Leaves* flat, cordate, deeply 5-lobed, obsoletely notched with short blunt notches, hairy on both sides, very soft to the touch, much nerved underneath, the nerves reticulately branched: *lobes* distant, spreading, very broad and rounded. *Petioles* slightly flattened on the upper side and rounded on the lower, thickly clothed with spreading villous hairs and soft down intermixed, as are the peduncles, bractes, and calyx. *Stipules* broadly cordate, acute, the margins reflexed. *Peduncle* cylindrical, generally 6-flowered. *Involucre* of 6 or 8 broadly lanceolate taper-pointed bractes, all united into one at the base. *Pedicles* very short, hairy. *Calyx* 5-cleft, upper segment ovate, the others lanceolate, all reflexed. *Petals* 5, cuneate; the two upper ones broadest, brick-coloured with two dark brown spots in the centre, between them and the base are numerous purple branched lines on nearly a white ground; lower petals of rather a lighter colour. *Filaments* 10, united at the base, seven bearing anthers, which are generally imperfect. *Style* pale-coloured, very long, hairy at the base and smooth upwards. *Stigmas* 5, pale purple, spreading.

Our drawing of this pretty plant was taken last summer in the collection of Robert Henry Jenkinson, Esq. It is of hybrid origin, but what its real parents were it is difficult to determine. The leaves are nearer like P. *Breesianum* than any other, and the flowers are not very different from P. *Broughtoniæ*. We have no doubt but it is the produce of hybrids for several generations.

A very free-growing plant, thriving well in a mixture of light turfy loam, peat, and sand, or any other light vegetable soil, producing its elegant flowers all the summer, and till late in autumn; and may be readily increased by cuttings, planted in pots in the same sort of soil, and placed in a sheltered situation.

253.

E. D. Smith del. Pub by J. Ridgway 169. Piccadilly Ap. 1. 1825. S. Watts sc.

PELARGONIUM Dobreeanum.

Mrs. Dobree's Stork's-bill.

P. *Dobreeanum,* caule fruticoso ramoso: ramis gracilibus villosis, foliis cordatis oblongis sinuatis v. profunde 7-lobis undulatis obsolete dentatis pubescentibus subviscosis: lobis apice reflexis, umbellis subsexfloris, petalis patentibus.

Pelargonium Dobreeanum. *Swt. hort. brit. p.* —. *n.* 320. *ined.*

Stem shrubby, branching: branches slender, spreading, thickly clothed with unequal soft villous hairs. *Leaves* oblong, cordate at the base, the sinus generally overlapped, pinnatifidly sinuate or deeply 5 to 7-lobed, much undulate, and toothed with very small teeth, more or less pubescent, slightly viscid: lobes rounded, a little reflexed at the points; sinuses rounded. *Petioles* slightly flattened on the upper side and rounded on the lower, thickened at the base, thickly covered with unequal villous hairs, as are the peduncles, calyx, and nectariferous tube. *Stipules* short, cordate, taper-pointed, villous and fringed. *Peduncles* stout, thickened at the base. *Umbels* 5 or 6-flowered. *Involucre* of several lanceolate, acute bractes. *Pedicles* short, villous. *Calyx* 5-cleft, upper segment erect, the others reflexed. *Nectariferous tube* unequal in length, longer than the calyx. *Petals* 5, the 2 upper ones, broadly obovate, cuneate, of a bright orangy scarlet, with a dark spot in the centre, and a white mark below it, from which branch numerous short dark lines: lower petals oblongly obovate, of rather a lighter colour, much spreading. *Filaments* 10, connected at the base, 7 bearing anthers, which are sometimes perfect, but often sterile; when perfect, the flowers are always much larger. *Style* hairy at the base, and smooth upwards. *Stigmas* 5, reflexed.

This handsome plant is of hybrid origin, and was raised by Mrs. Dobree, of Guernsey, from a seed of P. *ignescens* that had been fertilized by the pollen of P. *glutinosum;* it was raised about the year 1818, and a drawing of it was sent to the Horticultural Society in 1820, so that it was amongst the first of the fine scarlet hybrids that was raised. We believe only Sir R. C. Hoare's P. *ignescens* and P. *scintillans*, and perhaps P. *nanum*, preceded it: we have named it in compliment to the lady who raised it; we understand it was nearly lost again, after it had flowered, the old plant dying, but was preserved by a cutting. It is as near as possible intermediate between its two parents; the flowers have the colour of P. *ignescens*, but their number, and the habit of the plant, and form of the leaves, is nearer P. *glutinosum;* it is also slightly viscous.

Our drawing was taken from a plant at the Nursery of Mr. Colvill, that had been procured for him by the kindness of S. Pearce, Esq. of Guernsey. At present it continues scarce; and as it is not a fast grower, will not soon be very common; like its allies, it succeeds best in a light sandy soil, and care must be taken not to overwater it. Cuttings root readily, if planted in pots, and placed on a shelf in the greenhouse.

254

E. D. Smith del. Pub. by J. Ridgway 169 Piccadilly Ap. 1. 1825. J. Watts sc.

PELARGONIUM flavum.

Yellow Carrot-leaved Stork's-bill.

P. *flavum*, subcaulescens, foliis decomposite laciniatis hirsutis; laciniis linearibus, umbellis multifloris. *DC. prodr.* 1. *p.* 662.

Pelargonium flavum. *Hort. Kew. ed.* 1. *v.* 2. *p.* 418. *ed.* 2. *v.* 4. *p.* 166. *Willden. sp. pl.* 3. *p.* 651. *Pers. syn.* 2. *p.* 228.

Geranium flavum. *Linn. f. suppl.* 257.

Geranium daucifolium. *Murr. gœtt.* 1780. *p.* 13. *t.* 4. *Cav. diss.* 4. *t.* 120. *f.* 2.

Root very large, tuberous, clothed with a brown cracked bark. ***Stem*** very short, decumbent. ***Leaves*** doubly compound, much branched, laciniate, very hairy, of a pale yellowish green: leaflets and segments very small, linear, bluntish, the points curved inwards, bearded. ***Stipules*** roundly ovate, membranaceous, fringed. ***Scape*** simple, swollen at the base, thickly clothed with spreading unequal hairs, producing a single umbel of flowers. ***Umbel*** many-flowered. ***Flowers*** delightfully fragrant in the evening and at night, but without scent during the day, of a greenish yellow colour. ***Involucre*** of several unequal, lanceolate, bluntish bractes. ***Calyx*** 5-cleft, upper segment largest, erect, concave, bluntish, the others narrower, reflexed. ***Nectariferous tube*** more than three times the length of the calyx, sessile, hairy. ***Petals*** 5, a little reflexed, the two upper ones rather largest, broadly obovate; lower ones of the same shape, but narrower, of a greenish yellow, faintly striped with brown. ***Filaments*** 10, united at the base, one of them a broad spatulate one, which produces no anther, 6 bearing perfect anthers. ***Style*** very short. ***Stigmas*** 5, purple, reflexed or revolute.

This curious plant is an old inhabitant of our greenhouses, having been introduced from the Cape in 1724; it is, however, seldom to be met with at present, most probably from its not being so showy as others of the genus, yet we think its singularity and delightful fragrance entitle it to a place in any collection. We have not yet seen any hybrid produced from the present plant, but believe some very curious ones might be obtained. Its time of flowering is generally in Autumn, after many of its more showy competitors have done blooming for the season; like the other plants of this section, it succeeds best in a very light sandy soil, and a dry airy situation in the greenhouse; it may be increased by the little tubers from the roots, or from seeds, which ripen plentifully, if some pollen be attached to the stigmas when in bloom.

Our drawing was taken from a plant in the select collection of Robert Henry Jenkinson, Esq.

255.

E. D. Smith del. Pub by J. Ridgway 169 Piccadilly Ap. 1. 1825. F. Watts sc.

PELARGONIUM comptum.

Decked Stork's-bill.

P. *comptum*, caule erecto carnoso ramoso pubescente, foliis rotundato-reniformibus obsolete lobatis crenato-dentatis: supra glabris subpubescentibus subtus tomentosis, stipulis acuminatis subpersistentibus, umbellis multifloris subpaniculatis, tubo nectarifero calyce quadruplo longiore.

Pelargonium comptum. *Swt. hort. brit. p. —. n. 59. inedit.*

Stem shrubby, erect, branched, succulent, clothed with a hard brown bark, pubescent. *Leaves* kidney-shaped, rounded, slightly lobed, unequally and rather deeply notched, with blunt rounded teeth, of a glossy green, but slightly pubescent on the upper side, and tomentose underneath. *Petioles* slender, nearly cylindrical, swollen at the base, thickly clothed with short villous hairs. *Stipules* narrowly lanceolate, taper-pointed, villous, hardening into a sort of spine, and continuing for a considerable time. *Flower-stem* paniculately branched, thickly clothed with long spreading villous hairs and short down intermixed. *Peduncles* villous. *Umbels* many-flowered. *Involucre* of 6 or 7 lanceolate, acute, villous bractes. *Pedicles* very short, often wanting. *Calyx* 5-cleft, villous, segments unequal, the back one ovate or broadly lanceolate, blunt, concave, erect, the others narrower, reflexed. *Nectariferous tube* slender, about 4 times the length of the calyx, thickly clothed with unequal, soft, villous hairs. *Petals* 5, nearly obcordate; the upper ones very little larger than the others, of a bright pink, light at the base, and a dark purple spot in the centre, with numerous short purple stripes below it: lower petals darker, also marked with a purple spot, and obsoletely lined from the base. ***Filaments*** 10, united at the base, one of them a broad spatula-shaped one, which produces no anther; 6 bearing anthers. ***Style*** short, smooth. ***Stigmas*** 5, purple, reflexed.

This grand flowering plant is of hybrid origin, and was raised in 1821 at the Nursery of Mr. Colvill, from a seed of P. ***cortusæfolium***, the flowers of which had been fertilized by the pollen of P. ***sæpeflorens***. It is by far a much handsomer plant than either of its parents, and also more hardy, producing its handsome flowers in abundance all the Summer, and till late in Autumn; those also remain several days without dropping, so that the whole umbel is seen in flower at once; the only care it requires, is that it does not get too much water in Winter, but in Summer it requires a regular supply. It succeeds best in a light sandy soil, or an equal mixture of light turfy loam, peat, and sand, will suit it very well. Cuttings will also strike root readily, planted in pots in the same sort of soil, and placed on a shelf in the greenhouse, letting them remain without water for a few days after planting, that the wound may dry up, or they will be liable to rot; it may also be increased by the tubers of its roots.

256.

E. D. Smith del. Pub by J. Ridgway 169 Piccadilly Ap. 1. 1825. J. Watts sc.

PELARGONIUM ringens.

Ringent-flowered Stork's-bill.

P. ***ringens***, subcaulescens, foliis pinnatis pinnatifidisque canescenti-pubescentibus, foliolis segmentisque cuneatis pinnatifido-laciniatis grosse dentatis, scapo folioso paniculato, petalis inferioribus concavis subconniventibus.

Pelargonium ringens. *Colv. catal. ed. 2. p. 22. col. 2.*

Root tuberous, scaly, branching out into numerous small tubers. ***Stem*** very short, erect, branching a little, rough and rugged, occasioned by the remains of the leaves that are fallen. ***Leaves*** long and spreading, pinnate or pinnatifid, and clothed with a soft hoary pubescence: leaflets or segments wedge-shaped, unequally cut and toothed with large roundish teeth, lower ones pinnatifid. ***Petioles*** long and rather slender, flattened a little on the upper side, and rounded on the lower, more or less clothed with soft spreading white hairs. ***Stipules*** attached to the base of the petioles, ovately-lanceolate, taper-pointed. ***Scape*** leafy, branching, villosely hairy, as are the peduncles and calyx. ***Umbels*** many-flowered. ***Involucre*** of 6 broadly lanceolate, acute bractes. ***Calyx*** 5-cleft, upper segment erect, concave, bluntish; the others reflexed, and more acute. ***Nectariferous tube*** unequal in length, sometimes scarcely longer than the calyx, at others more than double the length, hairy. ***Flowers*** of a light scarlet, ringent, upper petals oblong, reflexed, marked at the base with a few dark, branching lines: lower ones smaller, concave, more or less connivent. ***Filaments*** 10, connected, 7 bearing anthers, which in our specimens were all imperfect. ***Style*** short. ***Stigmas*** 5, reflexed.

A handsome plant, also a hybrid production, raised in the collection of Robert Henry Jenkinson, Esq. from a seed of P. ***fulgidum*** that had been mixed with the pollen of ***Hoarea corydaliflora***, or some nearly related plant. It is of very free growth, and continues in bloom all the Summer, beginning to flower the early part of April; like the others to which it is nearest related, it thrives best in a mixture of light turfy loam, peat, and sand, and the pots to be well drained with potsherds broken small, that the water may pass readily off, nothing being so injurious to the tuberous rooted species, as the mould to get sodden in the pots. When they have done flowering, and their leaves begin to decay, they should be kept quite dry, till they show an inclination to begin to grow again; they should then be shifted into other pots in fresh mould, and watered sparingly at first, and as they begin to grow they require a more constant supply, but never so much as the shrubby species. It is readily increased by the little tubers from the root.

257.

E. D. Smith del. Pub. by J. Ridgway 169 Piccadilly May. 1, 1825 J. Watts sc.

PELARGONIUM Chærophyllum.

Cow-Parsley-leaved Stork's-bill.

P. ***Chærophyllum***, caule erecto suffruticoso carnoso squamoso, foliis pinnatifidis bipinnatifidisque pubescentibus: segmentis laciniatis dentatis obtusis, stipulis cordato-ovatis acutis subpersistentibus, scapo flexuoso paniculato-ramoso, umbellis multifloris, tubo nectarifero calyce subtriplo longiore.

Pelargonium Chærophyllum. ***Swt. hort. brit. p. —. n. 23. ined.***

Stem suffruticose, erect, succulent, somewhat scaly, occasioned by the subpersistent stipules and cracked bark. ***Leaves*** pinnatifid, thickly clothed on both sides with short hairs, very soft to the touch; segments pinnatifid or deeply laciniate, toothed, obtuse. ***Petioles*** slightly flattened on the upper side and rounded on the lower, a little thickened at the base, densely clothed with short hairs, and soft down intermixed. ***Stipules*** cordately ovate, acute, partly remaining persistent, joined to the base of the petioles. ***Scape*** long, somewhat flexuose, paniculately branched, leafy at the point. ***Peduncles*** cylindrical, many-flowered. ***Involucre*** of several linearly-lanceolate, taper-pointed, hairy bractes. ***Pedicles*** slender, longer than the bractes. ***Calyx*** 5-cleft, segments unequal, the upper one erect, ovately-lanceolate, acute, concave, keeled, much longer than the others, which are lanceolate, acute, and slightly reflexed. ***Nectariferous tube*** about 3 times longer than the calyx, flattened and keeled on each side, gibbous at the base, slightly hairy. ***Petals*** 5, obovate, the 2 upper ones about double the size of the others, of a bright scarlet, tinged with dark brown, and marked from the base with several dark lines that are slightly branched; lower ones also marked with 2 dark lines near the base, and between them tinged with dark brown. ***Filaments*** 10, united at the base, 7 bearing anthers, which are always fertile: no spatulate one, as might be expected from its habit. ***Pollen*** pale yellow. ***Style*** pale flesh-colour, hairy. ***Stigmas*** 5, pale red, reflexed.

A very curious hybrid production, raised at the Nursery of Mr. Colvill, in 1822, from a seed of P. *fulgidum* that had been fertilized by the pollen of P. *sanguineum*, and it is as near as possible intermediate between its two parents; its flowers are not to be surpassed in brilliancy of colour, by any with which we are acquainted; and by its singularity and decided difference from all others, makes it truly desirable. It requires precisely the same kind of management, as others of the same tribe; a mixture of light turfy loam, peat, and sand, suit it very well; and cuttings taken off when in a free growing state, will soon strike root, if planted in pots in the same kind of soil, and placed on a shelf in the green-house, giving them no water for the first 2 or 3 days, till the cut is dried up, or they will be apt to rot. It may also be increased from the little tubers of its roots.

258.

E. D. Smith del.   Pub. by J. Ridgway 169 Piccadilly May 1. 1825.   J. Watts sc.

PELARGONIUM veniflorum.

Veined-flowered Stork's-bill.

P. ***veniflorum***, caule erecto ramoso, foliis basi cuneatis ovatis quinquelobis acutis inciso-dentatis, stipulis lanceolatis acutis, umbellis 3-4-floris, petalis venosis patentibus, tubo nectarifero calyce paulo longiore.

Pelargonium veniflorum. ***Swt. hort. brit. p.* —. *n.* 222. *inedit.***

Stem shrubby, erect, branching; branches slender, clothed with unequal spreading hairs. *Leaves* ovate, acute, wedge-shaped at the base, 5-lobed, unequally and sharply cut and toothed, slightly hairy. *Petioles* about the length of the leaves, flattened on the upper side and convex on the lower, a little widened at the base, thickly clothed with unequal spreading hairs, as are the peduncles and calyx. *Stipules* lanceolate, acute. *Peduncles* 2 to 4-flowered. *Involucre* of 4 to 6 lanceolate, acute, fringed bractes. *Pedicles* about the length of the nectariferous tube, slender. *Calyx* 5-cleft, segments long, lanceolate, taper-pointed. *Nectariferous tube* a little longer than the calyx, broadly flattened on each side, and gibbous at the base. *Petals* 5, spreading, the 2 upper ones obovate, slightly emarginate, white, with a dark purple patch in the centre, and numerous purple veins branching in all directions: lower ones obovately oblong, rounded, also marked with purple veins. *Filaments* 10, united at the base, 7 bearing perfect anthers: *pollen* orange-coloured. *Style* purple, hairy at the base, and smooth upwards. *Stigmas* 5, purple, reflexed or revolute.

This is also a hybrid production, and was raised at the Nursery of Mr. Colvill, in 1822, from a seed of P. ***Hoareanum***, that had been fertilized with the pollen of P. ***striatum;*** it is a very pretty plant, and as hardy as any of the tribe to which it is related, thriving well in a mixture of turfy loam, peat, and sand, or any light vegetable soil; it will also succeed well in a smallish sized pot, as its roots are not so luxuriant as many of the stronger growing sorts; the cuttings do not root so freely as some of the other kinds, particularly if they are allowed to get too ripe before they are taken off; the young shoots will strike root much more freely; those must be planted in pots, and placed on a shelf in the green-house.

259

E. D. Smith. del. Pub by J. Ridgway 169 Piccadilly May 1. 1825. S. Watts. sc.

PELARGONIUM cynosbatifolium.

Cynosbati-leaved Stork's-bill.

P. ***cynosbatifolium***, caule fruticoso ramoso; ramis confertis brevissimis, foliis cordatis trilobis obtusis denticulato-crenatis pilosis: lobo medio trilobo, stipulis cordatis acuminatis, pedunculis 2-5-floris, petalis subæqualibus, tubo nectarifero brevissimo calyce triplo breviore.

Pelargonium cynosbatifolium. ***Willden. hort. berol.*** *t.* 78. ***Enum.*** *v.* 2. *p.* 708. ***Link enum.*** *v.* 2. *p.* 193. ***DC.*** ***prodr.*** 1. *p.* 654. ***Hort. sub. lond.*** *p.* 152.

Geranium oxoniense. ***Andrews's geran. c. ic. et Hortulanorum.***

Stem shrubby, much branched: ***branches*** very short, crowded, spreading, thickly clothed with spreading villous hairs, as is every other part of the plant, except the corolla. ***Leaves*** cordate, deeply 3-lobed or nearly pinnatifid, obtuse, roughish, margins finely but bluntly notched or toothed, underneath prominently nerved, the nerves branching in all directions: middle lobe 3-lobed; side ones entire, or sometimes shortly 2-lobed. ***Petioles*** much flattened, and furrowed on the upper side, and convex on the lower, widened at the base. ***Stipules*** cordate, taper-pointed, sometimes toothed, ciliate. ***Peduncles*** short and stiff, cylindrical, from 2 to 5-flowered. ***Involucre*** of 6 or 7 ovate or broadly lanceolate concave pointed bractes. ***Pedicles*** longer than the bractes. ***Calyx*** 5-cleft, segments erect or slightly spreading, oblongly-lanceolate, concave, pointed. ***Nectariferous tube*** very short, (in some flowers wanting,) about 3 times shorter than the calyx. ***Petals*** 5, nearly equal, the 2 upper ones rather largest, (sometimes increased to 6 or 7,) roundly obovate, of a light rose or pink, the upper ones marked with a bright violet spot, from which to the base are 2 forked dark purple lines, that are slightly branched: lower petals faintly striped. ***Stamens*** 10, erect, connected at the base, 5 to 7 bearing anthers, sometimes more in the many-petaled flowers. ***Style*** short, pale, all over hairy. ***Stigmas*** 5, purple, about the length of the style, reflexed.

This plant is an old inhabitant of our green-houses, where it has generally passed under the name of the Oxford Geranium, having, we believe, been first raised from seed at the Botanical Garden at Oxford. We have no doubt but it is a hybrid production, and one of its parents must have been P. ***quercifolium***, but what the other was is not so easily ascertained; we suspect it might be P. ***adulterinum;*** it varies with 5 to 10 petals, and also very much in the number of its stamens, according to the strength of the plant; the stamens are generally sterile, another circumstance indicative of its hybrid origin. We suppose the name of P. ***oxaloides***, by which it is commonly known by the German gardeners, has originated from a confusion of P. ***oxoniense***, by which name they most probably received it from this country. It is a pretty little snug growing bushy plant, and produces abundance of bloom when grown well, succeeding best in light rich soil, and the pots well drained, as it is very liable to suffer from too much moisture. Cuttings of it strike root readily, if planted in pots, and placed on a shelf in the green-house.

Our drawing was taken last Summer, from a plant sent us by Mr. William Smith, from the collection of the Earl of Liverpool, Coombe-wood.

HOAREA Colvillii.

Colvill's Hoarea.

H. ***Colvillii***, subacaule, radice tuberoso, foliis ternatis pinnatifidisque utrinque hirsutis: foliolis inferioribus bilobis; lobis cuneatis rotundato-dentatis: terminali maximo ovato sinuato-lobato obtuse dentato, scapo folioso ramoso, umbellis multifloris, petalis patentibus, tubo nectarifero calyce duplo longiore.

Hoarea Colvillii. *Swt. hort. brit. p. —. n.* 38.

Root tuberous. ***Stem*** none, or very short. ***Leaves*** embracing each other and spreading in a radiate form, ternate, or pinnatifid, very hairy on both sides: lower leaflets 2-lobed, lobes cuneate, spreading, rounded at the points, and toothed with 2 or 3 large bluntly rounded teeth; terminal leaflet very large, ovate, sinuately lobed, and toothed with large bluntly rounded teeth. ***Petioles*** very hairy, much flattened on the upper side and rounded on the lower, widened at the base. ***Stipules*** broadly lanceolate, taper-pointed, joined to the base of the petioles. ***Scape*** long, branching, leafy at the base of the peduncles, thickly clothed with long spreading white hairs, as are the peduncles and calyx. ***Peduncles*** long, cylindrical. ***Umbels*** many-flowered. ***Involucre*** of numerous narrowly lanceolate, acute, villous bractes. ***Pedicles*** unequal in length, some as long, others not half the length of the bractes. ***Calyx*** 5-cleft, segments lanceolate, bluntish, the upper one broadest, erect, the others reflexed. ***Nectariferous tube*** slender, flattened on each side, about twice the length of the calyx. ***Petals*** 5, spreading, of a bright crimson, tinged and marked with dark brown: upper ones broadly ligulate, slightly bent from about the middle, lower ones not half so broad, linearly ligulate. ***Filaments*** 10, connected at the base, every other one bearing anthers, points of the sterile ones curved inwards. ***Style*** pale red, very hairy. ***Stigmas*** 5, red, reflexed.

This grand flowering plant is a hybrid production, and was raised at the Nursery of Mr. Colvill, in 1823, from a seed of H. ***melanantha***, that had been fertilized by the pollen of P. ***ardens***. It is a very free growing plant, and begins flowering early in April, and, if well managed, will continue to bloom till late in Autumn; the habit of the plant is as near as possible intermediate between its two parents, but it far surpasses them both in beauty. It succeeds well in a mixture of light turfy loam, peat, and sand, the same as recommended for the other tuberous rooted species; but this does not require to be kept long without water, as many of the others do, as it continues but a very short time in a dormant state, but is growing nearly all the year. The best method of increasing it, is by the little tubers from the root.

261
E. D. Smith del.
Pub. by J. Ridgway 169 Piccadilly June 1. 1825.
J. Watts sc.

PELARGONIUM acidum.

Sour-leaved Stork's-bill.

P. *acidum*, subacaule, radice tuberoso, foliis ovatis integris trifidisve sinuatis dentatis glabris, stipulis petiolo adhærentibus ovato-lanceolatis acuminatis subdentatis, umbellis multifloris, involucro polyphyllo, tubo nectarifero calyce reflexo subtriplo longiore.

Pelargonium acidum. *Swt. hort. brit. p.* —. *n.* 17. *inedit.*

Root tuberous, almost stemless, or stem very short. *Leaves* embracing each other at the base, ovate, some entire, others trifid, more or less sinuate and toothed, rather succulent, smooth and glossy, of a sour taste like *Rumex acetosa*, or sorrel; teeth rounded, bluntly mucronate. *Petioles* nearly cylindrical, or slightly flattened on the upper side, thickly clothed with short white down, and a few longer hairs intermixed, dilated at the base. *Stipules* large, joined to the base of the petioles, ovately lanceolate, taper-pointed, generally toothed. *Scape* long, not much branched, leafy, thickly clothed with soft white hairs. *Peduncle* long, cylindrical, villosely hairy. *Involucre* of numerous linear taper-pointed bractes. *Pedicles* very short, scarcely any. *Calyx* 5-cleft, segments lanceolate, acute, all reflexed. *Nectariferous tube* nearly 3 times longer than the calyx, flattened and keeled on each side, a little gibbous at the base. *Petals* 5, spreading, of a dark velvet on a crimson ground: upper ones obovate, slightly emarginate, reticulately veined near the base; lower ones spatulately ligulate, rounded. *Filaments* 10, united at the base, 7 of them bearing anthers, which in our specimen were all sterile; one of the filaments a broad spatulate one, which makes it belong to the same section as P. *sanguineum.* ***Style*** flesh coloured, pubescent near the base, and smooth upwards. ***Stigmas*** 5, pale red, reflexed.

A very curious hybrid production, raised at the Nursery of Mr. Colvill in 1823, from a seed of P. *sanguineum* that had been fertilized by the pollen of ***Hoarea*** *undulæflora*; its habit is nearer the latter parent, but its smoothness and the colour of its flowers are more like the former: nothing, we imagine, can surpass them in brilliancy when in full bloom; those are produced in succession from May to September, and sometimes later. Before the present plant flowered, we could scarcely believe that the number stick was right in the pot, it was so very different from its parent, but we are now convinced that it was quite correct. We have also seen another plant in flower, raised from seed collected at the same time, and from the same plant, that is still more singular; the petals are very narrow, and nearly black, with scarlet margins, and the habit of the plant is exactly that of ***Hoarea***, but it still belongs to this section. Some other very curious plants, that were raised at the same time from seeds collected from the same parent, and have not yet flowered, are very singular; one in particular, has a leaf very like P. *echinatum*, and a succulent stem resembling P. *cortusæfolium.*

The present subject succeeds well in an equal mixture of turfy loam, peat, and sand, as already recommended for plants of this tribe, giving it scarcely any water in Winter, and none when in a dormant state. The best method of increasing it is by the little tubers from its roots.

262
1
2
Pub by J. Ridgway 169 Piccadilly June 1. 1825.

HOARREA rosea.

Rose-coloured Hoarea.

H. *rosea*, acaule, foliis laciniato-lobatis obtusis dentatis tomentosis, scapo simplici longissimo, umbellis multifloris, petalis concoloribus inferioribus multo minoribus, tubo nectarifero calyce reflexo quadruplo longiore.

Hoarea rosea. *Swt. hort. brit. p. —. n.* 62. *inedit. Supra, fig.* 1.

Pelargonium roseum. *DC. prodr.* 1. *p.* 651. *n.* 31. *Hort. Kew. ed.* 2. *v.* 4. *p.* 161.

Pelargonium condensatum. *Pers. syn.* 2. *p.* 227.

Geranium roseum. *Andrews's reposit. t.* 173.

Root tuberous. *Stemless. Leaves* crowning the root, radiately spreading, sinuately lobed, very blunt, more or less toothed with blunt rounded teeth, and clothed with a white downy tomentum. *Petioles* furrowed on the upper side and rounded on the lower, clothed with soft spreading hairs, as are the scapes, pedicles, and calyx. *Scape* very long, simple, nearly cylindrical. *Umbel* compact, many flowered. *Involucre* of several linear, acute, fringed bractes. *Pedicles* short, about the length, or scarcely as long as the bractes. *Calyx* 5-cleft, segments lanceolate, the upper one erect, concave; the others reflexed. *Nectariferous tube* unequal in length, from 3 to 4 times as long as the calyx. *Petals* 5, of a bright rose colour, the 2 upper ones much the largest, obovate, slightly emarginate, a little recurved; lower ones spatulately oblong, obtuse, spreading. *Stamens* 10, united in a tube, 5 only bearing anthers. *Style* flesh-coloured, longer than the stamens. *Stigmas* 5, more or less reflexed.

This beautiful species, which was raised from Cape seeds by Mr. Colvill, in 1792, has now, we believe, quite disappeared from all the collections of this country, although Mr. Colvill informs me that it grew very freely, and that he had once the greater part of a house filled with it; but at that time the Heaths were more in fashion than any other plants, so that it got neglected, and at last was lost altogether. We have published this figure, to induce collectors to try to introduce it again to this country, as it would certainly be a valuable acquisition. Mr. Colvill remembers several other very fine species, raised at the same time, which have never been published, one in particular that flowered with him in large panicles of yellow flowers, which he named *speciosissimum;* this, as well as most of the others, have now disappeared. Our figure was copied from an original drawing, done by the late Mr. Sydenham Edwards, and now in the possession of Mr. Colvill. We have added, at the bottom of our plate, a single flower of another very splendid plant, the *Geranium Grenvilliæ* of Andrews, which has also been lost to our collections for some years, and which we propose as a distinct genus under the name of GRENVILLEA.

GRENVILLEA. *Calyx* 5-partitus: laciniis subæqualibus, suprema desinente in tubum nectariferum. *Corolla* 5-petala, irregularis: 2 superiora multo majora, longe unguiculata. *Filamenta* 10, basi connata: 4 antherifera declinata apice adscendentia. 6 sterilia abbreviata subulata recta.

G. *conspicua*, acaule, foliis spathulato-ovatis obovatisve grosse crenatis villosis, scapo longissimo subramoso, umbellis multifloris, petalis superioribus emarginatis, tubo nectarifero calyce subtriplo longiore.

Grenvillea conspicua. *Swt. hort. brit. p. —. inedit. Supra* 262. *f.* 2.
Geranium Grenvilliæ. *Andrews geran. c. ic.*

This fine species is mentioned by Mr. Andrews as a native of Africa, near the Namaqua Land, and from thence was introduced, in 1810, by the Right Honourable Lord Grenville; we do not know that it ever was for sale at any of the Nurseries, and has now entirely disappeared.

263.
E. D. Smith del.
Pub. by J. Ridgway 169 Piccadilly June 1 1825.
S. Watts sc.

HOAREA undulæflora.

Wave-flowered Hoarea.

H. *undulæflora*, foliis hirsutis: inferioribus simplicibus rotundato-ovatis; superioribus trifidis ternatisque raro pinnatifidis, umbellis compositis multifloris, calycibus villosis apice barbatis, petalis undulatis patentibus.

Hoarea undulæflora. *Swt. hort. brit. p. —. n. 35. inedit.*

Root tuberous, divided into several crowns at the top. ***Leaves*** very variable, spreading in a radiate form, hairy: *lower ones* simple, roundly oval, very obtuse: *upper ones* ternate or trifid, the middle leaflet of the size and shape of the lower leaves, side ones much smaller, oblong, obtuse: *the leaves* at the base of the scape, pinnatifid. ***Petioles*** long and flexible, slightly flattened on the upper side and rounded on the lower, winged nearly half way up by the stipules, thickly clothed with unequal hairs, as are the scape and peduncles. ***Stipules*** attached to the petioles, the points subulate. ***Scape*** proceeding from the crown of the root, generally producing a small leaf and 3 or 4 bractes at the base of the peduncles. ***Umbels*** many-flowered. ***Involucre*** of several subulately linear villous bractes. ***Calyx*** 5-cleft, villous, and bearded with a little tuft of white hairs, segments linearly lanceolate with membranaceous margins, upper one erect, the others reflexed. ***Nectariferous tube*** slightly flattened, thickly covered with unequal hairs tipped with a white pellucid gland. ***Petals*** 5, the 2 uppermost widest, all narrowly spatulate, very much undulate, obtuse, spreading, from the middle reflexed, of a dark brown, or nearly black, with white ungues. ***Filaments*** 10, united into a tube; 5 fertile ones of nearly the same length, the uppermost rather shortest, all bearing perfect anthers: barren ones very short, and curved inwards. *Pollen* orange-coloured. *Germen* villous. *Style* pale flesh-coloured, very hairy. *Stigmas 5*, revolute.

Several plants of the present species were received from the Cape, by Mr. Colvill, about four years ago, and they have continued to grow and flower freely ever since. We were at first inclined to consider them as varieties of H. *dioica*, but we are now convinced that they are perfectly distinct both from that species and H. *melanantha*. Several very curious mules have also been raised from them at Mr. Colvill's Nursery. Like the rest of its tribe, it succeeds well in a mixture of light turfy loam, peat, and sand, keeping it dry when in a dormant state; and it is readily increased by seeds, or by the little tubers of its roots.

264

E. D. Smith del. Pub. by J. Ridgway 169 Piccadilly June 1. 1825. J. Watts sc.

PELARGONIUM Scottii.

Sir Claude Scott's Stork's-bill.

P. *Scottii*, caule fruticoso ramoso: ramis patentibus villosis, foliis cordatis quinquelobis undulato-plicatis utrinque hirsutis margine incurvis, stipulis ovatis margine recurvis, umbellis plurifloris, tubo nectarifero calyce villoso subæquali v. paulo longiore.

Pelargonium Scottii. *Swt. hort. brit. p.* —. *n.* 335. *inedit.*

Stem shrubby, much branched: *branches* spreading, rather slender, thickly clothed with long spreading villous unequal hairs, as is every other part of the plant except the corolla. *Leaves* cordate, deeply 5-lobed, strongly and numerously nerved underneath, margins much curled and plaited, bent inwards, unequally toothed with rigid rounded teeth; sinuses rounded, often overlapped. *Petioles* short and stout, flattened on the upper side and rounded on the lower, thickened at the base. *Stipules* ovate, acute, sometimes toothed, ciliate, margins reflexed. *Umbels* several flowered. *Peduncle* cylindrical, swollen at the base. *Involucre* of 6 lanceolate acute villous bractes, their margins recurved. *Pedicles* about the length of the bractes. *Calyx* 5-cleft, segments lanceolate, acute, strongly veined, the upper one erect, the others reflexed. *Nectariferous tube* about the length of, or a little longer than the calyx, much flattened on each side, and gibbous at the base. *Petals* 5, the 2 upper ones ovate, oblique at the base, of a bright scarlet, with a dark purple spot in the centre, betwixt it and the base are several slightly branched purple lines; lower ones ligulate, spreading, of a lighter colour. *Filaments* 10, united at the base, 7 bearing anthers, which are seldom perfect. ***Style*** purple, hairy at the base, and smooth upwards. ***Stigmas*** 5, purple, reflexed.

This fine plant is of hybrid origin, and was raised in 1822, at the Nursery of Mr. Colvill, from a seed of P. ***Murrayanum***, that had been fertilized by the pollen of P. ***ignescens***, and it is as near as possible intermediate; we have named it in compliment to Sir Claude Scott, a distinguished Horticulturist, and a liberal promoter of the Science of Botany.

Like its nearest allies, the present plant succeeds well in a mixture of light turfy loam, peat, and sand, and requires to be kept in a warm light situation in Winter, at which season it requires but little water; its best season of flowering is in Summer, and early in Autumn, the Spring flowers not being near so large. Cuttings strike root without difficulty, planted in pots in the same sort of soil, and placed on a shelf in the greenhouse.

265.

Pub by J. Ridgway 169 Piccadilly July 1. 1825.

PELARGONIUM signatum.

Marked-leaved Stork's-bill.

P. *signatum,* caule fruticoso ramoso; ramis gracilibus erecto-patentibus villosis, foliis cordatis oblongis acutis 5-7-lobis acute dentatis piloso-pubescentibus: lobis planis divaricatis acutiusculis, stipulis cordato-ovatis acuminatis, umbellis 4-6-floris, tubo nectarifero calyce subæquali.

Pelargonium signatum. *Swt. hort. brit. p. —. n.* 322. *ined.*

Stem shrubby, branching, of a woody texture: *branches* slender, erect or slightly spreading, thickly clothed with long, spreading, villous, unequal hairs, as are the petioles, peduncles, bractes, and calyx. *Leaves* cordately oblong, acute, flat or slightly waved, 5 or 7 lobed, toothed with numerous sharp rigid teeth, covered on both sides with a hairy pubescence, roughish and slightly viscid, marked in the centre with a dark brown mark, sometimes much stronger than at others; lobes broad, distant, divaricately spreading, acute. *Petioles* long and slender, flattened on the upper side and rounded on the lower, widened at the base. *Stipules* cordately-ovate, taper-pointed, fringed. *Peduncles* cylindrical, 4 to 6-flowered. *Involucre* of 6 ovate or lanceolate acute fringed bractes, all united at the base. *Pedicles* unequal in length, some not so long, others longer than the bractes. *Calyx* 5-cleft, segments broadly lanceolate, acute, the upper one largest, erect; the others reflexed. *Nectariferous tube* about the length of the calyx, flattened on each side and gibbous at the base. ***Petals*** 5, the 2 upper ones broadly cuneate, of a reddish pink, marked at the base with numerous branching purple lines, lower ones narrower, of a pale pink. ***Filaments*** 10, united at the base, hairy, 7 bearing perfect anthers. ***Style*** purple, slightly hairy at the base, and smooth upwards. ***Stigmas*** 5, purple, reflexed or revolute.

This pretty plant is of hybrid origin, and appears to be intermediate between P. *glutinosum* and perhaps P. *rubescens,* but it is quite impossible to speak with any degree of certainty. It was raised from seed by Mr. Smith, in the collection of the Earl of Liverpool at Coombe Wood: it is a very distinct plant from any other, and is one of the earliest flowering sorts, which makes it the more desirable. P. *chrysanthemifolium*, P. ***Palkii***, and the present plant, we observed this Spring in full flower, for nearly a month before any of the other sorts began to bloom, which we consider very well worth noticing. The present plant is of free growth, though it never attains a large size, but makes a nice compact bush; it is also amongst the hardiest of the red flowered tribe, and thrives well in a mixture of sandy loam and peat. Cuttings strike root readily planted in pots in the same kind of soil, and placed in a sheltered situation.

266.

E. D. Smith del. Pub. by J. Ridgway 169 Piccadilly July 1.1825. J. Watts sc.

CAMPYLIA variegata.

Variegated-flowered Campylia.

C. *variegata*, caule suberecto ramoso; ramis patentibus, foliis ovalibus undulatis inæqualiter dentatis apice truncatis tomentoso-velutinis, stipulis ovatis acutis, pedunculis paniculatis, umbellis 3-5-floris, petalis superioribus rotundatis inferioribus ovato-oblongis, tubo nectarifero brevissimo calyce duplo breviore.

Campylia variegata. *Swt. hort. brit. p.* —. *n.* 2. *ined.*

Stem shrubby, nearly erect, branching; branches spreading, thickly clothed with dense wool, and short reflexed hairs. *Leaves* oval, rounded at the base, sometimes auriculate, the point truncate, toothed with numerous unequal short bluntish teeth, strongly and numerously nerved, the nerves much branched, thickly clothed on both sides with short close pressed silky hairs, which gives them a velvetty appearance. *Petioles* long and slender, slightly flattened on the upper side, and rounded on the lower. *Stipules* ovate, taper-pointed, keeled, clasping the stem, sometimes bifid. *Peduncles* panicled, thickly clothed with short tomentum, and small hairs intermixed. *Umbels* 3 to 5-flowered. *Involucre* of six bractes, all united at the base; bractes short, ovate, obtuse, fringed. *Pedicles* long and spreading, bent near the flower, thickly clothed with unequal spreading hairs. *Calyx* 5-cleft, segments erect, ovate, obtuse, concave, keeled at the back, with red margins, villous, bearded at the points. *Petals* 5, the 2 upper ones broad, nearly round or slightly emarginate, eared just above the short unguis, beautifully variegated with white and purple, with a dark velvet patch at the base:

lower ones of an oblong oval, of a bright lilac, with a purple spot at the base. ***Stamens*** 10, united at the base, 5 bearing anthers, which in our specimens were all imperfect, 2 upper sterile ones, elongated and recurved, of a dark purple. ***Style*** clothed at the base with unequal, spreading hairs, the upper part smooth. ***Stigmas*** 5, purple, reflexed.

This very handsome plant is a hybrid production, and is intermediate between C. *cana* and C. *holosericea;* it was raised at the Nursery of Mr. Colvill from seed, in 1823, and flowered this Spring for the first time, and we consider it the most beautiful plant of the tribe that has yet been raised; like its relatives, it grows freely in a mixture of turfy loam, peat, and sand; and cuttings strike root readily, if taken off in the young wood, and planted in pots in the same sort of soil, and placed on a shelf in the greenhouse.

267.

E. D. Smith del. Pub. by J. Ridgway 169 Piccadilly July 1. 1825. J. Watts sc.

PELARGONIUM delicatum.

Delicate Stork's-bill.

P. *delicatum*, caule erecto ramoso: ramis patentibus, foliis cuneatis 5-lobis incisis dentatis planis, pedunculis 2-3-floris, petalis patentibus inferioribus spatulato-ligulatis, tubo nectarifero calyce longiore.

Pelargonium delicatum. *Hoare Mss. Colv. catal. ed. 2. p. 23. col. 2. Swt. hort. brit. p. —. n. 237. ined.*

Stem shrubby, very much branched: *branches* weak and slender, scarcely strong enough to support their own weight when grown long and in flower, which often causes them to be bent and crooked, thickly clothed with soft villous hairs, as are the petioles, peduncles, and calyx. *Leaves* flat, wedge-shaped, 5-lobed, incised and toothed with pointed teeth; lower lobes deep and spreading; upper ones shallow. *Petioles* flattened and channelled on the upper side and convex on the lower, dilated at the base. *Stipules* ovately lanceolate, oblique, broad at the base, taper-pointed and ciliate. *Peduncles* slender, 2 to 3-flowered. *Involucre* of, from 4 to 6 narrow, subulately-linear, taper-pointed, fringed bractes. *Pedicles* long and slender, unequal in length. *Calyx* 5-cleft, segments lanceolate, acute, the upper one erect, the others spreading. *Nectariferous tube* unequal in length, sometimes double the length of the calyx, at other times but little longer, flattened and furrowed on each side. *Petals* 5, unguiculate, the 2 upper ones obovate, oblique at the base, of a rosy lilac, with a dark purple spot in the centre, and several dark lines branching from it: lower petals spatulately ligulate, of a lighter colour. *Filaments* 10, united at the base, 7 bearing anthers. *Germen* and *aristæ* villous. *Style* very hairy. *Stigmas* 5, revolute.

Our drawing was taken from a plant sent us by Sir R. C. Hoare, under the name that we have adopted; it is of hybrid origin; but what its parents were, is not easy to be ascertained; it is related to P. *hermannifolium*, or perhaps to P. *ternatum*, and has most probably been mixed with one of the larger leaved sorts; it is an abundant bloomer, and its habit, leaves, and flowers, are dissimilar to any other with which we are acquainted; this makes it the more desirable; it is also of free growth, thriving well in any rich light soil, or a mixture of sandy loam and peat suits it very well; cuttings soon strike root, potted in the same sort of soil, and placed in a sheltered situation.

268.

Smith del. Pub by J. Ridgway 169 Piccadilly July 1. 1825. Watts sc.

GERANIUM lividum.

Wrinkled-leaved Cranes-bill.

G. *lividum,* caule simplici tereti erecto, foliis radicalibus novemlobis: lobis patentibus obtusis inciso-dentatis; caulinis 5-7-lobis acutis, calycibus simplicibus pilosis, petalis planis margine undulatis.

Geranium lividum. *L'Herit. ger. t.* 39. *Willden. sp. pl.* 3. *p.* 701. *Pers. syn.* 2. *p.* 235. *Hort. Kew. ed.* 2. *v.* 4. *p.* 186.

Geranium patulum. *Vill. dauph.* 3. *p.* 371. G. subcæruleum. *Schleich. cat.* 25.

Perennial, herbaceous. *Stems* several from the same root, from eighteen inches to 3 feet in height; simple, not forked, cylindrical, thickly clothed with unequal villous hairs. *Root-leaves* with long petioles, very large, 9-lobed, rugose or wrinkled, the lobes spreading, wedge-shaped, obtuse, unequally cut and toothed, entire at the base, the teeth bluntly rounded: *petioles* nearly cylindrical, villosely hairy: *Stem-leaves* on shorter petioles, the upper ones nearly sessile, lower ones 7-lobed, upper ones 5-lobed, villosely hairy on both sides, lobes deeply divided, much spreading, more acute, and the teeth rather sharper: *petioles* nearly cylindrical, swollen at the base. *Peduncles* opposite to the leaves, 2-flowered, rather slender, nearly cylindrical, thickened at the base, thickly clothed with short hairs, and longer ones intermixed. *Involucre* of 4 small, oblong, membranaceous, blunt, fringed bractes. *Pedicles* cylindrical, thickened just below the flower. *Calyx* of 5 sepals, which are ovately-lanceolate, concave, bluntish, and terminated by a very short blunt point, clothed with spreading villous hairs. ***Petals*** 5, roundly obcordate, flat, with undulate margins, slightly emarginate, of a bluish lilac, lighter toward the base, where they are streaked with light blue. ***Stamens*** 10, all fertile, united at the base, ***filaments*** dilated downwards, fringed with long hairs near the base, and smooth upwards. ***Style*** green, slightly pubescent. ***Stigmas*** 5, spreading. ***Carpella*** 5, very hairy, transversely ribbed.

This fine herbaceous perennial has been considered by some authors as a variety of G. *phæum*, from which we consider it as distinct as any species in a natural genus had need be; this, as far as we have observed, always produces long simple stems, whereas, those of G. *phæum* are always forked; this is also a much stronger growing plant, its leaves are larger, more divided, and more pubescent; besides other distinctions, whether G. *fuscum* be as distinct or not, we have not yet ascertained, but when growing together they appear to us very different; the present plant is a very fine hardy perennial, thriving well in the open ground, in the common garden soil, where it continues to bloom for a considerable time, and ripens plenty of seed, by which it may be readily increased; it may also be propagated by dividing at the root. Our drawing was taken from a plant communicated by Mr. Anderson, from the Garden belonging to the Apothecaries' Company at Chelsea, in May last.

269

E. D. Smith del. Pub. by J. Ridgway 169 Piccadilly Aug 1. 1825 J. Watts sc.

PELARGONIUM Couttsiæ.

Mrs. Coutts's Stork's-bill.

P. *Couttsiæ*, foliis cordatis subtrilobis undulatis inæqualiter et rigide dentatis pubescentibus, umbellis plurifloris, calycibus reflexis, petalis inferioribus obovato-oblongis undulatis, tubo nectarifero calyce parum longiore.

Pelargonium Couttsiæ. *Swt. hort. brit. p. —. n.* 293.

Stem shrubby, erect, not much branched. ***Leaves*** cordate, generally 3-lobed, more or less undulate, rather succulent, and of a greasy appearance, rather rough to the touch, unequally toothed with numerous sharp rigid teeth, of a bright green on the upper side and paler underneath, strongly 3-nerved from the base, the nerves more or less branched. ***Petioles*** flattened on the upper side and convex on the lower, thickly clothed with unequal, spreading, long, soft hairs, as are the peduncles, bractes, and calyx. ***Stipules*** lanceolate, acute, broad at the base. ***Umbels*** several-flowered. ***Peduncle*** cylindrical. ***Involucre*** of 6 to 9 bractes, which are imbricate, ovate, acute, concave, and fringed. ***Pedicles*** more than double the length of the bractes, hairy. ***Calyx*** 5-cleft, upper segment ovate, acute, erect, the others unequal, oblong or lanceolate, reflexed. ***Petals*** 5, the 2 upper ones oblongly-obovate, oblique at the base, a little rugged, of a red salmon colour, with a purple spot in the centre more or less conspicuous, or sometimes wanting, and from it to the base is a large white stripe, from which branch several dark purple stripes, and also some across it: lower petals oblong, inclining to obovate, much undulate, strongly veined, of a lighter colour.

Filaments 10, united at the base, 7 bearing anthers: *pollen* orange-coloured. *Germen* villous. *Style* quite smooth, purple. *Stigmas* 5, purple, spreading, their points revolute.

This fine plant is of hybrid origin, and was raised from seed, at the Nursery of Mr. More, in the King's Road, Chelsea, where our drawing was made last Autumn. We cannot speak with precision as to its parents; but from its habit it appears to be nearly intermediate between P. *triumphans* and P. *rubescens*: it is a fine strong-growing plant and a free flowerer, and continues to bloom the greater part of the Summer; it is also as hardy as any of the tribe, and grows readily in any rich light soil, or a mixture of sandy loam and peat will suit it very well. Cuttings root freely, planted in pots in the same sort of soil, and placed in a sheltered situation.

Mr. More has succeeded in raising several other very fine hybrid sorts, which we shall soon take the opportunity of publishing; one in particular, that is intermediate between P. *ignescens* and a variety of P. *quercifolium*, and which he calls his Victory, is of a most brilliant colour, which we should suppose was scarcely to be surpassed.

270.

E. D. Smith del. Pub. by J. Ridgway 169 Piccadilly Aug. 1. 1825. F. Watts sc.

PELARGONIUM Belladonna.

Smith's painted lady Stork's-bill.

P. ***Belladonna***, caule fruticoso erecto ramoso, foliis planis basi trinerviis acute serrato-dentatis glabriusculis; inferioribus reniformibus quinquelobis; superioribus cuneatis 3-5-lobis acutis, umbellis 3-5-floris, petalis superioribus ovatis calyce duplo longioribus, tubo nectarifero calyce acuto paulo longiore.

Pelargonium Belladonna. *Swt. hort. brit. p. —. n.* 278.

Stem shrubby, erect, branching: ***branches*** spreading, glossy, thickly clothed with long unequal spreading white hairs, as are the petioles, peduncles, and nectariferous tube. ***Leaves*** flat, strongly three-nerved at the base, the nerves much branched, deeply and sharply toothed with very unequal sharp rigid teeth, smooth and glossy, the nerves and margins a little hairy: lower ones kidney-shaped, 5-lobed, rather broader than long: upper ones wedge-shaped, acute, 3 to 5-lobed, deeply and sharply toothed, slightly fringed. ***Petioles*** broad, flattened and furrowed on the upper side, and convex on the lower, widened at the base and point. ***Stipules*** ovately lanceolate, acute, sometimes toothed, densely fringed. ***Peduncles*** long and slender, 3 to 5-flowered. ***Involucre*** of 6 lanceolate, taper-pointed, fringed bractes. ***Pedicles*** about the length of the bractes. ***Calyx*** 5-cleft, segments long and slender, lanceolate, taper-pointed, slightly hairy and fringed. ***Nectariferous tube*** longer than the calyx, flattened on each side and gibbous at the base. ***Petals*** 5, the 2 upper ones ovate, of a pale blush, shaded with rose, and a faint rosy patch in the centre, and many purple lines below it, more or less branched; lower ones oblong, obtuse, nearly white. ***Filaments*** 10, united at the base, 7 bearing anthers. ***Style*** flesh-coloured, hairy below, and smooth upwards. ***Stigmas*** 5, purple, revolute.

This pretty plant is also a hybrid production, and was raised from seed by Mr. Smith, at the Earl of Liverpool's Garden, Coombe Wood; it is one of the lateral descendants of P. *grandiflorum*, that has probably been muled for several generations, so that it would be quite impossible to speak with certainty as to its origin; in habit and character it comes nearest to P. *amplissimum* of any we know described; but there are plenty of distinguishing marks to keep it distinct from all with which we are acquainted; its colours are variable, and very pleasing; it is also a very free grower, and its flowers are produced in abundance. It succeeds well in any rich light soil, or a mixture of turfy loam and peat will suit it very well. Cuttings strike root freely, planted in pots in the same sort of soil, if placed in a sheltered situation.

Drawn from a strong plant in the select collection of R. H. Jenkinson, Esq. last Autumn, at which season the flowers are in the greatest perfection.

271
E. D. Smith del.
Pub by J. Ridgway 169 Piccadilly. Aug 1. 1825.
S. Watts sc.

GERANIUM macrorhizon.

Long-rooted Crane's-bill.

G. *macrorhizon*, caule basi suffruticoso apice dichotomo, foliis glabris 5-partitis: lobis apice dentatis, calycibus globoso inflatis, petalis integris, staminibus nutantibus. *DC. prodr. syst. nat.* 1. *p.* 640.

Geranium macrorhizum. *Willden. sp. pl.* 3. *p.* 699. *Pers. syn.* 2. *p.* 235. *Hort. Kew. ed.* 2. *v.* 4. *p.* 185. *Jacq. coll.* 1. *p.* 258. *Ic. rar.* 1. *t.* 134. *Cav. diss.* 4. *p.* 212. *t.* 25. *Sims bot. mag.* 2420.

Stem suffrutescent at the base, often a foot in length and branched, scaly. *Leaves* peltate, deeply 5 or 7-parted, smoothish above, densely pubescent underneath; segments deeply toothed, with blunt rounded teeth terminated with a small mucro: *upper leaves* 3-parted, slightly toothed. *Petioles* long, slightly flattened on the upper side and rounded on the lower, swollen at the base, attenuated upwards, slightly pubescent. *Stipules* lanceolate, keeled, mucronate. *Flower-stem* dichotomous, pubescent, of a purplish colour, longer than the leaves. *Peduncles* clustered, dichotomously panicled, 2-flowered. *Bractes* 4, very short, lanceolate, pointed. *Pedicles* short, hairy. *Calyx* globular, inflated: *sepals* 5, unequal in size, strongly 3-ribbed, purplish, mucronate. *Petals* 5, spreading or reflexed, roundly obovate, entire, of a reddish purple, reticulately veined with lighter veins. *Stamens* 10, all bearing anthers, very long, declining, remaining some time after the petals are dropt. *Style* longer than the stamens, smooth, purple. *Stigmas* 5, purple, spreading.

This fine hardy perennial plant is a native of the South of Europe, and differs from most others of the genus by its long filaments, and its suffruticose stem, which approaches to G. *anemonefolium:* it thrives well in almost any soil or situation, but it grows strongest in a rich light ground, where it produces an abundance of flowers, from May to July; it also ripens plenty of seeds, by which it is readily increased. We believe, with a little pains, that some handsome and interesting mules might be raised in this genus, which would be well worth the trouble, as they would all prove hardy, and be an acquisition to our flower gardens. Our drawing was taken from a plant given us by Mr. William Anderson, Curator of the Apothecaries' Garden at Chelsea.

272

E. D. Smith del. Pub. by J. Ridgway 169 Piccadilly Aug 1.1825 J. Watts sc.

PELARGONIUM Bishopæ.

Mrs. Bishop's Stork's-bill.

P. ***Bishopæ***, caule erecto ramoso: ramis patentibus villosissimis, foliis cordatis profunde 5-7-lobis rotundato-obtusis undulatis crenatis hirsutis, umbellis subquinquefloris, pedunculis calycibusque villosis, calycibus reflexis, petalis omnibus obovatis, tubo nectarifero calyce subæquali aut parum longiore.

Pelargonium Bishopæ. *Swt. hort. brit. p. —. n.* 321.

Stem shrubby, of a woody texture, upright, much branched: ***branches*** spreading, very thickly clothed with unequal spreading, white, villous hairs. ***Leaves*** cordate at the base, oblong, roundly obtuse, more or less undulate, deeply 5 or 7-lobed, more or less notched with round shallow notches, strongly nerved underneath, the nerves much branched, hairy on both sides: lobes rounded, spreading, sometimes imbricate: the upper leaves and their lobes more acute, and clothed with longer hairs, of a darkish green colour. ***Petioles*** much flattened on the upper side and convex on the lower, widened at the base, thickly clothed with unequal spreading villous hairs. ***Stipules*** short, cordate, acute, villous, the margins reflexed or revolute. ***Umbels*** generally 5-flowered. ***Peduncles*** short and stout, cylindrical, a little swollen at the base, thickly clothed with unequal villous hairs, as are the bractes, pedicles, and calyx. ***Involucre*** of 6 ovate, acute, imbricate, fringed bractes. ***Pedicles*** short, about the length of, or a little longer than the bractes. ***Calyx*** 5-cleft, segments broadly lanceolate, scarcely acute, the upper one broadest, erect, keeled, the others reflexed. ***Necta-***

riferous tube about the length of, or a little longer than the calyx, much flattened and furrowed on each side, gibbous at the base, villosely hairy. ***Petals*** 5, all obovate, the 2 upper ones rather largest, slightly emarginate, oblique at the base, of a deep bright scarlet, with a dark purple spot in the centre, and numerous dark lines below it, which branch in various directions; lower petals of a lighter colour. ***Filaments*** 10, united at the base, 7 bearing anthers. ***Style*** flesh-coloured, all over hairy. ***Stigmas*** 5, purple, reflexed.

This very beautiful plant is a hybrid production, and is intermediate between P. *ignescens major* and P. *quercifolium*, partaking in an equal degree of both; the shape and size of the flowers, and also the form of the leaves, are nearer the latter parent; but the brilliant colour of the flowers is that of the former. We have named it in compliment to Mrs. Bishop, of Dorking, Surrey, in whose collection it was raised from seed. We are informed that it is in fine bloom at Messrs. Young's Nursery at Epsom, said to be much finer than the specimen from which our drawing was made; it is a free bushy growing plant, and flowers continually all through the Summer and till late in Autumn; it is therefore a very desirable plant for all collections. A mixture of turfy loam, peat, and sand, is a very good soil for it; and young cuttings strike root freely, planted in pots in the same sort of soil, and placed on a shelf in the greenhouse.

273
Pub by J. Ridgway 170 Piccadilly Sep 1. 1825.
S. Watts sc.

273

MONSONIA lobata.

Broad-leaved Monsonia.

M. *lobata,* foliis cordatis 5-7-lobis: lobis obtusis serrato-dentatis subtus petiolis calycibusque pilosiusculis.

Monsonia lobata. *DC. prodr.* 1. *p.* 638. *Willd. sp. pl.* 3. *p.* 718. *Botan. magaz. t.* 385.

Stem herbaceous, or scarcely suffruticose, rather succulent, 2 or 3 forked, generally very crooked, procumbent if not supported. *Leaves* cordate or cordately ovate, 5 or 7-lobed, smooth and glossy on the upper side, and slightly hairy underneath, strongly 5-nerved, the nerves branched: lobes blunt, serrately toothed, with small rather bluntish teeth. *Petioles* nearly cylindrical, long and slender, slightly hairy. *Stipules* lanceolate, acute, slightly fringed. *Peduncles* very long, cylindrical, clothed with short unequal hairs, all tipped with a small gland. *Involucre* of 6 narrowly lanceolate, taper-pointed, keeled, and fringed bractes. *Calyx* of 5 sepals, connected at the base, or more properly of one sepal deeply 5-parted. *Sepals* nearly equal, lanceolate, acute, 3-nerved, with membranaceous margins. *Petals* 5, widely spreading, not imbricate, obovate, with a longish unguis, deeply 5-toothed, the teeth bluntish, underneath of a greenish yellow, marked with 5 longitudinal purple lines that are slightly branched; upper side of a pale blush, redder near the base. *Stamens* 15, in 5 sets, 3 in each, all connected at the base, and surrounding the stigmas: *filaments* dark purple, flattened and fringed: *pollen* orange-coloured. *Stigmas* 5, dark purple, revolute.

Our drawing of this ornamental plant was taken at the Nursery of Mr. Colvill, in June last; it is an old inhabitant of our gardens, having been introduced into them from the Cape, ever since the year 1774; but it is still far from being common, and is not so much cultivated as it deserves to be, probably from want of a proper mode of treatment. The best soil, to have it thrive and flower well, is an equal mixture of turfy loam, peat, and sand, and the pots to be well drained with potsherds broken small, or they will be liable to suffer with moisture in winter, at which season it requires but very little water; but in summer, when it is growing freely, it requires a constant supply. The best method of propagating it is by cuttings of the root, planted with their tops above the surface of the mould; those require no water for the first 2 or 3 days, until the wound is dried over; they must then be supplied with a little, and they will soon make nice young plants.

We have lately received seeds of M. *ovata* brought from the Cape by Mr. W. Synnet, who had been residing there, in the interior, for four years; we have also received from him seeds of that rare and little known plant, *Grielum laciniatum*, which we have long been wishing to procure, and plants of it are already growing; the styles in it were not hardened into a spine, as in G. *tenuifolium*, though they were very rigid and persistent; the calyx is also persistent and hardened, but not so much as in the latter species. From the same gentleman we have received both seeds and roots of several other curious Geraniaceæ, which we hope soon to flower, and to have an opportunity of publishing. Mr. Colvill has also procured from him a fine collection of bulbs, consisting of different species of Gladiolus, Ixia, Moræa, and other genera belonging to Irideæ, Asphodeleæ, and Melanthaceæ; amongst them, we believe, there are some curious new genera.

274
E. D. Smith del.
Pub. by J. Ridgway 170 Piccadilly. Sept 1825.
S. Watts sc.

PELARGONIUM polytrichum.

Many-haired Stork's-bill.

P. *polytrichum,* foliis cordatis utrinque pilosis: inferioribus undulato-lobatis inæqualiter cartilagineo-dentatis, superioribus cuneato-cochleatis sublobatis inciso-dentatis, stipulis oblongis acutis subdentatis ciliatis, pedunculis plurifloris, tubo nectarifero calyce reflexo subæquali.

Pelargonium polytrichum. *Swt. hort. brit. p. —. n.* 385.

Stem shrubby, erect or a little flexuose, branching, thickly clothed with unequal long spreading villous white hairs, as is every other part of the plant, except the corolla. *Leaves* cordate, acute, hollow at the base; lower ones very large and spreading, very much undulate, obsoletely 5 or 7-lobed, flaccid, unequally toothed with numerous rigid cartilaginous teeth; strongly and numerously nerved underneath, the nerves branching: upper ones wedge-shaped or spoon-shaped, lobed or incised, deeply and sharply toothed with rigid unequal teeth. *Petioles* long, much flattened on the upper side, and convex on the lower. *Stipules* oblong or ovately lanceolate, taper-pointed, generally toothed, and fringed with numerous long spreading hairs. *Peduncles* long, cylindrical, several-flowered. *Involucre* cup-shaped, consisting of 6 or 7 broad ovate, acute, keeled bractes, some of which are frequently toothed. *Pedicles* longer than the bractes. *Calyx* 5-cleft, segments broadly lanceolate, acute, the upper one erect, the others reflexed. *Nectariferous tube* about the length of the calyx, flattened on each side, and gibbous at the base. *Petals* 5, the 2 upper ones obovate, oblique at the base, with a longish unguis, white, tinged with blush, and marked with a dense cluster of dark purple lines, terminated in lilac, which are much branched, and extend above half way over the petals; lower ones oblong, blunt, the margins slightly notched, or uneven, of a pure white. ***Filaments*** 10, united at the base, 7 bearing anthers. ***Style*** purple, all over hairy. ***Stigmas*** 5, purple, reflexed.

This pretty plant is of hybrid origin, and was raised from seed at the Nursery of Mr. More, in the King's Road, Chelsea, where our drawing was made in June last; one of its parents, we should suspect, was P. *involucratum maximum*, and the other, one of the smaller growing sorts; but it is not easy to determine with certainty the precise species. It is a free growing plant, and as hardy as any one in the genus; it is also a good flowerer, and thrives well in any rich light soil, or a mixture of turfy loam and peat will suit it very well. Cuttings will strike root freely, if planted in pots in the same sort of soil, and placed in a sheltered situation.

275.

PELARGONIUM mucronatum.

Mucronated Stork's-bill.

P. *mucronatum,* ramis subflexuosis patulis hirsutis, foliis subcordatis quinquelobis grosse dentatis glabris, pedunculis 3-5-floris, calycibus patentibus, tubo nectarifero calyce subæquali.

Pelargonium mucronatum. *Swt. hort. brit. p. —. n.* 297.

Stem shrubby, branching: *branches* spreading, flexuose, thickly clothed with short spreading hairs, and longer ones intermixed. *Leaves* slightly cordate at the base, 5-lobed, deeply and sharply toothed, with long sharp-pointed cartilaginous teeth, smooth and glossy, or very slightly pubescent, the margins slightly ciliate, underneath punctate with innumerable very minute dots, strongly nerved, the nerves not much branched. *Petioles* rather slender, nearly cylindrical, or a little flattened on the upper side, also unequally hairy. *Stipules* broadly lanceolate, taper-pointed, concave, hairy and fringed. *Peduncles* bent, unequally hairy, 3 to 5-flowered. *Involucre* of about 6 broadly lanceolate, concave, mucronate, hairy bractes. *Pedicles* scarcely longer than the bractes, villous. *Calyx* 5-cleft, segments very long, lanceolate, acute, of a brown colour, upper one rather broadest, erect, the others more or less spreading, villosely hairy. *Nectariferous tube* broad, and flattened on each side, gibbous at the base, about the length of the calyx, also irregularly hairy. *Petals* 5, the 2 upper ones obovate, oblique at the base, of a purplish red, with a large dark spot in the centre, and numerous dark purple lines branching nearly all over the petals; above the spot are lighter veins: lower petals oblong, obtuse, of a bright lilac. ***Filaments*** 10, united at the base, 7 bearing perfect anthers. ***Style*** purple, hairy at the base, and smooth upwards. ***Stigmas*** *5*, purple, fringed and revolute.

Also a hybrid production, raised from seed by Mr. W. Smith, at the Earl of Liverpool's, Coombe Wood; from its habit and appearance we should pronounce one of its parents to be P. ***Smithii***, and the other P. ***macranthon***, as it is exactly intermediate between the two. It is very distinct from any other sort with which we are acquainted, and is, in our opinion, as desirable a plant as any of the tribe, the colour of the flowers being different from all others; it is also a free strong growing sort, and produces a great abundance of bloom; a mixture of sandy loam and peat suits it very well; and cuttings strike root freely, planted in pots in the same kind of soil, and placed on a shelf in the greenhouse.

276

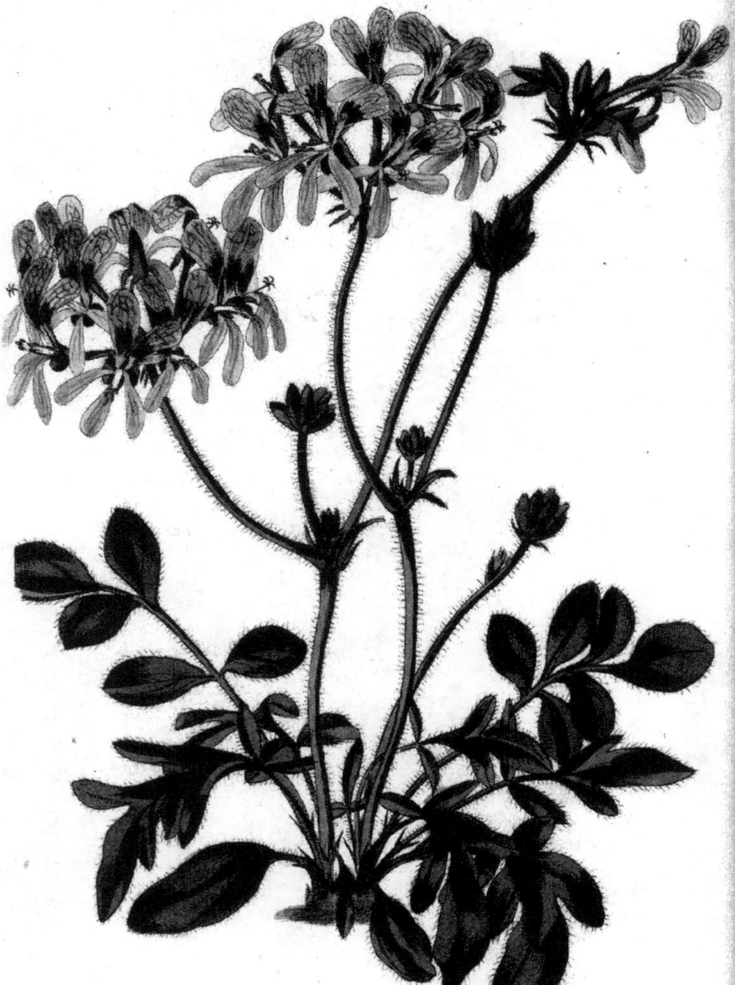

Smith del. Pub by J Ridgway 170 Piccadilly Sep 1 1825 S Watts sc

HOAREA labyrinthica.

Labyrinth-flowered Hoarea.

H. *labyrinthica,* foliis piloso-canescentibus: inferioribus simplicibus ovatis ternatisque; superioribus pinnatifidis pinnatisque: foliolis segmentisque oblongo-ovatis oppositis alternisque utrinque pilosis canescentibus, scapo ramoso, umbellis multifloris, tubo nectarifero calyce reflexo sesquilongiore.

Hoarea labyrinthica. *Swt. hort. brit. p. —. n.* 61.

Root tuberous. ***Stemless.*** ***Leaves*** variable, hairy and canescent; lower ones simple and ovate, trifid or ternate; upper ones pinnatifid or pinnate: *leaflets* opposite and alternate, oblong or ovate, bluntish, hairy and canescent. ***Petioles*** slender, villosely hairy. ***Stipules*** lanceolate, acute, joined at the base of, and decurrent a good way up the petiole. ***Scapes*** branching, and producing several umbels of flowers, thickly clothed with soft unequal hairs, as are the peduncles, calyx, and nectariferous tube. ***Peduncles*** cylindrical. ***Involucre*** of several linear, acute, fringed bractes. ***Umbels*** many-flowered. ***Pedicles*** very short, or altogether wanting. ***Calyx*** 5-cleft, segments lanceolate, acute, upper one erect, concave, the others narrower and reflexed. ***Nectariferous tube*** about half as long again as the calyx. ***Petals*** 5, the 2 upper ones spatulately ligulate, reflexed from about the middle, much veined, the veins crossing each other, marked with a dark purple spot near the bend, which extends into some of the veins: lower ones narrower, of a lighter colour, and scarcely veined. ***Filaments*** 10, united at the base, 5 bearing anthers: barren filaments bent inwards at the points. ***Style*** purple, thickly covered with short stiff hairs. ***Stigmas 5***, purple, reflexed.

This neat little plant is of hybrid origin, and is the produce of ***Dimacria pinnata*** that had been fertilized by H. ***reticulata***; it is related to H. ***venosa***, already published by us, but is sufficiently distinct; it is an abundant flowerer, beginning to bloom in March, and continuing in flower till August; like the other plants of this genus, it succeeds best in an equal mixture of light turfy loam, peat, and sand, requiring no water when in a dormant state; but as soon as it shows an inclination to grow, it should be shifted into fresh mould, and as it grows, will need a constant supply of water; the best method of propagating it is by the little tubers of its roots.

Drawn at the Nursery of Mr. Colvill, last Autumn, where it was raised from seed in 1823.

[illegible]

GERANIACEÆ

[illegible] NATURAL ORDER OF GERANIA[illegible]

[illegible]

277

E. D. Smith del. Pub. by J. Ridgway 169 Piccadilly Oct 1. 1825 J. Watts sc.

PELARGONIUM affine.

Related Stork's-bill.

P. *affine,* caule fruticoso ramoso; ramis villosis, foliis cordatis undulato-lobatis rigidis cartilagineo-dentatis utrinque pilosis, stipulis ovatis acuminatis ciliatis, umbellis plurifloris subpaniculatis, tubo nectarifero calyce reflexo sesquilongiore.

Pelargonium affine. *Colv. catal. ed. 2. p. 23. col. 2. Swt. hort. brit. p.* 79. *n.* 103.

Stem shrubby, erect, branching: ***branches*** erect or slightly spreading, thickly clothed with unequal spreading villous hairs, as is every other part of the plant except the corolla. ***Leaves*** cordate, very much undulate, more or less lobed, rigid, and sharply toothed with brown cartilaginous teeth, fringed round the edges. ***Petioles*** a little flattened on the upper side, and convex on the lower, stoutest at the base. ***Stipules*** ovate, taper-pointed, undulate and fringed. ***Peduncles*** cylindrical, several-flowered, in a sort of panicle. ***Involucre*** of 6 ovately lanceolate, acute bractes. ***Pedicles*** about the length of the bractes, sometimes scarcely as long. ***Calyx*** 5-cleft, upper segment broadest, ovate, acute, erect; the others lanceolate and reflexed. ***Nectariferous tube*** about half as long again as the calyx, much flattened on both sides. ***Petals*** 5, the 2 upper ones obovate, very much oblique at the base, of a dark reddish scarlet, marked with a dark velvetty patch in the centre, from which to the base are several short dark lines, more or less branched, the unguis white: lower petals ligulately oblong, of a lighter colour and much spreading. ***Filaments*** 10, united at the base, 7 bearing anthers. *Germen* and *aristæ* villous. *Style* purple, with a few hairs near the base, the upper part smooth and glossy. *Stigmas* 5, purple, reflexed or revolute.

Our drawing of this plant was taken at the Nursery of Mr. Colvill, where it was raised from seed: it is of hybrid origin, and the seed was produced by P. *involucratum* ε *lilacinum* that had been fertilized by P. *ignescens;* several plants that have been raised by the same parents, have all proved precisely the same, without the least variation; in the same manner as we have noticed by the produce of P. *Mostynæ* mixed with P. *ignescens,* which have invariably produced P. *flammeum,* without variation; we have noticed the same in several other mule productions, so that if any sort should happen to be lost by inattention or otherwise, it might be again raised, if its original parents are known.

The present plant is of very free growth, and an abundant bloomer, and continues to flower the greater part of the year; a mixture of turfy loam, peat, and sand, is a very proper soil for it; and cuttings root readily, planted in pots in the same sort of soil, and placed in a sheltered part of the Greenhouse.

278

E. D. Smith del. Pub. by J. Ridgway 169 Piccadilly Oct. 1 1825. S. Watts sc.

PELARGONIUM limonium.

Lemon-scented Stork's-bill.

P. *limonium,* caule fruticoso ramosissimo, foliis sparsis cordatis 3-5-lobis crispis: lobis divaricatis rotundato-cuneatis inæqualiter dentatis, pedunculis subtrifloris, calycibus reflexis, tubo nectarifero calyce longiore.

Pelargonium limonium. *Swt. hort. brit. p.* 81. *n.* 252.

Stem shrubby, very much branched: *branches* erect or slightly spreading, thickly clothed with short unequal hairs. *Leaves* scattered, cordate at the base, broader than long, 3 to 5-lobed, margins much curled, unequally toothed with short rigid teeth, underneath strongly nerved, the nerves branching, clothed on both sides with short hairs, of a pleasant scent like lemon: lower lobes divaricately spreading, roundly wedge-shaped, slightly 2-lobed: upper one widened upwards, more or less 3-lobed, the point slightly reflexed. *Stipules* small, cordate, acute, sometimes toothed, ciliate. *Peduncles* opposite to a leaf, cylindrical, 2 or 3-flowered, clothed with short unequal hairs. *Involucre* of 6 ovately-lanceolate, acute, fringed bractes. *Pedicles* longer than the nectariferous tube, clothed with short spreading unequal hairs. *Calyx* 5-cleft, upper segment ovate, acute, erect, slightly keeled, the others lanceolate, acute, reflexed, all of them hairy and fringed. *Nectariferous tube* longer than the calyx, much flattened on each side, and gibbous at the base, hairy. *Petals* 5, with long unguis, the two upper ones obovate, slightly oblique, of a bright lilac, tinged with purple, with a large velvetty mark in the centre, and several dark lines below it, and running through it, more or less branched:

lower ones narrowly spatulate, pale lilac. ***Filaments*** 10, united at the base, 7 bearing anthers: pollen orange-coloured. ***Style*** pale flesh-coloured, very hairy, but smooth upwards. ***Stigmas*** 5, bright purple, reflexed.

This pretty little plant is a hybrid production, and is related to P. *crispum*, or some of the Citron scented species; but what its real parents were, is not now to be determined. Our drawing was taken from plants sent to us by Sir R. C. Hoare, from his interesting and extensive collection of Geraniaceæ, at Stourhead; the scent of the leaves is very pleasant, very much resembling that of Lemon; it makes a snug compact little bush, and our plants have been covered with bloom ever since last April, which makes it a very desirable plant; it is also as hardy as any of the genus, thriving well in any rich light soil; or a mixture of loam and peat suits it very well. Cuttings root freely if taken off in the young wood, and planted in pots, and placed in a shady situation.

279
E. D. Smith del.
Publd. by J. Ridgway 170 Piccadilly Oct. 1. 1825
J. Watts sc.

279

PELARGONIUM rutaceum.

Rue-scented Stork's-bill.

P. *rutaceum*, caule carnoso nodoso subsimplici, foliis pinnatis glaucescentibus glabris carnosis: foliolis pinnatifidis: segmentis oblongis acutis inciso-dentatis, petiolis pedunculisque sparse pilosis, umbellis multifloris, floribus pentandris, tubo nectarifero subsessili calyce reflexo 3-4-plo longiore.

Pelargonium rutaceum. *Swt. hort. brit. p.* 84. *n.* 389.

Root large, branching out into numerous tubers, of various shapes and sizes. ***Stem*** fruticose, succulent, knotted unequally in irregular large swellings at the joints, of a brownish glaucous colour, the upper part thickly clothed with long spreading white hairs, and producing a few long slenderish flowering branches. ***Leaves*** like a large fern or umbelliferous plant, the upper ones like Rue, to which the scent also bears a strong resemblance, succulent, glaucous: lower ones very large and spreading, decompoundly divided; others pinnate, the leaflets pinnatifid or bipinnatifid; segments oblong, or sometimes lanceolate, acute, incised or sharply toothed, or sometimes entire. ***Petioles*** nearly cylindrical, swollen at the base, thinly clothed with long spreading hairs, very slender when compared with the large leaf, which it can scarcely support without assistance. ***Stipules*** variable, some broadly cordate, and others lanceolate, acute, slightly hairy and fringed. ***Peduncles*** very long, slightly angular, glaucous, also hairy. ***Involucre*** of numerous lanceolate, acute, fringed bractes, their points terminated by a little tuft of bristly hairs. ***Pedicles*** very short, not half the length of the bractes. ***Calyx*** 5-cleft; segments ovate, bluntish, pubescent, all tipped with a tuft of long white hairs. ***Nectariferous tube*** pubescent, a little flattened on each side, more than 3 times longer than the calyx. ***Petals*** 5, roundly obovate, the 2 upper ones largest; the upper part of a dark chocolate colour, edged with yellow, the lower part also pale yellow: lower ones narrower, dark chocolate colour, edged with yellow. ***Filaments*** 10, united at the base, 5 bearing perfect anthers, the back one a large spatulate one, as in the Section Monospatalla, two back sterile ones a little reflexed; those, also, make an attempt at anthers, but it is very imperfect; the other 3 incurved, as in its parent. ***Style*** green, slightly hairy. ***Stigmas*** 5, yellowish, reflexed.

This curious plant is a hybrid production, and was raised in 1823 at the Nursery of Mr. Colvill, from a seed of P. *multiradiatum* that had been fertilized by the pollen of P. *gibbosum*; it is intermediate between both parents in every part of the plant; even the character of the flowers are intermediate between the two sections, having the 5 fertile anthers of P. *multiradiatum*, with the spatulate filament of P. *gibbosum*, and an attempt at the other two anthers: like its two parents, its flowers are without scent during the day, and in the evening are very strongly scented, and most pleasant at a little distance; the scent of the flowers, as well as the leaves, partake a good deal of the Rue, which is rather too powerful to be near; in the natural arrangement it must be placed with P. *multiradiatum*, in Decandolle's Section Polyactium, to stand next to our Section Monospatalla.

The habit of the present plant is altogether different from any other, which makes it the more desirable; two plants were raised from seeds at the same time, and we cannot perceive the slightest difference in them; they also came in flower together for the first time, in July last; being of a succulent nature, it does not require much water, except when in flower or growing freely; like the other succulent species, it succeeds well in an equal mixture of turfy loam, peat, and sand; and cuttings root freely on a shelf in the Greenhouse.

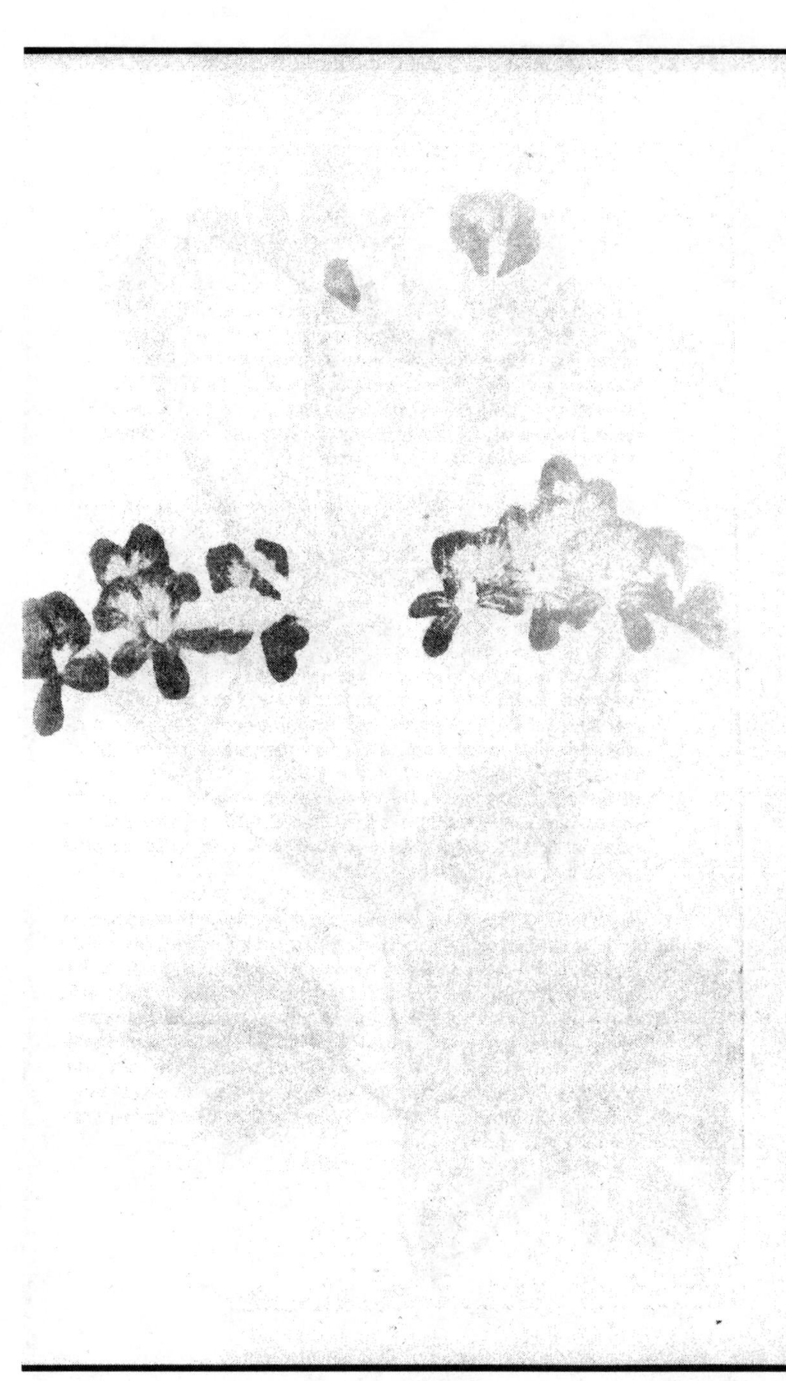

280
E. D. Smith del.
Pub by J. Ridgway 169 Piccadilly Oct. 1. 1825.

PELARGONIUM variifolium.

Various-leaved Stork's-bill.

P. *variifolium,* caule subflexuoso erecto ramoso: ramis gracilibus ad geniculis nodosis, foliis inferioribus cordatis tripartitis inciso-dentatis; superioribus cuneato-ovatis, stipulis lanceolatis acutis, calycibus reflexis, petalis superioribus obovato-rotundatis: inferioribus cuneatis, tubo nectarifero calyce sesquilongiore.

Pelargonium variifolium. *Swt. hort. brit. p.* 84. *n.* 393.

Stem shrubby, erect, branching; ***branches*** slender, swollen at the joints, and clothed with short unequal hairs. ***Leaves*** incised or sharply toothed with large teeth, pubescent on both sides: *lower ones* cordate, deeply 3-parted; lower segments 2-lobed, sharply and unequally toothed; terminal segment generally 5-lobed and sharply toothed: *upper leaves* ovate or cuneate, sharply cut or deeply toothed. ***Petioles*** flattened a little on the upper side, and rounded on the lower, thickly clothed with spreading unequal hairs. ***Stipules*** lanceolate, taper-pointed, clothed with short hairs. ***Peduncles*** cylindrical, axillary, or opposite to a leaf, clothed with spreading unequal hairs. ***Umbels*** several flowered. ***Involucre*** of 6 lanceolate taper-pointed bractes. ***Pedicles*** unequal in length, generally longer than the bractes. ***Calyx*** 5-cleft, segments lanceolate, acute, upper one largest, erect, the others reflexed. ***Nectariferous tube*** about half as long again as the calyx, flattened and furrowed on each side, thinly clothed with hairs. ***Petals*** 5, the two uppermost roundly obovate, attenuated to the base, of a bright scarlet, with an interrupted velvetty patch in the centre, and numerous dark lines that branch nearly all over the petals: lower petals unguiculate, wedge-shaped, of a bright scarlet, with 2 dark lines from the base. ***Filaments*** 10, joined in a tube at the base, 7 bearing anthers, which are generally imperfect. ***Style*** pale coloured, slightly hairy at the base, and smooth upwards. ***Stigmas*** 5, purple, reflexed.

This very pretty and bright flowering plant, which, we are sorry to say, cannot be done justice to by the artist, is a hybrid production, and we believe is the produce of P. *fulgidum*; but what its other parent was, is not so easy to be determined; we should suppose, from its knotted joints, that it is somewhat related to P. *sanguineum*, or to some hybrid species that has been produced by it.

Like the plants to which the present is nearest akin, it succeeds well in an equal mixture of turfy loam, peat, and sand, and continues to bloom successfully all the summer, and until late in autumn; care must be taken, not to sodden it with too much wet, as it is rather impatient of moisture. Cuttings strike root readily, planted in pots, and placed on a shelf in the Greenhouse.

Our drawing was taken from a fine healthy plant, covered with its splendid flowers, in the collection of Robert Henry Jenkinson, Esq. where it was raised from seed.

281

PELARGONIUM luridum.

Lurid Stork's-bill.

P. *luridum*, radice tuberoso maximo rugoso-corticata squamoso, foliis ovatis obtuse dentatis incisisve glabris subpubescentibus, scapo simplici, umbellis multifloris patentissimis, floribus longissime pedicellatis, petalis subæqualibus obovatis demum reflexis, tubo nectarifero calyce quintuplo longiore.

Pelargonium luridum. *Colv. catal. ed. 2. p. 22. col.* 1. *Swt. hort. brit. p.* 78. *n.* 45.

Geranium luridum. *Andrews's geran. c. ic.*

Pelargonium huræfolium *Colv. catal. ed.* 1. *p.* 21. *col.* 2.

Root tuberous, very large, oval or oblong, and clothed with a thick hard woody bark, that is cracked irregularly, and scales off like the bark of a tree. ***Stems*** very short, or none. ***Leaves*** broadly ovate, rounded at the base, or sometimes cuneate, bluntish, incised, and toothed with large bluntly rounded teeth, of a glossy green on the upper side, the underside and margins slightly hairy. ***Petioles*** unequally hairy. ***Stipules*** subpersistent, ovately lanceolate, acute, turning dark brown by age. ***Scapes*** simple, several from one root, sometimes with a leaf or two near the base, at other times without; about the size of a Raven's quill, clothed with very short unequal, almost gland-like hairs, or short pubescence. ***Involucre*** of numerous small taper-pointed bractes. ***Umbels*** from 15 to 24-flowered, divaricately spreading. ***Pedicles*** very long, thickly clothed with short, but unequal hairs, a little swoln and transparent where joined to the nectariferous tube.

Calyx 5-cleft, segments pubescent, all reflexed; upper and lower one broadest, oblong or ovate, obtuse, the other 3, lanceolate and more acute. ***Petals*** 5, nearly equal, obovate, with long unguis, of a straw colour, tinged with brownish copper, spreading when first open, afterwards all reflexed. ***Filaments*** 10, united at the base, 7 bearing anthers, one of them a large spatula shaped one, which produces an anther about half the size of the others. ***Style*** short, smooth, and straw coloured. ***Stigmas*** 5, spreading.

Several roots of this very distinct and curious species, were received from the Cape, by Mr. Colvill, in the year 1820, and was named by us P. ***huræfolium*** in Mr. Colvill's Catalogue, published in 1821, as we had not then seen their flowers; the following year they produced flowers, but not in perfection, though sufficiently so, for us to determine it to be the ***Geranium luridum*** of Mr. Andrews, drawn from a plant at Mr. Lee's, which we recollect having been pointed out to us as a great rarity, as far back as 1811; when we were also informed that there was no means of propagating it; the method now generally adopted of fertilizing the stigmas with the pollen, being at that time scarcely ever attended to: and they seldom produce any offsets to their tubers, so that there is scarcely any means of propagating them, except by seeds.

Mr. Colvill's plants have flowered in great profusion this autumn, when our drawing was made. Like the other plants of this section, it succeeds well in an equal portion of light turfy loam, peat, and sand, requiring no water when in a dormant state, and not a great deal at any time; as it makes but few fibrous roots, the pots must also be well drained with small potsherds, that the water may pass readily off, so that the mould do not get sodden: seeds of it ripen readily, if pains be taken to fertilize the stigmas with the pollen when in bloom.

282

E. D. Smith del. Pub. by J. Ridgway 169 Piccadilly Nov. 1 1825 J. Watts sc.

PELARGONIUM rhodanthum.

Rose-coloured Stork's-bill.

P. *rhodanthum*, ramis pilosis, foliis subcordatis acutis quinquelobis undulato-plicatis argute dentatis ciliatis: supra glabris nitidis: subtus nervisque pilosis, stipulis oblongis acuminatis subdentatis, umbellis laxis plurifloris, petalis lato-obovatis imbricatis, tubo nectarifero calyce reflexo subæquali aut parum longiore.

Pelargonium rhodanthum. *Swt. hort. brit. p.* 84. *n.* 396.

Stem shrubby, flexuose, much branched, thickly clothed with spreading unequal white hairs. ***Leaves*** slightly cordate, acute, 5-lobed, much undulate and plaited, more or less cucullate, sharply toothed with very unequal rigid teeth, and fringed with short hairs, of a smooth glossy green on the upper side, the under side and nerves thinly clothed with spreading white hairs: *upper leaves* inclining to wedge-shaped, 3 to 5-lobed, and very sharply toothed. ***Petioles*** stout, unequal in length, flattened on the upper side, and convex on the lower, thinly clothed with spreading hairs. ***Stipules*** oblong, or sometimes lanceolate, taper-pointed, often toothed and ciliate. ***Peduncles*** long, cylindrical, thinly clothed with spreading hairs. ***Umbels*** several-flowered, loosely spreading. ***Involucre*** of 6 or 8 lanceolate, acute, fringed bractes. ***Pedicles*** unequal in length, sometimes about the length of, at other times twice as long as the bractes. ***Calyx*** 5-cleft, segments lanceolate, reflexed or revolute, very hairy and ciliate, the upper one broadest, more erect and slightly keeled. ***Nectariferous tube*** broadly flattened, and gibbous at the base, about the length of, or a little longer than the calyx. ***Petals*** 5, very broad and much imbricate, roundly obovate; the two upper ones broadest, oblique at the base, of a bright rose colour, a little stained in the centre, and several purple lines from the base, branching in various directions: lower petals rather lighter, about half the breadth of the upper ones. ***Filaments*** 10, united at the base, 7 bearing anthers. ***Style*** flesh-coloured, slightly hairy at the base, and smooth upwards. ***Stigmas*** 5, purple, reflexed, or revolute.

This fine plant is a hybrid production, and has been raised from seed at the Nursery of Mr. More, in the King's Road, where our drawing was made last summer; it is very different from any other of the hybrid sorts to which it is nearest related, and is readily distinguished by its broad petals; we believe, from the shape of those, and the habit of the plant altogether, that one of its parents is P. *macranthon*, and the other is one of the red flowering sorts, but which, it is not easy to guess: it makes a fine appearance when in bloom, as it is a strong growing plant, and its flowers are very large, and produced in great abundance; the colour is also different from most others, being of a lively rose; it is also amongst the hardiest of the red flowering sorts, and grows freely in any light rich vegetable soil, or a mixture of light turfy loam, peat, and sand, will suit it very well. Cuttings will also root freely, if planted in pots, in the same sort of soil, and placed on a shelf in the Greenhouse.

283.

E. D. Smith del. Pub. by J. Ridgway 169 Piccadilly Nov. 1. 1825. S. Watts sc.

ERODIUM glaucophyllum.

Glaucous-leaved Heron's-bill.

E. *glaucophyllum,* caule erecto ramoso: ramis nodoso-articulatis glabris, foliis oblongo-ovatis sublobatis crenatis subcarnosis glaucescentibus glabris subtus nervisque subpubescentibus, pedunculis plurifloris, petalis ellipticis distinctis patentibus, aristis à medio ad apicem longè plumosis.

Erodium glaucophyllum. *DC. prodr.* 1. *p.* 648. *Hort. Kew. ed.* 1. *v.* 2. *p.* 416. *ed.* 2. *v.* 4. *p.* 158. *Willden. sp. pl.* 3. *p.* 636. *Pers. syn.* 2. *p.* 225.

Geranium glaucophyllum. *Cav. diss.* 4. *p.* 221. *t.* 92. *f.* 2. *Dill. elth.* 150. *t.* 124. *f.* 150.

Geranium crassifolium. *Forskahl descr.* 23.

Perennial? herbaceous. *Stem* erect, much branched: *branches* spreading, smooth, knotted at the joints, lengthening out and becoming slender at the points. *Leaves* oblongly ovate, bluntish, slightly lobed, unequally crenate or notched, smooth and glaucous, or slightly pubescent underneath and on the nerves. *Petioles* slender, thickened at the base, slightly flattened on the upper side, scarcely pubescent. *Stipules* elliptic or lanceolate, acute, soon withering and turning brown. *Peduncles* slender, cylindrical, scarcely pubescent, from 2 to several flowered. *Involucre* of several membranaceous scariose bractes. *Pedicles* slender, pubescent, erect when in flower, but reflexed when in seed, the calyx and seed ascending. *Calyx* of 5 sepals, which are oblongly lanceolate, mucronate, strongly nerved and furrowed, with scariose membranaceous margins. ***Petals*** 5, elliptic, distinctly spreading, longer than the calyx, strongly fringed at the base, of a bluish lilac. ***Filaments*** 10, united at the base, 5 bearing anthers; fertile ones winged at the base with subulate points. ***Stigmas*** 5, short and flat, sessile, spreading, dark purple. ***Arista's*** very long, spiral at the base, from the middle to the point feathered, with long white feathered hairs.

This curious and rare plant is generally considered as an annual, but the one from which our drawing was taken has already survived two years, and appears likely to prove perennial, as it is now making strong young shoots, below the flower stems, that are all dying away, so that if the plant was only biennial, we suspect it would have went off altogether at the same time, instead of making young healthy shoots.

Our plant was raised from a seed given us by Mr. Hunneman, who received it from Germany; whether or not it will prove hardy enough to survive our winters in the open air, remains to be ascertained, as the last one can scarcely be called a winter at all, but we intend to try it, as our plant has produced abundance of seeds.

Pub by J. Ridgway 169 Piccadilly Nov 1.1823.

PELARGONIUM volatiflorum.

Flying-flowered Stork's-bill.

P. *volatiflorum*, ramis flexuosis gracilibus, foliis 3-partitis subcanescenti-pubescentibus: segmentis divaricatis dentatis; lateralibus bilobis terminalibus 3-5-lobis inciso-dentatis, stipulis cordato-ovatis acutis, umbellis plurifloris paniculatis, petalis patentissimis, tubo nectarifero calyce subæquali.

Pelargonium volatiflorum. *Swt. hort. brit. p. 84. n. 392.*

Stem shrubby, when large, clothed with a rough cracked bark, much branched: *branches* rather slender, flexuose, more or less spreading, thickly clothed with short spreading unequal white hairs. *Leaves* deeply 3-parted, thickly clothed on both sides with short white hairs, which gives them a hoary appearance: segments divaricately spreading, toothed with very unequal teeth, and tipped with bristle-like hairs: side ones 2-lobed: terminal one 3 to 5-lobed; unequally toothed or cut, teeth more or less acute. *Petioles* a little flattened on the upper side, and convex on the lower, thickly clothed with short spreading unequal hairs. *Stipules* cordately ovate, taper-pointed, very hairy and fringed. *Peduncles* 3 to 7-flowered, in a sort of panicle, thickly clothed with short hairs and a few longer ones intermixed. *Involucre* of 6 lanceolate, acute, fringed bractes. *Pedicles* shorter than the bractes. *Flowers* leaning forwards. *Calyx* 5-cleft, hairy, segments reflexed, acute, the upper one largest, oblong, keeled; the others lanceolate or linear, the margins scariose or membranaceous. *Petals* 5, widely spreading, having an appearance of flying; 2 upper ones narrowly spathulate, reflexed from about the middle, of an orangy scarlet, marked with numerous dark lines and spots, which branch nearly all over the petals: lower petals about half the width, of the same colour, marked with two dark lines near the base, which are also slightly branched. *Filaments* 10, united into an inflated tube, 7 bearing anthers. *Style* pale, very hairy. *Stigmas* 5, purple, revolute, or reflexed.

This very singular plant is a hybrid production, and was raised in the superb collection of R. H. Jenkinson, Esq. from a seed of P. *fulgidum*, which, from the appearance of the present plant, we should suspect had been fertilized by the pollen of P. *verbenæfolium*, as it seems to be exactly intermediate between the two, although its flowers are not so large as many others, yet their number, and the brilliancy of their colour, makes up for that deficiency; the flowers are produced in panicles, so that the upper part of the plant is oftentimes covered with its singular blossoms, which may not unaptly be compared to flying insects, to which, in our opinion, when the petals are spread out, they bear a great resemblance, and from which our specific name is derived.

Like its nearest allies, the present plant succeeds well in an equal mixture of turfy loam, peat, and sand, and cuttings root readily, planted in pots in the same sort of soil, and placed on a shelf in the Greenhouse.

285.

Edwin Smith del. Pub. by J. Ridgway 169 Piccadilly Decr. 1825. J. Watts sc.

PELARGONIUM Moreanum.

More's Victory Stork's-bill.

P. *Moreanum*, caule fruticoso ramosissimo, ramis diffuso-patentibus villosis, foliis cordatis pinnatifido-lobatis utrinque pilosis plicato-crispis: segmentis oblongis sublobatis rotundato dentatis obtusiusculis, stipulis brevi-cordatis acutis subdentatis, pedunculis plurifloris, petalis cuneatis, tubo nectarifero calyce subæquali.

Pelargonium Moreanum. *Swt. hort. brit. p.* 84. *n.* 388.

Stem shrubby, flexuose, very much branched, clothed with a brown rough bark: *branches* more or less bent, very much spreading in all directions, thickly clothed with leaves, and with unequal spreading villous white hairs. *Leaves* cordate, oblong, pinnatifidly divided or deeply lobed, hairy on both sides, strongly nerved underneath and furrowed on the upper side, the nerves much branched: segments plaited, scarcely acute, very much curled, sometimes lobed, and unequally toothed with numerous small rounded teeth. *Petioles* flattened and furrowed on the upper side, and convex on the lower, unequally villous. *Stipules* short, cordate, acute, entire or sometimes sharply toothed, villous and fringed. *Umbels* 5 to 7-flowered. *Peduncles* thickly clothed with unequal spreading villous hairs, as are the bractes, calyx, and nectariferous tube. *Involucre* of 6 broadly lanceolate, acute, keeled, and ciliated bractes. *Pedicles* short, villous. *Calyx* 5-cleft, upper segment erect, ovate, concave, obtuse; the others narrower, oblong or lanceolate, more acute, the margins sometimes scariose or membranaceous, spreading or reflexed. *Petals* 5, all cuneate or wedge-shaped, the two upper ones nearly double the breadth of the lower ones, of a bright orangy scarlet, with a dark velvetty spot in the centre, below which are some shortly branched dark lines; lower petals regularly spreading, 2-nerved from the base. ***Filaments*** 10, connected at the base, 7 bearing anthers, which in our specimens were all imperfect. ***Style*** hispidly hairy. ***Stigmas*** 5, purple, reflexed.

This very fine plant is of hybrid origin, and was raised from seed by Mr. More, in 1823; the seed was produced by P. *ignescens* ε *sterile*, that had been fertilized by P. *dianthiflorum*; the habit and foliage of the plant is altogether that of the latter parent, but the flowers partake in the colour of the former, but they far exceed it in brilliancy: its flowers are also produced in great abundance, frequently 7 on an umbel, and it continues to bloom in succession all the Summer, and till late in Autumn: it also makes a compact bushy plant, and may be grown with advantage in a small pot, where room is of consequence. It requires precisely the same sort of treatment as those to which it is nearest related, succeeding well in a rich light sandy soil, or a mixture of turfy loam, peat, and sand, will suit it very well, being careful not to overwater it in Winter. Cuttings root as freely as any others, if planted in pots, and placed on a shelf in the greenhouse. Our drawing was taken at the Nursery of Mr. More, in August last, and we received a plant of it in full bloom in October.

286

OTIDIA alternans.

Parsley-leaved Otidia.

O. *alternans,* caule fruticoso subcarnoso; ramis pilosis, foliis pinnatisectis; segmentis petiolulatis subalternis cuneiformibus apice inciso-dentatis, umbellis paucifloris. *DC. prodr.* 1. *p.* 655.

Otidia alternans. *Swt. hort. brit. p.* 75. *n.* 6. *Colv. catal. ed.* 2. *p.* 22.

Pelargonium alternans. *Wendl. h. herren.* 1. *p.* 14. *t.* 9. *Willden. sp. pl.* 3. *p.* 687. *Pers. syn.* 2. *p.* 233. *Hort. Kew. ed.* 2. *v.* 4. *p.* 182.

Pelargonium alternatim-pinnatum. *Wendl. obs. p.* 53.

Stem succulent, very much branched: *branches* short, erect, succulent, rough and knotted, compact, clothed with a brown glossy bark; the young shoots thickly clothed with short densely villous hairs. *Leaves* pinnate, thickly clothed with long white hairs: *leaflets* petiolate, generally alternate, cuneate, 3-lobed or 3-parted, the points curled or undulate, more or less cut or toothed, the teeth bluntish. *Petioles* slender, slightly flattened on the upper side and rounded on the lower, thickly clothed with long spreading white hairs, of very unequal lengths. *Stipules* short, cordately ovate, acute, rather succulent, but soon becoming brown and scariose. *Peduncles* 2 to 4-flowered, terminal, thickly clothed with unequal, spreading hairs. *Involucre* of 6 narrow lanceolate, very hairy bractes, points bearded. *Pedicles* very short. *Calyx* 5-cleft, the segments lanceolate, concave, acute, very hairy and fringed, longer than the nectariferous tube, spreading or slightly reflexed. *Nectariferous tube* short, flattened on each side, gibbous at the base. *Petals* 5, nearly equal in size, narrowly spatulate, white: the 2 upper ones narrow at the base, reflexed from about the middle, with 2 red lines near the centre, eared a little above the base. *Stamens* 10, united at the base, the 5 fertile ***filaments*** very long and straight; ***pollen*** orange-coloured. ***Style*** very short, hairy at the base, and smooth upwards. ***Stigmas*** 5, purple, spreading or reflexed.

The present curious plant is an original species from the Cape, and was introduced to our collections about the year 1791; it differs in the form of its flowers from the other species of this genus, but is nevertheless a true congener, agreeing precisely with the character by which the genus is distinguished. Another fine species of this genus is P. *crithmifolium* of Smith's Icones, the P. *paniculatum* of Jacquin; this we have not seen flower so perfect as we wish, or we should have published a figure of it before this: we believe there are also some new species in Mr. Colvill's collection, lately raised from seeds brought by Mr. Synnet from the interior of the Cape; a great many plants of this family are raised from seeds brought by him, some of which are already showing bloom; and plants of the rare and little known *Grielum laciniatum* are thriving very well at Mr. Colvill's, both from seeds and dried roots; and we are in hopes of seeing them flower early next Spring. From the same collection were procured a great quantity of Cape bulbs; many of those have already bloomed, and they are chiefly either new or very rare species; several very distinct species of Ventenat's genus HOMERIA have flowered, and three quite new and very different species of FERRARIA; of those and of many new and interesting species of MORÆA, BABIANA, IXIA, LAPEYROUSIA, GLADIOLUS, &c. we have had fine drawings made, which we intend publishing in our BRITISH FLOWER GARDEN, with an account of their management, and the best manner of cultivating them in the open ground, where, with a little attention, they may be grown as freely as Hyacinths or Tulips, and will flower stronger and much finer than in pots.

The above plant, from which our drawing was made, was sent to us some time back, by the kindness of Sir R. C. Hoare; but we waited an opportunity of its flowering in good perfection, before we had it drawn; it requires exactly the same sort of treatment, as the other species of Otidia already published.

E. D. Smith del. Pub by J. Ridgway 169 Piccadilly Dec 1 1825. S. Watts sc.

287

PELARGONIUM biflorum.

Two-flowered Stork's-bill.

P. *biflorum*, caule fruticoso ramosissimo, foliis cordatis rotundato-ovatis acute dentatis subtus multinerviis utrinque pubescentibus, stipulis ovato-lanceolatis acutis ciliatis, pedunculis bifloris, petalis omnibus obovatis, tubo nectarifero calyce parum breviore.

Stem shrubby, of a woody texture, clothed with a brown rough bark, very much branched: *branches* slender, rigid, flexuose, thickly clothed with unequal spreading villous hairs, as are the petioles, peduncles, bractes, and calyx. *Leaves* nearly as broad as long, cordate, roundly ovate, flat or sometimes concave, not lobed, but toothed with numerous unequal small sharp teeth, strongly and numerously nerved underneath, and furrowed on the upper side, clothed on both sides with a short pubescence, the nerves hairy. *Petioles* slender, flattened a little on the upper side and convex on the lower. *Stipules* small, ovate or lanceolate, acute, hairy and fringed. *Peduncles* slender, generally two-flowered. *Involucre* of 6 short, broadly ovate, concave, taper-pointed bractes. *Pedicles* long and slender, villosely hairy. *Calyx* 5-cleft, segments all reflexed, the upper one broadest, ovately lanceolate; the others lanceolate, all acute. *Nectariferous tube* a little shorter than the calyx, flattened on both sides. *Petals* 5, all obovate, white tinged with blush, the two upper ones broadest, with a faint red spot in the centre, below which are a few short bright red and purple lines, a little branched. *Filaments* 10, united at the base, 7 bearing anthers. *Style* slender, longer than the stamens, of a bright purple, very hairy on the lower part, and smooth on the upper. *Stigmas* 5, purple, reflexed or revolute.

This very pretty and abundant flowering plant, is a hybrid production, and was raised from seed by Sir R. C. Hoare, who was so kind as to send us cuttings of it from his fine collection, some time since, but without a name or number, only marked H. S. or Hoare's Seedling; this we have supplied with P. *biflorum*, as its peduncles are generally 2-flowered: it is nearest in habit to P. *betulinum*, which is probably one of its parents; but it is readily distinguished by its cordate pubescent leaves and villous stems, also by the shape of its flowers; and it is very different from any other with which we are acquainted. It is a very free grower, and a very hardy sort, and makes a compact bushy plant, continuing to flower all the Summer and till late in Autumn; it thrives well in any light vegetable soil, or a mixture of turfy loam and peat will suit it very well; young cuttings, planted in pots in the same kind of soil, will soon strike root, if placed on a shelf in the greenhouse. Our drawing was taken in October last, at the same time as *Otidia alternans*.

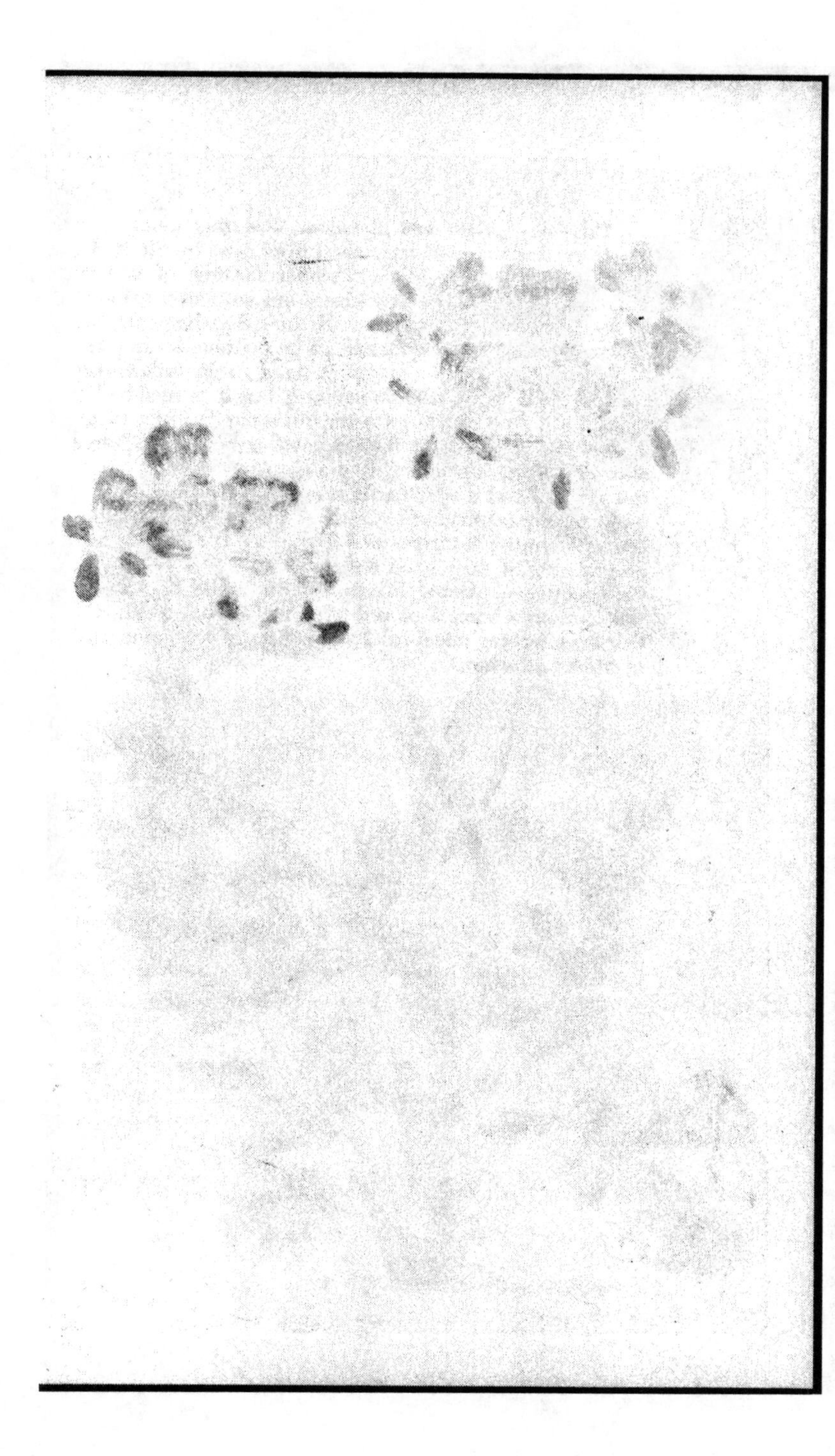

E. D. Smith del. Pubd by J. Ridgway 169 Piccadilly Dec 1 1825 S. Watts sc.

PELARGONIUM mundulum.

Spruce Stork's Bill.

P. ***mundulum***, subcaulescens, scapo gracili longe ramoso, umbellis sub-8-floris, foliis pinnatifidis pinnatisque canescentibus: foliolis segmentisque inferioribus 2-3-partitis 2-3-lobisve: superioribus simplicibus lanceolatis ovatisque integerrimis acutis omnibus sericeo-canescentibus, tubo nectarifero calyce duplo longiore.

Pelargonium mundulum. *Swt. hort. brit. p.* 84. *n.* 394.

Root tuberous, branching. *Stem* short, producing several short stout branches. *Leaves* pinnate, or pinnatifid, thickly clothed with a short silky canescence: *leaflets* or *segments* lanceolate or ovate and acute, the lower ones 2 or 3-parted, or 2 to 3-lobed: the upper ones entire, all clothed with a silky canescence. *Petioles* slender, nearly cylindrical, or slightly flattened on the upper side, densely clothed with short hairs and a few longer ones intermixed. *Stipules* lanceolate, acute, hairy and fringed with very short hairs, joined a good way up to the petioles. *Scapes* several, long and slender, and producing several umbels of flowers, leafy at the base of the peduncles, thickly clothed with white spreading hairs, very unequal in length. *Peduncles* cylindrical, long and slender, generally producing an umbel of 8 flowers, also clothed with spreading unequal hairs. *Involucre* of several lanceolate, acute, hairy and fringed bractes, some double the size of the others. *Pedicles* very short, or altogether wanting. *Calyx* 5-cleft, segments lanceolate, acute; the upper one largest, erect, the others spreading or slightly reflexed, all densely clothed with soft woolly hairs. *Nectariferous tube* about double the length of the calyx, slightly flattened on each side, and thickly clothed with spreading hairs. ***Petals*** 5, the 2 upper ones slightly retuse, narrowly cuneate, of an orangy scarlet, white at the base, and marked from there to the middle with a few short branched dark purple lines: ***lower petals*** about half the width of the upper ones, of rather a lighter colour, and white from below the middle ***Filaments*** 10, united at the base, 7 bearing anthers. ***Style*** short, purple, thickly clothed with short hairs. ***Stigmas*** 5, purple, reflexed.

A very pretty hybrid plant, raised in 1823 at the Nursery of Mr. Colvill, from the seed of a mule from ***Dimacria pinnata***, that had been fertilized by the pollen of P. ***ardens***; the leaves and the colour of the flowers are very similar to its former parent, but its habit, loose growth, and form of the flowers, is more like the latter: it is a very free growing sort, and an abundant bloomer, beginning to flower the latter part of February or the beginning of March, and our plant was very fine in flower the beginning of November: like its nearest relatives, it succeeds best in a light sandy soil, and requires very little water after it has done flowering: an equal mixture of light turfy loam, peat, and sand, is a very proper soil for it; and the pots must be well drained with potsherds broken small, that the moisture may pass readily off: the best method of increasing it is by the little tubers of its roots; the most proper time for taking those off, is when the plants are in a dormant state, as they can then be kept quite dry till the wound is dried up; they would otherwise be liable to rot: the roots must be planted with their tops above the surface of the mould, to prevent their rotting; and as soon as the cut is dried up, they may be regularly watered, and they will soon make nice young plants, and will flower the first Summer.

289

E. D. Smith del. Pub. by J. Ridgway 169 Piccadilly Jan. 1. 1826 J. Watts sc.

PELARGONIUM schizophyllum.

Deeply cut-leaved Stork's-bill.

P. *schizophyllum*, caule fruticoso ramoso; ramis nodosis flexuosis glaucescentibus, foliis tripartitis pinnatifido-laciniatis acutis glaucescentibus acute inciso-serratis, stipulis ovato-lanceolatis acutis, umbellis multifloris, tubo nectarifero longe pedicellato calyce sesquilongiore.

Pelargonium schizophyllum. *Swt. hort. brit. p.* 82. *n.* 295.

Stem shrubby, branching: *branches* spreading, flexuose, swollen at the joints, glaucous, slightly pubescent. *Leaves* ternate, or deeply 3-parted, acute, more or less glaucous, sharply cut and toothed, clothed on both sides with very short hairs: lower leaflets or segments deeply 2-parted, divaricate; terminal one pinnatifid or deeply laciniated, the sinuses acute. *Petioles* slender, nearly cylindrical, or slightly flattened on the upper side, pubescent. *Stipules* ovate or lanceolate, taper-pointed. *Peduncles* cylindrical, glaucous, slightly pubescent, in a sort of panicle, many-flowered. *Involucre* of from 6 to 8 linearly lanceolate acute bractes. *Pedicles* long and slender, transparent at the base and apex, longer than the nectariferous tube. *Calyx* 5-cleft, segments erect, lanceolate, acute, keeled and ciliate. *Nectariferous tube* about half as long again as the calyx, flattened on both sides, pubescent. *Petals* 5, of a red salmon colour, the 2 upper ones erect, wedge-shaped, and marked from the base with purple slightly branched lines: lower ones spreading, ligulate, also faintly marked with red lines from the base. *Filaments* 10, united at the base, 5 only bearing anthers in the specimens that we have examined, and those were very imperfect. ***Style*** green, very hairy. ***Stigmas*** 5, purple, reflexed.

Our drawing was taken from a fine plant in the superb collection of R. H. Jenkinson, Esq. where it was first raised from seed: it is of hybrid origin, and was raised in 1822 from the seed of P. *fulgidum* that had been fertilized by the pollen of P. *grandiflorum*: its nearest relative is P. *Barnardianum*, which was raised from the seed of P. *grandiflorum* mixed with P. *fulgidum*. The present plant is of much readier growth; its leaves are much more divided, and it bears a far greater number of flowers in the umbels, which are produced in a sort of panicle, and continue to bloom till late in Autumn; it is therefore a very desirable plant, particularly as it is so different from all the others of this numerous tribe. It succeeds well in an equal mixture of light turfy loam, peat, and sand, or any other light sandy soil; it also strikes root readily from cuttings planted in pots, and placed on a shelf in the greenhouse; it may also be increased by pieces of the roots, planted with their tops above the surface, that they may not rot; those will soon make nice young plants, and will flower the same season, if planted early in Spring; as soon as they begin to make shoots, they must be planted separately in small pots, leaving only one shoot to each root; for if more are left, they will weaken each other, and will not succeed so well.

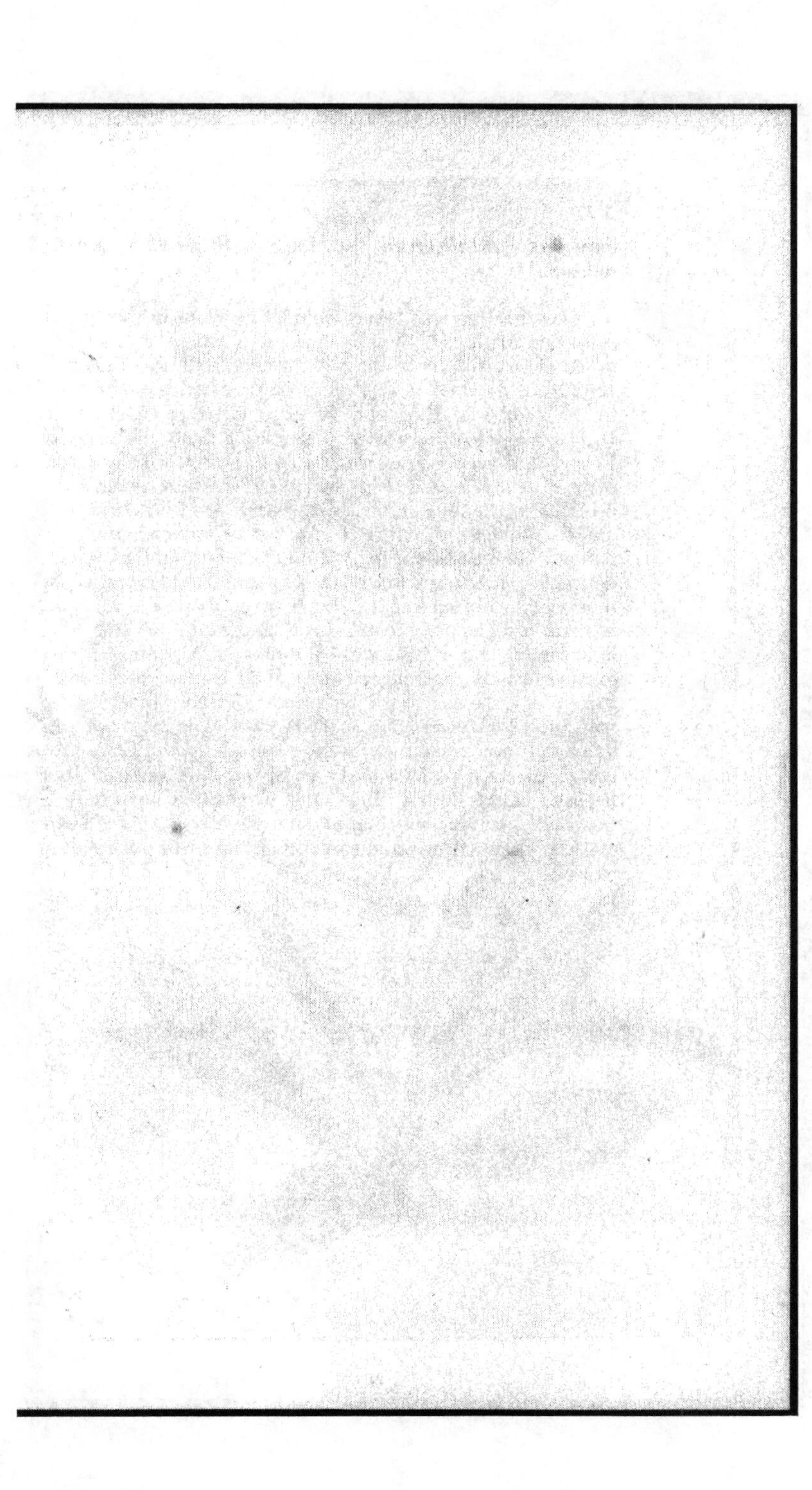

290

E. D. Smith del. Pub. by J. Ridgway 169 Piccadilly Jan. 1. 1826. S. Watts sc.

DIMACRIA depressa.

Depressed umbelled Dimacria.

D. *depressa*, acaulis, foliis oblongo-lanceolatis integerrimis acutis glabris basi involutis attenuatis margine breviter ciliatis, stipulis barbatis, umbella composita depressa multiflora, pedicellis demum reflexis, floribus tetrandris, filamentis 6 sterilibus erectis, petalis longis linearibus, tubo nectarifero villoso calyce duplo longiore.

Hoarea depressa. *Swt. hort. brit. p.* 76. *n.* 24.

Pelargonium depressum. *Jacq. ic. rar.* 3. *t.* 520. *Pers. syn.* 2. *p.* 226. *DC. prodr.* 1. *p.* 649.

Root tuberous, fusiform. *Stem* none. *Leaves* crowning the root, and spreading round or sometimes erect, oblongly lanceolate, acute, entire, smooth, but dotted with numerous small dots, attenuated towards the base and down the petiole, where it is a little involute, the margins a little fringed with short hairs. *Petioles* long and slender, flattened and furrowed on the upper side, and convex on the lower, slightly pubescent, more so towards the base. *Stipules* linear, acute, attached to the base of the petioles, and densely bearded with long white hairs. *Scapes* several, erect, pubescent, each producing 2 to 4 umbels of flowers; at the base of the peduncles is a whorl of linear, taper-pointed, very hairy bractes. *Peduncles* cylindrical, unequal in length, thickly clothed with short rigid spreading hairs, that are all tipped with a small gland. *Umbels* from 8 to 12-flowered, spreading flat. *Involucre* of numerous linear taper-pointed fringed bractes. *Pedicles* very short, or altogether wanting. *Calyx* 5-cleft, segments lanceolate, acute, all reflexed, very hairy, the hairs all tipped with transparent glands. *Nectariferous tube* unequal in length, generally 2 or 3 times longer than the calyx, thickly clothed with short spreading hairs; when in flower, bent downwards, which gives the depressed appearance to the umbel. *Petals* 5, linear, reflexed from about the middle, of a pale sulphur colour, the two upper ones largest, obtuse or sometimes emarginate, marked from the middle downwards with a dark velvetty patch. *Filaments* 10, slightly connected at the base, 4 only bearing perfect anthers, with sometimes a sterile one, or attempt at a fifth, two of the fertile ones rather longer than the other two, the sterile ones subulate and erect: *pollen* orange-coloured. *Style* very short, hairy, light purple. *Stigmas* 5, light purple, spreading.

Our drawing of this rare and very handsome species was taken from some fine plants at the Nursery of Mr. Tate, in Sloane Street, Chelsea, where we saw a great many of them in flower without the least variation. They were received in 1824 from the Cape, and had been collected near Algoa Bay for Mr. Tate, with many other curious bulbs: we had also received a fine specimen of the same species, sent us from the collection of A. Arcedeckne, Esq. of Glevering Hall, Suffolk, but the petals had all dropped off before their arrival. Before we had an opportunity of examining the plant, we thought, from its near resemblance to *Hoarea radicata*, that it would belong to the same genus, under which we had arranged it in our Hortus Britannicus above quoted; but we now find it to be a genuine species of *Dimacria*, as is also *longifolia* and *longiflora*, and perhaps *auriculata?* and some other species that are there arranged under that genus, which can only be satisfactorily distinguished by the examination of perfect specimens; we believe several of the species are now in our collections, which have been lately reintroduced by Mr. Synnet from the Cape with many new ones.

The present plant requires the same treatment as the other tuberous rooted species, succeeding well in an equal mixture of turfy loam, peat, and sand, and the pots to be well drained with small potsherds; it should be kept quite dry all the Winter, until it shows an inclination to grow afresh, when it should be fresh potted, and watered regularly; it may be increased readily by seeds, or by the little tubers at its roots.

291

Smith del. Pub. by J. Ridgway 169 Piccadilly Jan. 1 1826. J. Watts

PELARGONIUM rhodolentum.

Rose-smelling Stork's-bill.

P. *rhodolentum*, ramis petiolis pedunculis calycibusque villosis, foliis cordatis profunde trilobis undulatis inæqualiter argute dentatis utrinque leviter pilosis, calycibus cordato-lanceolatis acutis ciliato-barbatis, pedunculis subtrifloris, petalis omnibus obovatis, tubo nectarifero calyce parum breviore.

Pelargonium rhodolentum. *Swt. hort. brit. p.* 84. *n.* 395.

Stem shrubby, much branched: *branches* spreading, thickly clothed with spreading white unequal hairs, as are the petioles, peduncles, and calyx. *Leaves* small, about as broad as long, cordate, deeply 3-lobed, very much undulate, scarcely acute, unequally but sharply toothed, side lobes acute, terminal one sometimes slightly 3-lobed, and more rounded, thinly clothed on both sides with short hairs. *Petioles* flattened and furrowed on the upper side, and convex on the lower, about the length of the leaf. *Stipules* cordately lanceolate, acute, bearded, or strongly fringed with long white hairs. *Peduncles* cylindrical, generally 3-flowered. *Involucre* of 6 lanceolate, taper-pointed bractes, which are much fringed. *Pedicles* rather longer than the nectariferous tube, stout, villous. *Calyx* 5-cleft, segments lanceolate, taper-pointed, the upper one broadest, erect, 3-nerved, the others more or less reflexed or spreading. *Nectariferous tube* scarcely as long as the calyx, flattened on each side, and gibbous at the base. *Corolla* of 5 petals, all obovate, the 2 upper ones largest, very oblique at the base, of a pale blush tinged with rose, and a large irregular purple patch in the centre, becoming lighter all round, between which and the base are several dark purple lines, branching in various directions: lower ones white, or tinged with blush. ***Filaments*** 10, united at the base, 7 bearing anthers. ***Style*** flesh-coloured, very hairy. ***Stigmas*** 5, purple, revolute.

This pretty plant is of hybrid origin, and was raised in 1823 at the Nursery of Mr. Colvill, from a seed of P. *dumosum* that had been fertilized by the pollen of P. *obscurum*; in its habit it is distinct from all others, and makes a handsome compact bush; the pleasant rose-like scent of its leaves also makes it a desirable plant for the greenhouse; it is also very hardy and of free growth, succeeding well in any rich light soil, or a mixture of turfy loam, peat, and sand, will suit it very well. Young cuttings will strike root freely, if planted under hand-glasses, or in pots, and then placed in the Greenhouse; hardened cuttings of the small leaved species do not root freely, they will remain a long time in the pots without rooting, although the bottom of the cutting is callosed over; whereas young cuttings will strike readily; this is the case with P. ***Hoareanum***, and many other nearly related sorts.

292

G. D. Smith del. Pub. by J. Ridgway 169 Piccadilly Jan 1 1826. J. Watts sc.

HOAREA sisymbriifolia.

Water-Rocket-leaved Hoarea.

H. ***sisymbriifolia***, acaulis, foliis oblongis ternatis pinnatifido-laciniatisque subhirsutis: foliolis segmentisque oblongo-lanceolatis acutis subdentato-incisis, stipulis lanceolatis acutis ciliatis, scapo ramoso pedunculisque villoso-pilosis, umbellis multifloris, tubo nectarifero calyce duplo longiore.

Hoarea sisymbriifolia. ***Swt. hort. brit. p. 76. n. 65.***

Root tuberous, branching into other small tubers. ***Stem*** none. ***Leaves*** radical, rather succulent, of a dark glossy green, ternate, pinnatifid or laciniate, slightly hairy: ***leaflets*** and ***segments*** oblong, oblongly lanceolate, or sometimes narrowly lanceolate, acute, deeply toothed or incised, or sometimes entire, the margins slightly fringed. ***Petioles*** slender, flattened on the upper side and convex on the lower, more or less clothed with unequal spreading hairs. ***Stipules*** lanceolate, acute, hairy and fringed, the points tipped with long bristle like hairs. ***Scapes*** branching, and producing several umbels of flowers, thickly clothed with unequal spreading villous hairs, as are the peduncles, and producing a leaf or two at the joint. ***Peduncles*** cylindrical, producing many-flowered umbels. ***Involucre*** of numerous linear or linearly lanceolate, acute, fringed bractes, that are also tipped with bristly points. ***Calyx*** 5-cleft, segments oblongly lanceolate, hairy, ciliate and bristle-pointed, the upper one broadest, erect, the others spreading, or slightly reflexed. ***Nectariferous tube*** sessile, or nearly so, about twice the length of the calyx, flattened on both sides, and clothed with short unequal hairs, that are tipped with a small pellucid gland. ***Petals*** 5, spreading, of a bright scarlet, clouded with a dark velvetty purple or nearly black, the 2 uppermost broadest, spathulate, with 2 or 3 dark lines near the base: lower ones about half the width, with a slender unguis. *Filaments* 10, united into a tube, 5 bearing anthers, sterile ones curved inwards. *Style* ascending, pale flesh colour, hairy at the base, and smooth upwards. *Stigmas* 5, the points reflexed.

The present very curious and pretty plant is a hybrid production, raised in 1823 at the Nursery of Mr. Colvill, from a seed of P. *sanguineum* that had been fertilized by the pollen of H. *varia;* it has entirely lost the habit of its former parent, and only resembles it in its glossy leaves, and the colour of its flowers; the habit and character is precisely that of *Hoarea:* we do not know any plant that mules more readily than P. *sanguineum;* we have some very singular productions both from it and P. *multiradiatum;* some of them have flowered, but not in such good perfection as we expect them to do next Summer.

Like the other tuberous rooted sorts, the present plant succeeds well in an equal mixture of turfy loam, peat, and sand, requiring but little water, and none when in a dormant state; but as soon as it begins to grow again, it will require to be shifted into another pot, and will need a regular supply; it may be readily increased by the little tubers from its roots.

293
E. D. Smith del.
Pub by J. Ridgway 169 Piccadilly Feb 1 1825.
J. Watts sc.

PELARGONIUM dilutum.

Diluted Stork's-bill.

P. *dilutum,* foliis cordatis trilobis undulato-plicatis cartilagineo-dentatis villoso-pilosis, stipulis ovatis acutis dentatis villosis, pedunculis multifloris, calycibus reflexo-patentibus, tubo nectarifero calyce subæquali aut paulo breviore.

Pelargonium dilutum. *Swt. hort. brit. p.* 84. *n.* 386.

Stem shrubby, erect, branching: *branches* thickly clothed with long spreading unequal villous hairs. *Leaves* cordate, 3-lobed, very much undulate or plaited, the edges more or less reflexed, sharply and rigidly toothed, with nearly equal cartilaginous teeth, clothed on both sides with soft villous hairs, strongly and numerously nerved underneath. *Petioles* broad and stout, flattened on the upper side and convex on the lower, widened at the base, thickly clothed with long spreading unequal villous hairs, as is every other part of the plant except the corolla. *Stipules* ovate, taper-pointed, more or less toothed and ciliate. *Umbels* many-flowered. *Peduncles* cylindrical. *Involucre* of several ovate, taper-pointed, concave, fringed bractes, which are more or less imbricate. *Pedicles* about the length of the bractes, or sometimes a little longer. *Calyx* 5-cleft, segments lanceolate, acute, spreading or slightly reflexed, of a brownish colour. *Nectariferous tube* about the length of, or scarcely as long as the calyx, flattened on each side, and gibbous at the base. *Petals* 5, the 2 upper ones obovate, oblique at the base, of a red purple, more or less stained, and marked with numerous dark lines, which branch and cross each other, below those are 2 white lines: lower petals oblong, obtuse, spreading, of a lighter colour, much veined with numerous branching light purple veins. ***Filaments*** 10, united at the base, 7 bearing anthers. ***Style*** purple, very hairy at the base, and smooth upwards. ***Stigmas* 5,** purple, revolute.

This very fine flowering plant is of hybrid origin, and was raised from seed at the Nursery of Mr. More, in the King's Road, where our drawing was taken last Autumn; we believe one of its parents to be P. ***Barringtonii***, or some nearly related sort, and the other is one of the red flowering hybrids, but which of them, would be difficult to ascertain; it is a strong free growing plant, and an abundant bloomer, and continues flowering in perfection till late in Autumn; it thrives well in any rich light soil, or a mixture of loam, peat, and sand, will suit it very well, being careful not to overwater it in Winter, as all this tribe are impatient of moisture at that season. Cuttings soon strike root, if planted in pots, and placed on a shelf in the greenhouse.

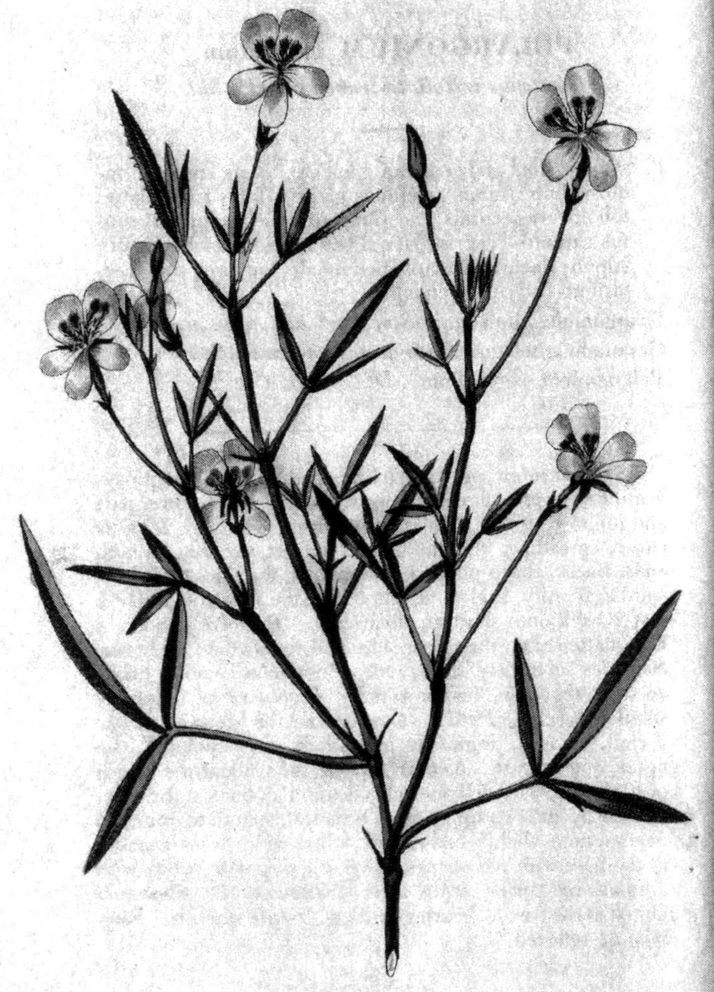
294
Pub by J. Ridgway 169 Piccadilly Feb 1. 1825

294

PELARGONIUM trifoliatum.

Glaucous trifoliate-leaved Stork's-bill.

P. *trifoliatum*, glaberrimum glaucum, caule fruticoso ramosissimo: ramis gracilibus glabris, foliis trifoliolatis; foliolis integerrimis linearibus utrinque acuminatis subtus carinatis scabris; lateralibus brevioribus divaricatis, stipulis lineari-subulatis, pedunculis unifloris, tubo nectarifero calyce subæquali.

Pelargonium trifoliatum. *Swt. hort. brit. p.* 82. *n.* 267.

Geranium trifoliatum. *Andrews's geran. c. ic.*

Pelargonium oxyphyllum. *DC. prodr.* 1. *p.* 667.

Stem shrubby, very much branched, smooth and glossy: *branches* slender, flexuose, swollen at the joints, lower part and joints very red. *Leaves* glaucous, trifoliate: *leaflets* entire, spreading, the middle one longest, tapering at both ends, linear, sharp-pointed, channelled, the sides folded inwards, sharply keeled at the back, the keel rough like a rasp: back ones shortest, divaricate. *Petioles* slender, a little flattened on the upper side, and rounded on the lower. *Stipules* subulately linear, red. *Peduncles* slender, thickened at the base, one-flowered. *Involucre* of 2 linearly subulate bractes. *Pedicles* shorter than the bractes. *Calyx* 5-cleft, smooth, segments lanceolate, taper-pointed, the upper one largest. *Nectariferous tube* about the length of the calyx, flattened on each side, and gibbous at the base. *Petals 5*, the two upper ones broadest, spatulate, rounded or sometimes slightly emarginate, white, more or less marked at the base with red stripes, lower ones ligulate, white with a small red stripe at the base. *Stamens* 10: *filaments* united at the base, 7 bearing anthers. *Style* smooth. *Stigmas 5*, reflexed.

Our drawing of this very distinct and curious species was taken from a plant at the Nursery of Mr. John Lee, at Hammersmith, last Summer; we were afraid that it had quite disappeared from our collections, as we had not seen it before for several years. M. Decandolle not being acquainted with Mr. Andrews's figure, supposed it to be an unpublished species, and has described it in his Prodromus by the very appropriate title of P. *oxyphyllum;* but as Mr. Andrews has given a good figure of it, and also a very proper name, which was published several years ago, we have adopted it as having the right of priority.

This species is nearly related to P. *glaucum,* and, like it, requires to be preserved in a good greenhouse in Winter; and being also of a succulent nature, care must be taken not to overwater it; the best soil for it is a mixture of turfy loam, peat, and sand, being careful that the pots are well drained with potsherds; young cuttings strike root freely, if planted in pots in the same sort of soil, and placed on a shelf in the greenhouse.

[illegible] the time of the very [illegible] was taken as a plant of the [illegible] [illegible]

[illegible]

E. D. Smith del. Pub by J. Ridgway 169 Piccadilly Feb 1. 1826 J. Watts sc.

CICONIUM micranthum.

Small-flowered Ciconium.

C. *micranthum*, caule fruticoso carnoso, foliis cordato-reniformibus orbiculatis breviter 5-lobis crenatis utrinque molliter pubescentibus, stipulis cordatis ciliatis, umbellis multifloris, petalis rotundato-obovatis subemarginatis calyce sesquilongioribus, tubo nectarifero calyce duplo longiore.

Ciconium micranthum. *Swt. hort. brit. p.* 85. *n.* 23.

Geranium coccineum, *var.* parviflorum. *Hoare geran. p.* 2.

Stem shrubby, succulent, branching: *branches* stiff, erect, glossy, but slightly pubescent, naked below, and producing a few leaves only at the extremities. *Leaves* cordately reniform, rounded, slightly 5-lobed, shallowly notched, very soft to the touch, and densely clothed on both sides with a short pubescence: lobes rounded. *Petioles* nearly cylindrical, swollen at the base, thickly clothed with short spreading hairs. *Stipules* short, cordate, fringed. *Peduncles* lateral, long, erect, thickly clothed with short spreading hairs. *Umbels* many-flowered. *Involucre* of 6 cordately ovate, acute, fringed bractes. *Pedicles* short, hairy. *Calyx* 5-cleft, segments erect, oblong, bluntish, concave, thickly clothed with unequal spreading villous hairs. *Nectariferous tube* about twice the length of the calyx, thickly clothed with short hairs. *Petals* 5, roundly obovate or cuneate, sometimes emarginate, of a bright scarlet, and imbricate, the two upper ones rather shortest and smallest. *Filaments* 10, very short and erect; sometimes 6, at other times 7, bearing anthers. *Style* short, quite smooth. *Stigmas* 5, light flesh-coloured, slightly spreading.

This pretty little plant is an old inhabitant of our collections; it is amongst one of the first plants that we can recollect; but when it was introduced, or from where, is now not easy to be ascertained, as it does not appear to have been taken notice of in any botanical publication with which we are acquainted; it is more tender than the rest of the tribe to which it belongs, and requires to be kept in a good greenhouse to have it in health; and as it is of a succulent habit, it requires very little water in Winter; for if it happens to get too much, it will soon throw off its leaves, and will not be easily recovered; when in good health, and covered with its neat little round flowers, it makes a pretty appearance, and is the more desirable by being so very different in flower from all others; a mixture of turfy loam, peat, and sand, is a very proper soil for it; and the pots must be well drained with potsherds, that the wet may pass off readily. Cuttings root freely, planted in pots in the same sort of soil, and placed on a shelf in the greenhouse.

Our drawing was taken in September last, from a plant that was raised from a cutting, kindly sent to us by Sir R. C. Hoare, from his magnificent collection of Geraniaceæ at Stourhead, and who observed that it was well deserving a figure, on account of its singularity.

296.

E. D. Smith del. Pub. by J. Ridgway 169 Piccadilly Feb. 1. 1826 S. Wa[illegible]

PELARGONIUM lasiophyllum.

Woolly divided-leaved Stork's-bill.

P. *lasiophyllum*, foliis cordatis pinnatifido-lobatis inciso-dentatis utrinque villoso-tomentosis: lobis divaricatis acutis, stipulis cordato-ovatis acutis, pedunculis villosissimis plurifloris subpaniculatis, tubo nectarifero calyce sesquilongiore.

Pelargonium lasiophyllum. *Swt. hort. brit. p.* 83. *n.* 341.

Stem shrubby, rather succulent, thickly clothed with unequal spreading white villous hairs, as is every other part of the plant except the corolla: *branches* nearly erect, or slightly spreading, densely villous. *Leaves* cordate, deeply 5 to 9-lobed, or nearly pinnatifid, densely clothed on both sides with white villous down, strongly nerved underneath, the nerves branched: lobes spreading, wedge-shaped, acute, incised or toothed with bluntish teeth. *Petioles* flattened a little on the upper side, and convex on the lower, densely villous. *Stipules* cordately ovate, acute, joined to the base of the petioles. *Peduncles* in a sort of panicle, several-flowered. *Involucre* of 6 lanceolate, acute, villous bractes. *Pedicles* about the length of the bractes. *Calyx* 5-cleft, segments unequal, oblongly lanceolate, reflexed. *Nectariferous tube* about half as long again as the calyx, flattened on each side, gibbous at the base, and widened upwards. *Petals* 5, the 2 upper ones obovate, a little oblique at the base, of a reddish brick colour, stained with purple, and a light stroke to the base, in the middle is 2 dark purple spots, that are connected by a reddish shade, and from them to the base are some short dark lines, which are more or less branched: lower petals ligulate, brick coloured. *Stamens* 10, connected at the base, 7 bearing anthers, which, as far as we have observed, have always been without pollen. *Style* purple, thickly clothed with long rigid hairs. *Stigmas* 5. purple, reflexed.

A very curious hybrid production, raised at the Nursery of Mr. Colvill, from a seed of P. *fulgidum* that had been fertilized by the pollen of P. *Vandesiæ;* it is as nearly as possible intermediate between the two, but we believe very few would guess its origin, had it not been known: it is a free strong growing plant, and is more hardy than many of its relatives, requiring nothing but a common greenhouse to keep it in good health: like the rest of that tribe, it succeeds best in a mixture of light turfy loam, peat, and sand, and the pots to be well drained; young cuttings strike root freely, if planted in pots, and placed on a shelf in the greenhouse.

297

PELARGONIUM confertifolium.

Close-leaved Stork's-bill.

P. *confertifolium*, caule suffruticoso ramoso; ramis brevibus erecto-adscendentibus confertis squamoso-rugosis: foliis confertis ternatis pinnatifidis simplicibus quinquelobisve molliter undique villosis: foliolis lobisque imbricatis obtusis crenato-dentatis, scapo simplici, umbella multiflora subprolifera, petalis omnibus obovatis, tubo nectarifero calyce reflexo duplo longiore.

Pelargonium confertifolium. *Swt. hort. brit. p.* 77. *n.* 27.

Geranium ardens, *minor. Andrews's geran. c. ic.*

Stem suffruticose, short and rugged, erect, about 4 or 6 inches in height, much branched: *branches* short, very much crowded, erect or ascending, very rugged and unequal, scaly, occasioned by the remains of the stipules and petioles, the upper part thickly clothed with soft villous hairs. *Leaves* very variable, some ternate or pinnatifid, others deeply 5-lobed and simple, covered all over with soft villous hairs: *leaflets, segments,* or *lobes,* obtusely rounded, and notched or toothed with blunt rounded teeth, imbricate or lapping over each other. *Petioles* slightly flattened on the upper side, and rounded on the lower, densely clothed with long, white, spreading, unequal, villous hairs. *Stipules* very short, broadly cordate, acute, fringed, and joined to the base of the petioles. *Scape* simple, cylindrical, elongated, thickly clothed with long spreading unequal hairs. *Umbel* many-flowered, generally proliferous. *Involucre* of several linear acute villous bractes. *Pedicles* long and slender, unequal in length, thickly clothed with unequal hairs. *Calyx* 5-cleft, segments lanceolate, scarcely acute, villous, the upper one broadest, erect, the others reflexed. *Petals* 5, all roundly obovate, the two upper ones broadest, of a bright scarlet, tinged with brown, and two dark lines running down them, that are slightly branched: lower petals of nearly the same colour, but the lines fainter. ***Filaments*** 10, connected at the base, one of them a broadish spatulate one, as in the other plants of this section, 6 or 7 bearing anthers. ***Style*** short, thinly hairy. ***Stigmas*** 5, purple, reflexed.

This curious little plant is of hybrid origin, and appears to be intermediate between P. *fulgidum* and P. *pulchellum*, and, like the latter parent, is rather shy in producing its flowers; we do not know by whom it was first raised, but we first saw it at the Nursery of Mr. Lee, at Hammersmith, as long ago as the year 1816; it is not so much cultivated in our collections as it deserves to be, which we believe is chiefly owing to its not being well managed, and therefore produces but few flowers; but when well grown and covered with its handsome little flowers, we think none can exceed it in brilliancy: the umbels are very often proliferous, which is also sometimes the case in P. *pulchellum;* it has certainly very little affinity with P. *ardens*, with which it has been confused, the habit of the plants being totally dissimilar, this being an erect suffruticose plant, producing innumerable leafy branches; whereas P. *ardens* is scarcely more than herbaceous, and produces very few leaves or branches, the leaves are also altogether different.

The best method of treating the present subject, is to pot it in an equal mixture of turfy loam, peat, and sand, and to have the pots well drained with potsherds, that it may not get sodden with too much wet; as the pot becomes filled with roots, it should be shifted into a larger one, to keep it growing freely, the only method of flowering it well: in Winter it requires very little water, and if allowed to get too much at that season, it will be very liable to rot off. Cuttings planted in pots, root readily, if planted in the same sort of soil, and placed on a shelf in the Greenhouse. Drawn at the Nursery of Mr. Colvill, in October last.

298

Em. D. Smith. del. Pub by J. Ridgway 169 Piccadilly Mar 1 1826. J. Watts sc.

PELARGONIUM nitidum.

Glossy Stork's-bill.

P. *nitidum*, caule erecto fruticoso subcarnoso squamoso, foliis tripartitis laciniato-lobatis nitidis margine subciliatis, stipulis persistentibus ovatis obtusis petiolo adhærentibus, umbellis multifloris subpaniculatis, petalis venosis, tubo nectarifero calyce duplo longiore.

Pelargonium nitidum. *Swt. hort. brit. p.* 77. *n.* 24.

Stem shrubby, erect, a little succulent, clothed with a brown glossy bark, and scaly, owing to the persistent stipules and base of the footstalks, very little branched. ***Leaves*** succulent, deeply 3-parted, or sometimes ternate, unequally lobed and jagged, smooth and glossy, the margins slightly fringed: leaflets or segments spreading, and toothed with unequal bluntish teeth. ***Petioles*** long, nearly cylindrical, or slightly furrowed on the upper side, thinly clothed with hairs. ***Stipules*** large, ovate, obtuse, a little concave, joined to the base of the petioles, and with them remaining persistent. ***Umbels*** many-flowered, in a sort of panicle. ***Peduncles*** swollen at the base, slightly hairy. ***Involucre*** of numerous lanceolate acute bractes. ***Pedicles*** nearly twice the length of the bractes, slightly pubescent. ***Calyx*** 5-cleft, hollow at the base; upper segment ovate, concave, erect; the others narrower, reflexed. ***Nectariferous tube*** about double the length of the calyx, gibbous at the base, scarcely pubescent. ***Petals*** 5, spreading, obovate, of a light scarlet, approaching to salmon colour, and elegantly marked with dark branching lines, the 2 upper ones about double the size of the others. ***Filaments*** 10, united at the base, seven bearing anthers, which were all imperfect in our specimens. ***Style*** longer than the stamens. ***Stigmas*** **5**, reflexed.

This plant is also of hybrid origin, and was raised in 1822, at the Nursery of Mr. Colvill, from a seed of P. *fulgidum*, that had been fertilized by the pollen of P. *sanguineum:* in habit it is nearly intermediate between its two parents, partaking of the glossy foliage of P. *sanguineum*, and the hollow calyx and nectariferous tube of P. *fulgidum:* like its two parents, it is an abundant bloomer, and requires precisely the same mode of treatment, thriving well in a mixture of turfy loam, peat, and sand, and requiring but little water in Winter. Cuttings of it strike root freely, if planted in pots in the same sort of soil, in Spring or Summer, but they will not succeed so well if planted in Autumn; it may also be increased by the little tubers of its roots.

299

PELARGONIUM odoratissimum.

Sweet-scented Stork's-bill.

P. ***odoratissimum***, caule carnoso squamoso brevissimo, foliis subrotundo-cordatis obtuse crenulatis mollissimis, ramis floriferis prostratis, umbellis plurifloris, petalis calyce parum longioribus, tubo nectarifero calyce paulo breviore.

Pelargonium odoratissimum. *Willden. sp. pl.* 3. *p.* 657. *Pers. syn.* 2. *p.* 229. *Hort. Kew. ed.* 2. *vol.* 4. *p.* 167. *DC. prodr.* 1. *p.* 659.

Geranium odoratissimum. *Andrews's geran. t.* 40. *Cav. diss.* 4. *p.* 241. *t.* 103. *f.* 1.

Stem suffruticose, very short, branching; ***branches*** very short, thickly crowded with leaves, ***flowering branches*** elongated, prostrate, and producing numerous umbels of flowers. ***Leaves*** roundly cordate or kidney-shaped, obtusely crenulate, covered on both sides with a white mealy pubescence, very soft to the touch. ***Petioles*** a little flattened on the upper side, and convex on the lower, dilated at the base, downy. ***Stipules*** cordate, acute, membranaceous. ***Peduncles*** cylindrical, downy, 3 to 8-flowered. ***Involucre*** of 6 or 7 lanceolate, taper-pointed bractes. ***Pedicles*** a little longer than the nectariferous tube, thickly clothed with soft villous hairs. ***Calyx*** 5-cleft, segments lanceolate, acute, upper one erect, the others spreading when the flower is expanded, very hairy. ***Nectariferous tube*** flattened on both sides, gibbous at the base, rather shorter than the calyx. ***Petals*** 5, nearly equal, ligulate, white, a little longer than the calyx. ***Filaments*** 10, united at the base, 7 bearing anthers. ***Germen*** silky. ***Style*** short, pale flesh colour, slightly hairy at the base, and smooth on the upper part. ***Stigmas*** 5, flesh coloured, reflexed.

This curious plant is an old inhabitant of our gardens, having been introduced into them from the Cape, ever since the year 1724; it has formerly been much prized for the singular strong scent of its foliage, which by most people is thought to be very agreeable, but some few consider it quite the reverse; it is now become rather scarce, as are most of the old original species, none of them being now much cultivated, except a few that are thought essential for producing the finest hybrids.

We think it very probable that P. *fragrans* is a hybrid production, between the present plant, and P *exstipulatum*, as it is as near as possible intermediate between the two. The present plant thrives best in a light sandy soil, or a mixture of loam, peat, and sand, will suit it very well. Cuttings root readily, planted in pots, and placed on a shelf in the Greenhouse; it may also be increased by cuttings of the roots. Our drawing was made at the Nursery of Mr. Colvill, in the King's-road, Chelsea.

E. D. Smith del. Pub. by J. Ridgway 169 Piccadilly Mar. 1 1825. J. Watts sc.

300

PELARGONIUM insignitum.

Marked-flowered Stork's-bill.

P. *insignitum*, caule fruticoso villoso, foliis cordatis lobatis inæqualiter obtuse dentatis villoso-pubescentibus, umbellis plurifloris, petalis ramoso-venosis patentibus; superioribus cuneato-obovatis: tubo nectarifero calyce paulo longiore.

Stem shrubby, branching, thickly clothed with unequal villous hairs. *Leaves* cordate, ovate, deeply but irregularly lobed, unequally toothed with bluntish teeth, clothed on both sides with soft villous hairs, more or less undulate, the margins often curved inwards. *Petioles* short, flattened on the upper side and convex on the lower, thickly clothed with unequal villous hairs. *Stipules* lanceolate, acute, villous and fringed. *Peduncles* stout, also villous. *Umbels* several flowered. *Involucre* of 6 or 7 lanceolate, acute, fringed and villous bractes. *Pedicles* about the length of or a little longer than the bractes. *Calyx* 5-cleft: upper segment ovate, concave, erect; the others narrower and spreading, all clothed with soft villous hairs. *Nectariferous tube* about the length of, or a little longer than the calyx. *Petals* 5, spreading: the 2 upper ones cuneately obovate, of a bright scarlet, with a large dark patch near the base, and numerous dark lines which spread all over the petals, and are much branched: lower petals broadly ligulate, of a bright scarlet, also marked with dark branching lines. *Filaments* 10, united at the base, 7 bearing anthers, which were all imperfect in the specimens that we examined. *Style* longer than the stamens, hairy below, and smooth upwards. *Stigmas* 5, purple, reflexed, or revolute.

This pretty marked flowered plant, is a hybrid production, and was raised in the fine collection of R. H. Jenkinson, Esq. from a seed that had been produced by P. *fulgidum*, intermixed with one known by the name of ***Black Prince*** in the gardens ; the habit of the plant is as near as possible intermediate between the two parents, partaking of the former in its general appearance, but of the latter in the shape and marking of the flowers ; like the rest of the tribe to which it belongs, it succeeds best in a light sandy soil, or a mixture of turfy loam, peat, and sand, will suit it very well, being careful not to overwater it in Winter. Cuttings root freely, planted in the same sort of soil, and placed on a shelf in the Greenhouse. Drawn from a plant in the Greenhouse of R. H. Jenkinson, Esq. in the Autumn of 1824.

SYSTEMATICAL INDEX TO VOLUME III.

ALPHABETICAL INDEX TO VOLUME III.

ENGLISH INDEX TO VOLUME III.

INDEX OF SYNONYMS TO VOLUME III.

ERRATA IN VOLUME III.

At folio 210, line 1st and 3d, for " PELARGONIUM fuscatum," read " PELARGONIUM fusciflorum."

Folio 272, line 1st, 3d, and 9th, for " PELARGONIUM Bishopæ," read " Pelargonium Bisshoppæ," and at line 2d, for " Mrs. Bishop's," read " Mrs. Bisshopp's."

GENERAL SYSTEMATICAL INDEX TO VOLUMES I. II. AND III.

GENERAL SYSTEMATICAL INDEX TO VOLUMES I. II. AND III.

GENERAL ALPHABETICAL INDEX TO VOLUMES I. II. AND III.

END OF VOL. III.

Tilling, Printer, Grosvenor Row, Chelsea.

March 1, 1824

Nº LI.

To be continued Monthly.

PRICE THREE SHILLINGS.

GERANIACEÆ,

OR

NATURAL ORDER OF GERANIUMS.

EACH NUMBER TO CONTAIN

FOUR COLOURED FIGURES;

WITH THEIR

SCIENTIFIC AND ENGLISH NAMES, AND RULES FOR CULTURE.

THE DRAWINGS TO BE MADE FROM LIVING PLANTS.

[illegible]

[illegible]

BY ROBERT SWEET, F.L.S.

[illegible]

LONDON:

[illegible]

[illegible]

July 1, 1824.

N° LV.

To be continued Monthly.

PRICE THREE SHILLINGS.

GERANIACEÆ:

OR

NATURAL ORDER OF GERANIUMS.

EACH NUMBER TO CONTAIN

FOUR COLOURED FIGURES,

WITH THEIR

SCIENTIFIC AND ENGLISH NAMES, AND MODE OF CULTURE.

THE DESIGNS TO BE MADE FROM LIVING PLANTS

IN THE COLLECTIONS OF THIS COUNTRY.

A Work intended for the Use of such as desire to become acquainted with this ornamental Tribe of Plants.

BY ROBERT SWEET, F.L.S.

Author of Hortus Suburbanus Londinensis, Botanical Cultivator, &c. &c.

LONDON:

PRINTED FOR JAMES RIDGWAY, PICCADILLY.

By S. Gosnell, Little Queen Street.

August 1, 1824.

N° LVI.

(To be continued Monthly.)

PRICE THREE SHILLINGS.

GERANIACEÆ.

[illegible]

NATURAL ORDER OF GERANIUMS.

[illegible]

FOUR COLOURED FIGURES,

[illegible]

SCIENTIFIC AND ENGLISH NAMES, AND MODE OF CULTURE.

THE DRAWINGS TO BE MADE FROM LIVING PLANTS.

[illegible]

[illegible]

BY ROBERT SWEET, F.L.S.

[illegible]

LONDON:

[illegible]

November 1, 1824.

N° LIX.

To be continued Monthly.

PRICE THREE SHILLINGS.

GERANIACEÆ,

OR

NATURAL ORDER OF GERANIUMS.

EACH NUMBER IS TO CONTAIN

FOUR COLOURED FIGURES,

WITH THEIR

SCIENTIFIC AND ENGLISH NAMES, AND MODE OF CULTURE.

THE DESIGNS TO BE MADE FROM LIVING PLANTS

IN THE COLLECTIONS OF THIS COUNTRY.

A Work intended for the Use of such as desire to become acquainted with this ornamental Tribe of Plants.

BY ROBERT SWEET, F.L.S.

Author of Hortus Suburbanus Londinensis, Botanical Cultivator, &c. &c.

LONDON:

PRINTED FOR JAMES RIDGWAY, PICCADILLY,

By S. Gosnell, Little Queen Street.

December 1, 1824.

Nº LX.

To be continued Monthly.

PRICE THREE SHILLINGS.

GERANIACEÆ,

OR

NATURAL ORDER OF GERANIUMS.

EACH NUMBER IS TO CONTAIN

FOUR COLOURED FIGURES,

WITH THEIR

SCIENTIFIC AND ENGLISH NAMES, AND MODE OF CULTURE.

THE DESIGNS TO BE MADE FROM LIVING PLANTS

IN THE COLLECTIONS OF THIS COUNTRY.

A Work intended for the Use of such as desire to become acquainted with this ornamental Tribe of Plants.

BY ROBERT SWEET, F.L.S.

Author of Hortus Suburbanus Londinensis, Botanical Cultivator, &c. &c.

LONDON:

PRINTED FOR JAMES RIDGWAY, PICCADILLY,

By S. Gosnell, Little Queen Street.

January 1, 1825.

N° LXI.

To be continued Monthly.

PRICE THREE SHILLINGS.

GERANIACEÆ,

OR

NATURAL ORDER OF GERANIUMS.

EACH NUMBER IS TO CONTAIN

FOUR COLOURED FIGURES,

WITH THEIR

SCIENTIFIC AND ENGLISH NAMES, AND MODE OF CULTURE.

THE DESIGNS TO BE MADE FROM LIVING PLANTS

IN THE COLLECTIONS OF THIS COUNTRY.

A Work intended for the Use of such as desire to become acquainted with this ornamental Tribe of Plants.

BY ROBERT SWEET, F.L.S.
Author of Hortus Suburbanus Londinensis, Botanical Cultivator, &c. &c.

LONDON:
PRINTED FOR JAMES RIDGWAY, PICCADILLY,
By S. Gosnell, Little Queen Street.

February 1, 1825.

Nº LXII.

To be continued Monthly.

PRICE THREE SHILLINGS.

GERANIACEÆ,

OR

NATURAL ORDER OF GERANIUMS.

EACH NUMBER IS TO CONTAIN

FOUR COLOURED FIGURES,

WITH THEIR

SCIENTIFIC AND ENGLISH NAMES, AND MODE OF CULTURE.

THE DESIGNS TO BE MADE FROM LIVING PLANTS

IN THE COLLECTIONS OF THIS COUNTRY.

A Work intended for the Use of such as desire to become acquainted with this ornamental Tribe of Plants.

BY ROBERT SWEET, F.L.S.

Author of Hortus Suburbanus Londinensis, Botanical Cultivator, &c. &c.

LONDON:

PRINTED FOR JAMES RIDGWAY, PICCADILLY,

By S. Gosnell, Little Queen Street.

March 1, 1825.

N° LXIII.

To be continued Monthly.

PRICE THREE SHILLINGS.

GERANIACEÆ,

OR

NATURAL ORDER OF GERANIUMS.

EACH NUMBER IS TO CONTAIN

FOUR COLOURED FIGURES,

WITH THEIR

SCIENTIFIC AND ENGLISH NAMES, AND MODE OF CULTURE.

THE DESIGNS TO BE MADE FROM LIVING PLANTS

IN THE COLLECTIONS OF THIS COUNTRY.

A Work intended for the Use of such as desire to become acquainted with this ornamental Tribe of Plants.

BY ROBERT SWEET, F.L.S.

Author of Hortus Suburbanus Londinensis, Botanical Cultivator, &c. &c.

LONDON:

PRINTED FOR JAMES RIDGWAY, PICCADILLY,

By S. Gosnell, Little Queen Street.

April 1, 1825.

N° LXIV.

To be continued Monthly.

PRICE THREE SHILLINGS.

GERANIACEÆ,

OR

NATURAL ORDER OF GERANIUMS.

EACH NUMBER IS TO CONTAIN

FOUR COLOURED FIGURES,

WITH THEIR

SCIENTIFIC AND ENGLISH NAMES, AND MODE OF CULTURE.

THE DESIGNS TO BE MADE FROM LIVING PLANTS

IN THE COLLECTIONS OF THIS COUNTRY.

A Work intended for the Use of such as desire to become acquainted with this ornamental Tribe of Plants.

By ROBERT SWEET, F. L. S.

Author of Hortus Suburbanus Londinensis, Botanical Cultivator, &c. &c.

LONDON:

PRINTED FOR JAMES RIDGWAY, PICCADILLY,

By J. Tilling, Grosvenor Row, Chelsea.

May 1, 1825.

N° LXV.

To be continued Monthly.

PRICE THREE SHILLINGS.

GERANIACEÆ,

OR

NATURAL ORDER OF GERANIUMS.

EACH NUMBER IS TO CONTAIN

FOUR COLOURED FIGURES,

WITH THEIR

SCIENTIFIC AND ENGLISH NAMES, AND MODE OF CULTURE.

THE DESIGNS TO BE MADE FROM LIVING PLANTS

IN THE COLLECTIONS OF THIS COUNTRY.

A Work intended for the Use of such as desire to become acquainted with this ornamental Tribe of Plants.

By ROBERT SWEET, F. L. S.

Author of Hortus Suburbanus Londinensis, Botanical Cultivator, British Flower Garden, & the British Warblers.

LONDON:

PRINTED FOR JAMES RIDGWAY, PICCADILLY,

By J. Tilling, Grosvenor Row, Chelsea.

June 1, 1825.

N° LXVI.

To be continued Monthly.

PRICE THREE SHILLINGS.

GERANIACEÆ,

OR

NATURAL ORDER OF GERANIUMS.

EACH NUMBER IS TO CONTAIN

FOUR COLOURED FIGURES,

WITH THEIR

SCIENTIFIC AND ENGLISH NAMES, AND MODE OF CULTURE.

THE DESIGNS TO BE MADE FROM LIVING PLANTS

IN THE COLLECTIONS OF THIS COUNTRY.

A Work intended for the Use of such as desire to become acquainted with this ornamental Tribe of Plants.

By ROBERT SWEET, F. L. S.

Author of Hortus Suburbanus Londinensis, Botanical Cultivator, British Flower Garden, & the British Warblers.

LONDON:

PRINTED FOR JAMES RIDGWAY, PICCADILLY,

By J. Tilling, Grosvenor Row, Chelsea.

WORKS

PUBLISHING BY J. RIDGWAY.

---

1. The BOTANICAL REGISTER, No. CXX. for February, 1825, (continued Monthly,) completed the Tenth Volume. Price 4s. With an Appendix, containing an Alphabetical Index to the Volume, a General Index to the Ten Volumes, &c. &c. Price 1s. By SYDENHAM EDWARDS, F.L.S. and others. Accompanied by their History, Mode of Treatment in Cultivation, &c.

Each Number contains EIGHT *coloured* PORTRAITS, *from Life, of the most beautiful and rare* EXOTIC PLANTS *cultivated in the public and private Collections of this Country.*

*** *The former Numbers, which were out of print, having been severally reprinted, may now be had to complete Sets.—Volumes handsomely half-bound, Price 2l. 15s. each, or 2l. 9s. in Numbers.*

"We look upon this Work (Edwards's Botanical Register) to be the only one of its class capable of bearing the inspection of the Botanist in all its departments; and for beauty of execution in its plates and typography it stands unrivalled by any whatever which have come under our notice. It cannot fail to please every lover of this fashionable and interesting science, as well as admirers of beautiful works in general."

2. GERANIACEÆ, or, NATURAL ORDER of the BEAUTIFUL FAMILY of GERANIUMS, Number LXV. for May 1825. Price 3s. To be continued Monthly. Each Number contains Four coloured Figures, highly and correctly finished, from living Plants, with their Scientific and English Names and Mode of Culture. By ROBERT SWEET, F.L.S. No. L. completed the Second Volume, Price 3l. 16s.; or handsomely half-bound, 4l. 2s.

3. HORTUS SUBURBANUS LONDINENSIS, or, a CATALOGUE of PLANTS CULTIVATED in the NEIGHBOURHOOD of LONDON, arranged according to the Linnean System; with the Addition of the natural Orders to which they belong, References to Books where they are described, their native Places of Growth, when introduced, Time of Flowering, and References to Figures. By ROBERT SWEET, F.L.S. Price 18s. boards, royal 8vo.

*** *This Catalogue contains several Hundred more Plants than any other published, besides various acknowledged Improvements in Arrangement.*

4. THE BOTANICAL CULTIVATOR, or, INSTRUCTIONS for the MANAGEMENT and PROPAGATION of the PLANTS cultivated in the HOTHOUSES, GREENHOUSES, and GARDENS of GREAT BRITAIN, disposed under their generic Names, and alphabetically arranged under their proper Heads in Horticulture. By ROBERT SWEET, F.L.S. Price 10s. 6d. boards.

5. A TREATISE on BULBOUS ROOTS; containing a BOTANICAL ARRANGEMENT and DESCRIPTION of the PLANTS heretofore included under the Genera Amaryllis, Cyrtanthus, Crinum, and Pancratium; with General Observations and Directions for their Cultivation. Illustrated with coloured Plates. Price 5s. By the Honourable and Rev. WILLIAM HERBERT.

*** *This Work forms an* APPENDIX *to the* BOTANICAL REGISTER *and* BOTANICAL MAGAZINE.

6. HORTUS GRAMINEUS WOBURNENSIS; or, An Account of the Results of various Experiments on the Produce and fattening Properties of different Grasses, and other Plants, used as the food of the more valuable domestic Animals; instituted by John, Duke of Bedford. By G. Sinclair, F.L.S. and F.H.S. Gardener to his Grace the Duke of Bedford, Corresponding Member of the Caledonian Horticultural Society of Edinburgh, and Corresponding Member of the Honourable the Board of Agriculture of Stuttgard. Dedicated, with permission, to T. W. Coke, Esq. M.P. Second Edition. Price 1l. 10s. plain; and coloured 2l. 2s. under the Author's immediate Inspection.

7. ROSARUM MONOGRAPHIA, or, a Botanical History of Roses. To which is added an Appendix, for the Use of Cultivators, in which the most remarkable Garden Varieties are systematically arranged. With Nineteen Plates. Eighteen beautifully coloured. By John Lindley, Esq., F.L.S. One vol. royal 8vo, 1l. 1s.

8. THE FRUIT GROWER'S INSTRUCTOR, or, A Practical Treatise on Fruit-trees, from the Nursery to Maturity; and a Description and Enumeration of all the best Fruits now in Cultivation, both for keeping and immediate Use; with useful Hints as to the planting for Orchards or in Gardens. To which is added, a full definition of the Apple-fly, commonly termed the American Blight, which causes the Canker in Apple-trees; its effectual Remedy and Prevention; together with some Practical Observations on Horticulture in general. A Work which will be found equally useful to the Gentleman, Nurseryman, or Gardener; and particularly adapted for those who cultivate or superintend the Cultivation of their own Gardens. The whole written entirely from Practice. By G. Bliss, Gardener. Price 6s.

9. PRACTICAL REMARKS on the IMPROVEMENT of GRASS LAND, by Means of Irrigation, Winter Flooding, and Drainage. In a Letter to the Owners and Occupiers of Land in the County of Essex. By C. C. Western, Esq., M.P. Price 1s. 6d.

10. A SYSTEM for MANAGING HEAVY and WET LANDS without SUMMER FALLOWS; under which a considerable Farm in Hertfordshire is kept perfectly clean, and made productive. By Thomas Greg, Esq. Third Edition. With an Appendix, pointing out how the infant Turnip may be protected from Insects by a critical Application of Lime: with Extracts from Letters from the Earl of Thanet, proving the Infallibility of the Plan. As presented to the Board of Agriculture, and now published at their Request. Price 4s.

11. A PRACTICAL TREATISE, EXPLAINING the ART and MYSTERY of BREWING PORTER, ALE, TWOPENNY, and TABLE BEER; recommending and proving the Ease and Possibility of every Man's Brewing his own Beer in any Quantity, from One Peck to a Hundred Quarters of Malt. Intended to reduce the Expenses of Families. By Samuel Child, Brewer. The Eleventh Edition, carefully revised. Price 1s.

12. A PRACTICAL TREATISE on BREEDING, REARING, and FATTENING POULTRY, &c. after Plans pursued with Advantage and Profit in France. Second Edition. Price 5s.

13. REMARKS upon PRISON DISCIPLINE, &c. &c. By C. C. Western, Esq., M.P. New Edition, with Plates and Plans of a Prison to contain Five Hundred Persons. Price 3s. 6d.

July 1, 1825.

N° LXVII.

To be continued Monthly.

PRICE THREE SHILLINGS.

GERANIACEÆ,

OR

NATURAL ORDER OF GERANIUMS.

EACH NUMBER IS TO CONTAIN

FOUR COLOURED FIGURES,

WITH THEIR

SCIENTIFIC AND ENGLISH NAMES, AND MODE OF CULTURE.

THE DESIGNS TO BE MADE FROM LIVING PLANTS

IN THE COLLECTIONS OF THIS COUNTRY.

A Work intended for the Use of such as desire to become acquainted with this ornamental Tribe of Plants.

By ROBERT SWEET, F. L. S.

Author of Hortus Suburbanus Londinensis, Botanical Cultivator, British Flower Garden, & the British Warblers.

LONDON:

PRINTED FOR JAMES RIDGWAY, PICCADILLY,

By J. Tilling, Grosvenor Row, Chelsea.

CISTINEÆ.

he Natural Order of CISTUS, or ROCK-ROSE.

On the 1st of July, 1825, will be published,

No. I.

TO BE COMPLETED IN ONE VOLUME.

A Number to be published every alternate Month.

Price THREE SHILLINGS.

Each Number will contain Four very full and elegantly coloured Figures of iandsome family of Plants, at present so little known, and so much confused e collections of this country; with their Scientific and English Names and riptions; the best Method of Cultivation and Propagation, the Soils and tion that suits them best, or any other information respecting them that may nsidered of importance.

The greater part of the Species may be cultivated with advantage in the open ers of the Flower Garden; others will succeed well against a wall, so as to overed with a mat in severe frost; and the remainder may be kept through Vinter in a common garden frame, or in the Greenhouse. Many Species are adapted for the ornamenting of Rock-work, where their lively blossoms make ndsome appearance. Plants in flower of any new or rare Species, will be cfully received by the Author, and taken care of, and the receipt of them will knowledged in the Publication; and several very rare and interesting Species already been received, and are drawn for the Work.

By ROBERT SWEET, F. L. S.

or of Hortus Suburbanus Londinensis, Botanical Cultivator, Geraniaceæ, The British Flower Garden, and the British Warblers.

Also in the Press, and by the same Author,

HORTUS BRITANNICUS;

Or a CATALOGUE of the Plants cultivated in the Gardens of Great ain, arranged according to the Natural Orders to which they belong, with ference to the Linnean Classes and Orders; their Scientific and English es, with references to the best Authorities; where native, when introduced, times of flowering, duration, and references to the books in which they are ed; with numerous other Improvements; the whole brought down to the ent time, and contains many hundreds of Plants not yet published in any logue of this Country.

Also in the Press, and speedily will be Published,

A SECOND EDITION

OF THE

BOTANICAL CULTIVATOR,

By the same Author.

Containing full Instructions for the Management and best Method of Cultiva- and Propagation of all the Plants cultivated in the Hothouses, Greenhouses, the open Air of Great Britain; with a full and particular account of the best iod of growing and flowering Hothouse and Greenhouse Bulbs; also, Epiden- is, and other Orchideous Genera, in which the Author has been particularly essful.

Published by JAMES RIDGWAY, 169, Piccadilly.

WORKS Publishing by J. RIDGWAY.

1. The BOTANICAL REGISTER, No. CXX, for February, 1825, (continu Monthly,) completed the Tenth Volume. Price 4*s*. With an Appendix, conta ing an Alphabetical Index to the Volume, a General Index to the Ten Volum &c. &c. Price 1*s*. By SYDENHAM EDWARDS, F. L. S. and others. Acco panied by their History, Mode of Treatment in Cultivation, &c.

Each Number contains EIGHT *coloured* PORTRAITS, *from Life, of the most beauti and rare* EXOTIC PLANTS *cultivated in the public and private Collections of t Country.*

*** *The former Numbers, which were out of print, having been severally reprint may now be had to complete Sets.—Volumes handsomely half bound, Price* 2*l*. 15*s*. *ea or* 2*l*. 9*s*. *in Numbers.*

"We look upon this Work (Edwards's Botanical Register) to be the only one its class capable of bearing the inspection of the Botanist in all its departmen and for beauty of execution in its plates and typography it stands unrivalled any whatever which have come under our notice. It cannot fail to please eve lover of this fashionable and interesting science, as well as admirers of beauti works in general."

2. GERANIACEÆ, or, NATURAL ORDER of the BEAUTIFUL FAMILY GERANIUMS, Number LXVI. for June 1825. Price 3*s*. To be continued Month Each Number contains Four coloured Figures, highly and correctly finished, fr living Plants, with their Scientific and English Names and Mode of Culture. ROBERT SWEET, F.L.S. No. L. completed the Second Volume, Price 3*l*. 16 or handsomely half-bound, 4*l*. 2*s*.

3. A TREATISE on BULBOUS ROOTS; containing a BOTANIC ARRANGEMENT and DESCRIPTION of the PLANTS heretofore included under Genera Amaryllis, Cyrtanthus, Crinum, and Pancratium; with General Obser tions and Directions for their Cultivation. Illustrated with coloured Plat Price 5*s*. By the Honourable and Rev. WILLIAM HERBERT.

*** *This Work forms an* APPENDIX *to the* BOTANICAL REGISTER *and* BOTANICAL MAGAZINE.

4. HORTUS GRAMINEUS WOBURNENSIS; or, An Account of the Resu of various Experiments on the Produce and fattening Properties of differe Grasses, and other Plants, used as the food of the more valuable domestic Anima instituted by JOHN, Duke of Bedford. By G. SINCLAIR, F.L.S. and F.H. Gardener to his Grace the Duke of Bedford, Corresponding Member of t Caledonian Horticultural Society of Edinburgh, and Corresponding Member of t Honourable the Board of Agriculture of Stuttgard. Dedicated, with permissi to T. W. COKE, Esq. M.P. Second Edition. Price 1*l*. 10*s*. plain; and colour 2*l*. 2*s*. under the Author's immediate Inspection.

5. ROSARUM MONOGRAPHIA, or, a BOTANICAL HISTORY of ROSES. which is added an Appendix, for the Use of Cultivators, in which the m remarkable Garden Varieties are systematically arranged. With Nineteen Plat Eighteen beautifully coloured. By JOHN LINDLEY, Esq. F.L.S. One v royal 8vo. 1*l*. 1*s*.

6. THE FRUIT GROWER'S INSTRUCTOR, or, A Practical Treatise Fruit Trees, from the Nursery to Maturity; and a Description and Enumerati of all the best Fruits now in Cultivation, both for keeping and immediate Us with useful Hints as to the planting for Orchards or in Gardens. To which added, a full definition of the Apple-fly, commonly termed the American Blig which causes the Canker in Apple Trees; its effectual Remedy and Preventi together with some Practical Observations on Horticulture in general. A Wo which will be found equally useful to the Gentleman, Nurseryman, or Garden and particularly adapted for those who cultivate or superintend the Cultivati of their own Gardens. The whole written entirely from Practice. By G. BLI Gardener. Price 6*s*.

7. PRACTICAL REMARKS on the IMPROVEMENT of GRASS LAN by means of Irrigation, Winter Flooding, and Drainage. In a Letter to the Own and Occupiers of Land in the County of Essex. By C. C. WESTERN, Esq. M. Price 1*s*. 6*d*.

8. A SYSTEM for MANAGING HEAVY and WET LANDS without SU MER FALLOWS; under which a considerable Farm in Hertfordshire is k perfectly clean, and made productive. By THOMAS GREG, Esq. Third Editi With an Appendix, pointing out how the infant Turnip may be protected fr Insects by a critical application of Lime: with Extracts from Letters from the E of Thanet, proving the infallibility of the Plan. As presented to the Board Agriculture, and now published at their Request. Price 4*s*.

August 1, 1825.

N° LXVIII.

To be continued Monthly.

PRICE THREE SHILLINGS.

GERANIACEÆ,

OR

NATURAL ORDER OF GERANIUMS.

EACH NUMBER IS TO CONTAIN

FOUR COLOURED FIGURES,

WITH THEIR

SCIENTIFIC AND ENGLISH NAMES, AND MODE OF CULTURE.

THE DESIGNS TO BE MADE FROM LIVING PLANTS

IN THE COLLECTIONS OF THIS COUNTRY.

A Work intended for the Use of such as desire to become acquainted with this ornamental Tribe of Plants.

By ROBERT SWEET, F. L. S.

Author of Hortus Suburbanus Londinensis, Botanical Cultivator, British Flower Garden, & the British Warblers.

LONDON:

PRINTED FOR JAMES RIDGWAY, PICCADILLY,

By J. Tilling, Grosvenor Row, Chelsea.

September 1, 1825.

N° LXIX.

To be continued Monthly.

PRICE THREE SHILLINGS.

GERANIACEÆ,

OR

NATURAL ORDER OF GERANIUMS.

EACH NUMBER IS TO CONTAIN

FOUR COLOURED FIGURES,

WITH THEIR

SCIENTIFIC AND ENGLISH NAMES, AND MODE OF CULTURE.

THE DESIGNS TO BE MADE FROM LIVING PLANTS

IN THE COLLECTIONS OF THIS COUNTRY.

A Work intended for the Use of such as desire to become acquainted with this ornamental Tribe of Plants.

By ROBERT SWEET, F. L. S.

Author of Hortus Suburbanus Londinensis, Botanical Cultivator, British Flower Garden, & the British Warblers.

LONDON:

PRINTED FOR JAMES RIDGWAY, PICCADILLY,

By J. Tilling, Grosvenor Row, Chelsea.

October 1, 1825.

No. LXX.

To be continued Monthly.

PRICE THREE SHILLINGS.

GERANIACEÆ,

OR

NATURAL ORDER OF GERANIUMS.

EACH NUMBER IS TO CONTAIN

FOUR COLOURED FIGURES,

WITH THEIR

SCIENTIFIC AND ENGLISH NAMES, AND MODE OF CULTURE.

THE DESIGNS TO BE MADE FROM LIVING PLANTS

IN THE COLLECTIONS OF THIS COUNTRY.

A Work intended for the Use of such as desire to become acquainted with this ornamental Tribe of Plants.

By ROBERT SWEET, F. L. S.

Author of Hortus Suburbanus Londinensis, Botanical Cultivator, British Flower Garden, & the British Warblers,

LONDON:

PRINTED FOR JAMES RIDGWAY, PICCADILLY,

By J. Tilling, Grosvenor Row, Chelsea.

November 1, 1825.

No. LXXI.

To be continued Monthly.

PRICE THREE SHILLINGS.

GERANIACEÆ,

OR

NATURAL ORDER OF GERANIUMS.

EACH NUMBER IS TO CONTAIN

FOUR COLOURED FIGURES,

WITH THEIR

SCIENTIFIC AND ENGLISH NAMES, AND MODE OF CULTURE.

THE DESIGNS TO BE MADE FROM LIVING PLANTS

IN THE COLLECTIONS OF THIS COUNTRY.

A Work intended for the Use of such as desire to become acquainted with this ornamental Tribe of Plants.

By ROBERT SWEET, F. L. S.

Author of Hortus Suburbanus Londinensis, Botanical Cultivator, British Flower Garden, & the British Warblers.

LONDON:

PRINTED FOR JAMES RIDGWAY, PICCADILLY,

By J. Tilling, Grosvenor Row, Chelsea.

Works publishing by James Ridgway, 169, Piccadilly.

SECOND EDITION, Price 12s.

1. The HOTHOUSE & GREENHOUSE MANUAL, or BOTANICAL CULTIVATOR; giving full Instructions for the Management and Propagation of the Plants Cultivated in the Hothouses, Greenhouses, and Borders, in the Gardens of Great Britain; also the Management of Plants in Rooms, &c. disposed under the Generic Names of the Plants, Alphabetically arranged under the Heads of the Departments of Horticulture to which they belong. Second Edition. By ROBERT SWEET, F.L.S. Author of Hortus Suburbanus Londinensis, Geraniaceæ, British Warblers, British Flower Garden, Cistineæ, &c. &c.

Also by the same Author, No. 3, for November, Price 3s.

To be continued the 1st of every alternate Month, and to form one handsome Volume, Royal 8vo.

2. CISTINEÆ, the Natural Order of CISTUS, or ROCK-ROSE.—Each Number will contain Four very full and elegantly coloured Figures of this handsome family of Plants, at present so little known, and so much confused in the collections of this country; with their Scientific and English Names and Descriptions; the best Method of Cultivation and Propagation, the Soils and Situation that suits them best, or any other information respecting them that may be considered of importance.

The greater part of the Species may be cultivated with advantage in the open borders of the Flower Garden; others will succeed well against a wall, so as to be covered with a mat in severe frost; and the remainder may be kept through the Winter in a common garden frame, or in the Greenhouse. Many species are well adapted for the ornamenting of Rock-work, where their lively blossoms make a handsome appearance. Plants in flower of any new or rare Species, will be thankfully received by the Author, and taken care of, and the receipt of them will be acknowledged in the Publication; and several very rare and interesting Species have already been received, and are drawn for the Work.

3. The BOTANICAL REGISTER, No. CXXIX, for November, 1825, Price 4s. (continued Monthly.) No. 120, completed the Tenth Volume. Also an Appendix, containing an Alphabetical Index to the Volume, a General Index to the Ten Volumes, &c. &c. Price 1s. By SYDENHAM EDWARDS, F.L.S. and others. Each Number contains Eight coloured Portraits, from Life, of the most beautiful and rare EXOTIC PLANTS, cultivated in the public and private Collections of this Country; accompanied by their History, Mode of Treatment in Cultivation, and any thing else considered of general interest.

⁂ The former Numbers, which were out of print, having been severally reprinted, may now be had to complete Sets.—Volumes handsomely half-bound, Price 2l. 15s. each.

4. THE FRUIT GROWER'S INSTRUCTOR, or a Practical Treatise on Fruit-trees, from the Nursery to Maturity; and a Description and Enumeration of all the best Fruits now in Cultivation, both for keeping and immediate Use; with useful Hints as to the planting for Orchards or in Gardens. To which is added, a full definition of the Apple-fly, commonly termed the American Blight, which causes the Canker in Apple-trees; its effectual Remedy and Prevention; together with some Practical Observations on Horticulture in general. A Work which will be found equally useful to the Gentleman, Nurseryman, or Gardener; and particularly adapted for those who cultivate or superintend the Cultivation of their own Gardens. The whole written entirely from Practice. By G. BLISS, Gardener. Price 6s.

Mr. SWEET has in the Press, to appear as early as possible,

5. HORTUS BRITANNICUS, or a Catalogue of the Plants cultivated in the Gardens of Great Britain, arranged according to the NATURAL ORDERS to which they belong, with a reference to the Linnean Classes and Orders; their Scientific and English Names, with references to the best Authorities; where native, when introduced, their times of flowering, duration, and references to the books in which they are figured; with numerous other Improvements; the whole brought down to the present time, and contains many hundreds of Plants not yet published in any Catalogue of this Country.

December 1, 1825.

No. LXXII.

To be continued Monthly.

PRICE THREE SHILLINGS.

GERANIACEÆ,

OR

NATURAL ORDER OF GERANIUMS.

EACH NUMBER IS TO CONTAIN

FOUR COLOURED FIGURES,

WITH THEIR

SCIENTIFIC AND ENGLISH NAMES, AND MODE OF CULTURE.

THE DESIGNS TO BE MADE FROM LIVING PLANTS *IN THE COLLECTIONS OF THIS COUNTRY.*

A Work intended for the Use of such as desire to become acquainted with this ornamental Tribe of Plants.

By ROBERT SWEET, F.L.S.

Author of Hortus Suburbanus Londinensis, Botanical Cultivator, British Flower Garden, & the British Warblers.

LONDON:

PRINTED FOR JAMES RIDGWAY, PICCADILLY,

By J. Tilling, Grosvenor Row, Chelsea.

January 1, 1826.

No. LXXIII.

To be continued Monthly.

PRICE THREE SHILLINGS.

GERANIACEÆ,

OR

NATURAL ORDER OF GERANIUMS.

EACH NUMBER IS TO CONTAIN

FOUR COLOURED FIGURES,

WITH THEIR

SCIENTIFIC AND ENGLISH NAMES, AND MODE OF CULTURE.

THE DESIGNS TO BE MADE FROM LIVING PLANTS
IN THE COLLECTIONS OF THIS COUNTRY.

A Work intended for the Use of such as desire to become acquainted with this ornamental Tribe of Plants.

By ROBERT SWEET, F.L.S.

Author of Hortus Suburbanus Londinensis, Botanical Cultivator, British Flower Garden, & the British Warblers.

LONDON:

PRINTED FOR JAMES RIDGWAY, PICCADILLY,

By J. Tilling, Grosvenor Row, Chelsea.

February 1, 1826.

No. LXXIV.

To be continued Monthly.

PRICE THREE SHILLINGS.

GERANIACEÆ,

OR

NATURAL ORDER OF GERANIUMS.

EACH NUMBER IS TO CONTAIN

FOUR COLOURED FIGURES,

WITH THEIR

SCIENTIFIC AND ENGLISH NAMES, AND MODE OF CULTURE.

THE DESIGNS TO BE MADE FROM LIVING PLANTS *IN THE COLLECTIONS OF THIS COUNTRY.*

A Work intended for the Use of such as desire to become acquainted with this ornamental Tribe of Plants.

By ROBERT SWEET, F.L.S.

Author of Hortus Suburbanus Londinensis, Botanical Cultivator, British Flower Garden, & the British Warblers.

LONDON:

PRINTED FOR JAMES RIDGWAY, PICCADILLY,

By J. Tilling, Grosvenor Row, Chelsea.

March 1, 1826.

No. LXXV.

To be continued Monthly.

PRICE THREE SHILLINGS.

APPENDIX, PRICE ONE SHILLING.

N.B.—*The Appendix is delivered with the present Fasciculus, and will continue to be added to the concluding Number of each Volume.*

GERANIACEÆ,

OR

NATURAL ORDER OF GERANIUMS.

EACH NUMBER IS TO CONTAIN

FOUR COLOURED FIGURES,

WITH THEIR

SCIENTIFIC AND ENGLISH NAMES, AND MODE OF CULTURE.

THE DESIGNS TO BE MADE FROM LIVING PLANTS

IN THE COLLECTIONS OF THIS COUNTRY.

A Work intended for the Use of such as desire to become acquainted with this ornamental Tribe of Plants.

By ROBERT SWEET, F.L.S.

Author of Hortus Suburbanus Londinensis, Botanical Cultivator, British Flower Garden, & the British Warblers.

LONDON:

PRINTED FOR JAMES RIDGWAY, PICCADILLY.

By J. Tilling, Grosvenor Row, Chelsea.

CPSIA information can be obtained
at www.ICGtesting.com
Printed in the USA
LVHW050012090123
736726LV00004B/188

9 781363 117888

מסורה

ArtScroll Mesorah Series®

Expositions on Jewish liturgy and thought

Rab[illegible]son Scherman / Meir Zlotowitz
General Editors

Shema Yisrael

THE THREE PORTIONS OF THE SHEMA
INCLUDING THE BEDTIME SHEMA / A NEW TRANSLATION WITH A COMMENTARY ANTHOLOGIZED FROM TALMUDIC, MIDRASHIC, AND RABBINIC SOURCES.

Published by

Mesorah Publications, ltd

סדר קריאת שמע
וקריאת שמע על המטה

Translation and Commentary by
Rabbi Meir Zlotowitz

An Overview / "A Declaration of Faith," by
Rabbi Nosson Scherman

FIRST EDITION
First Impression ... February, 1982

Published and Distributed by
MESORAH PUBLICATIONS, Ltd.
Brooklyn, New York 11223

Distributed in Israel by
MESORAH MAFITZIM / J. GROSSMAN
Rechov Bayit Vegan 90/5
Jerusalem, Israel

Distributed in Europe by
J. LEHMANN HEBREW BOOKSELLERS
20 Cambridge Terrace
Gateshead / Tyne and Wear
England NE8 1RP

ISBN
0-89906-187-7 (hard cover)
0-89906-188-5 (paperback)

סֵדֶר בַּמְּסֹרֶת
חֶבְרַת אַרְטְסְקְרוֹל בע״מ

Typography by Compuscribe at ArtScroll Studios, Ltd.
1969 Coney Island Avenue / Brooklyn, N.Y. 11223 / (212) 339-1700

Printed in the United States of America by Moriah Offset

An Overview / A Declaration of Faith

אָמַר לָהֶם הקב״ה לְיִשְׂרָאֵל, אַתֶּם עֲשִׂיתוּנִי חֲטִיבָה אַחַת בָּעוֹלָם שֶׁנֶּאֱמַר שְׁמַע יִשְׂרָאֵל ה׳ אֱלֹהֵינוּ ה׳ אֶחָד; וַאֲנִי אֶעֱשֶׂה אֶתְכֶם חֲטִיבָה אַחַת בָּעוֹלָם שֶׁנֶּאֱמַר וּמִי כְּעַמְּךָ יִשְׂרָאֵל גּוֹי אֶחָד בָּאָרֶץ.

The Holy One, Blessed is He, said to Israel, You have declared Me unique in the universe, as it says (Deuteronomy 6:4), Hear O Israel, HASHEM, is [now] our God, HASHEM [will be] One — and I shall declare you unique in the universe as it says (I Chronicles 17:21): And who is like Your people Israel — a unique nation on earth (Berachos 6a).*

Life's most meaningful moments are punctuated with the Shema.

Morning and night, the Jew shuts his eyes and proclaims the *Shema* — God is ours and He is One. Life's most meaningful moments are punctuated with the *Shema:* when the Jew prepares to read the Torah on Sabbaths and festivals, when he dedicates his new day and when he surrenders to helpless sleep in the unknown night, at the climax of Yom Kippur, and at the climax of life when his soul leaves its earthly host. In the *mezuzah* the *Shema* sanctifies his home and in his *tefillin* it sanctifies his intellect and strength. And God Himself thanks Israel, as it were, for declaring His uniqueness by means of the *Shema,* as though *He* becomes fulfilled through *us.* Let us explore, in an elementary way, the significance of the *Shema;* if we succeed we shall be both better servants of God and better people.

I. R' Akiva's Example

Source of Life

One of the Talmud's most moving narratives tells of Rabbi Akiva's last days. He lived in the century after the destruction of the Second Temple, a time when Roman cruelty had brought Jewish life to one of its

* The unfamiliar translation of the first verse of *Shema* follows *Rashi's* commentary to the Torah. He explains: although at present only Israel recognizes HASHEM as God, in time to come He will be acknowledged by all mankind. See commentary p. 15.

lowest ebbs ever. The Romans sought to eradicate Judaism as an independent culture, and their primary target was Torah education. To ordain rabbis and to teach Torah publicly were declared criminal offenses punishable by death. R' Akiva would not knuckle under. He was the teacher of thousands, the nation's greatest sage, and one of its most devoted leaders. He knew that he was one of Rome's prime targets, but at a time when Israel's faith was under assault [שְׁעַת הַשְּׁמַד], personal safety, even survival, cannot take priority to the survival of Torah and the needs of the people. If R' Akiva were to withhold his teaching and his personal example, he would become the passive ally of the Roman executioners.

If R' Akiva were to withhold his teaching and his personal example, he would become the passive ally of the Roman executioners.

R' Akiva knew what he had to do. He gathered large congregations publicly and taught them Torah.

His friend and colleague, Papus ben Yehudah, was appalled at R' Akiva's temerity.

'Akiva, aren't you afraid of the government?'

R' Akiva answered, 'I will explain our predicament with a parable. Once a fox was walking along a river bank when he saw schools of fish frenziedly swimming from one part of the river to another. He called out to the fish, "From what do you flee?"

'The fish answered, "We seek to escape the nets that fishermen put out to catch us."

'Feigning concern, the fox shouted, "If only you would come up on the dry land! Then you and I could live together as peaceful neighbors, just as our forebears did before humans came along to disturb our harmony."

'The fish responded, "Are you the fox, about whom it is said that you are the shrewdest of all animals? You are not shrewd, but a fool! If our lives are in danger even in the water which is our source of life, how much greater would be our peril on land where our death is certain?"

'We are in the same predicament,' R' Akiva told Papus. 'If we are in danger when we study the Torah, about which we are taught *for it is your life and the length of your days (Deuteronomy* 30:20), then our very survival will surely be in danger if we forsake the Torah!'

'If we are in danger when we study the Torah, then our very survival will surely be in danger if we forsake the Torah!'

Before long, Roman soldiers discovered R' Akiva and threw him into a dungeon — and not long afterward Papus ben Yehudah, too, was arrested and imprisoned together with him. Upon seeing his dear friend, Papus exclaimed, 'Akiva, how fortunate you are — *you* were arrested for the sake of Torah. But sad it is for Papus — I was arrested for a mere triviality.'

It was the time of the morning *Shema* reading when R' Akiva was taken out to be tortured to death publicly. The Romans tore his flesh with iron combs, but during his frightful ordeal he accepted God's sovereignty upon himself by reciting the *Shema*. He was joyous, oblivious to the pain. Turnus Rufus, the Roman commander who ordered the barbarous execution, was flabbergasted. 'Have you no feeling of pain that you can laugh in the face of such intense suffering!' he exclaimed. Even R' Akiva's own students wondered, 'Our teacher, even to this extent?'

The dying sage explained, 'All my life I was concerned over a phrase of the Torah. We are taught in the *Shema* to accept God's sovereignty and decrees upon ourselves בְּכָל נַפְשְׁךָ, *with all your soul* — even if He takes your life. I used to wonder if I would ever have the privilege of serving God to such a degree. Now that the chance has come to me, shall I not grasp it with joy?'

I used to wonder if I would ever have the privilege of serving God to such a degree. Now that the chance has come to me, shall I not grasp it with joy?'

He repeated the first verse of *Shema — Hear O Israel, HASHEM is* [*now*] *our God, HASHEM* [*will be*] *One* — and he drew out the word אֶחָד, *One,* until his soul left him.

A Heavenly voice was heard, saying, 'You are praiseworthy, R' Akiva, for your soul left you as you proclaimed God's Oneness! ... You are praiseworthy, R' Akiva, for you are ready to enter the life of the World to Come' *(Berachos* 61b; *Yerushalmi Berachos* 9:5).

R' Akiva remains one of the most inspirational figures in the last two thousand years. At the age of forty, he was still an ignorant, scholar-hating shepherd, when, thanks to the prodding and encouragement of an equally inspirational wife, he began learning how to read. Many years later he returned home surrounded by twenty-four thousand students and acclaimed as his people's leading scholar, but he accorded public honor to his poverty-stricken wife, telling his students, 'Whatever I have attained and whatever your have attained is due to her.' He became a leader of the military and spiritual resistance to Rome and, through his students, he became the dominant Torah figure of his turbulent, tormented era and the following generations.

He summed up his entire life in a final act of heroism: he placed the survival of Israel as a Torah nation ahead of personal safety.

But at the end, he summed up his entire life in a final act of heroism: he placed the survival of Israel as a Torah nation ahead of personal safety; and he taught one of his greatest lessons as his soul expired. It is a worthy life's goal — even for a life as rich as R' Akiva's — to end on a note of total dedication to God. All his life he had declared his willingness to submerge his individuality to the goal of sanctifying God's Name, but no man can know if he will be equal to the awful challenge when it comes. R' Akiva's rejoicing eclipsed his suffering because he had proven equal to the ideals he taught. Turnus Rufus, his executioner, thought he was mad, but who remembers Turnus Rufus today? He thought he was wiping R' Akiva off the ledger of history, but Turnus Rufus is remembered only because of his notorious act, while his victim's memory lives on as one of the greatest people of the last two thousand years.

Turnus Rufus, his executioner, thought he was mad, but who remembers Turnus Rufus today?

The Prerequisite

Judaism has no special commandments for its Abrahams, Davids, and Akivas. If R' Akiva took comfort from his suffering in having declared the Oneness of God, if he considered his life a success because he was able to end it with a declaration that ה׳ אֶחָד, *HASHEM is One* — and if the Talmud and the Heavenly voice put so much stress upon it — then we must draw the lesson that the attainment of such a conviction is the duty of every man, woman, and child. Indeed, the twice-daily reading of the *Shema* is not only commanded by the Torah, it is the basic expression of Jewish belief.

When God gave Israel the Ten Commandments at Sinai, all Israel heard the first two directly from Him. The first commandment was God's declaration that He is God: *I am HASHEM your God ...*, the second commandment was the precept against belief in any other deity: *You shall not recognize the gods of others before My presence.* These are the cardinal commandments of Judaism, that we believe absolutely in God's existence and that we not share His mantle with any other being or power. As the Sages put it, only after a king's subjects acknowledge his legitimate authority can he promulgate decrees. Unless a government is recognized, it has no legal standing and its laws have no force. The first commandment, therefore, must be to believe in God, for without that prerequisite nothing else in the Torah could be binding. The second commandment is, in effect, a corollary of the first, that Divinity has no partners; there is one God and none other.

The first commandment, therefore, must be to believe in God, for without that prerequisite nothing else in the Torah could be binding.

The reading of *Shema* is our daily fulfillment of the

first commandment: that we declare our firm belief in God's existence and indivisibility (*Ramban* and *R' Bachya* to *Deut.* 6:4; but cf. *Rambam, Sefer HaMitzvos, Aseh* 1,2; and *Ramban* to *Lo Sa'aseh* 5).

Why does the profession of our faith require a declaration of God's Oneness? Why did R' Akiva draw out the word אֶחָד, *One*, until his death? — obviously this aspect of his final moments was critical, for it was followed by a Heavenly voice praising him for giving up his soul as he proclaimed that God is One, and announcing that he was entering the World to Come.

II. Oneness — The Ultimate Goal

Uniqueness and Control

There are two aspects of God's Oneness: a) Nothing else is comparable to Him; b) nothing exists independently of Him.

When we say that God is One, we mean not only that there is none other, but that He is beyond comparison. *Rambam's* second Principle of Faith states:

> *I believe with perfect faith that the Creator, Blessed is His Name, is unique, and no uniqueness resembles His in any manner ...*

There is only one Mount Everest, but there are other mountains, though not so high. The Pacific is the largest ocean, but there are others. Moses was the greatest prophet and Solomon was the wisest man, and Scripture assures us that no one would ever equal them. Nevertheless, there have been many prophets and scholars of rare genius. Consequently any manifestation of physical, cultural, or intellectual greatness can be called 'unique' only in relative terms — it is great, greater, or greatest, but others, though inferior, can be compared to it. Not so God's uniqueness. He has no beginning or end, no limitations, no competitors or partners, no corporeality. We cannot comprehend any aspect of His existence because our conception and even our vocabulary is limited by our very humanness. Our ears cannot hear even most of the soundwaves audible to a dog, our vision is limited to what our most powerful telescopes can show us, and all the power of modern science cannot quell a hurricane or light up the night. An atomic explosion gives as much light as the sun for the barest instant and over a limited space, but the sun

We cannot comprehend any aspect of His existence because even our vocabulary is limited by our very humanness.

illuminates half a planet without stop, and our sun is smaller than millions of others in the solar system. Yet all the suns combined are but a small part of the universe and God created them all! When we think of such uniqueness, the very word 'unique' seems ludicrously inadequate to describe it.

When we think of such uniqueness, the very word 'unique' seems ludicrously inadequate to describe it.

The second aspect of God's Oneness is that God is the source of everything we know. Not only did He create the universe and endow its various components with the powers and instincts to function, reproduce, and be creative, He retains ultimate control over them. Even their apparent power extends only within the limits He places upon them. But this concept goes much deeper. God has a plan for the universe and every event somehow fits into this plan. There are variations, of course, because man has freedom of choice. Most of the time, we do not understand how the parts relate to the whole; often events seem so evil or incomprehensible that we cannot imagine how a merciful, rational Creator could have included them in His program. But even these apparent aberrations fit into the master plan. Sometimes, hindsight offers us a vantage point of a grand design.

He is King

If God rules everything and God, by definition, is all good, how can there be evil and sinners? Evil is a product of ignorance — ignorance of His Will and the concealment of His Presence. People don't stumble at high noon; they trip when night conceals the obstacles in their path, or when greed and passion persuade them to close their eyes. This is why 'night' and 'darkness' have become synonyms for suffering and evil and why it is said, in the words of *Tzeidah LaDerech*, מְעַט מִן הָאוֹר דּוֹחֶה הַרְבֵּה מִן הַחֹשֶׁךְ, *A little bit of light banishes much darkness.* Obviously if people were not blind to the truth, the achievement of God's goal would come much more quickly. That people do not see Him and are seduced by evil does not defeat His plan, however. One way or another, every epoch and event has its place. A nation can play a constructive role by being a force for good, but if it chooses to do otherwise, its eventual punishment and downfall can serve as a lesson that God's will cannot be flouted with impunity. In the longed-for time when God provides us with a true perspective on history will we will know how sinners failed, and that knowledge will sanctify His Name — clearly the sinful person or

Obviously if people were not blind to the truth, the achievement of God's goal would come much more quickly.

community would have played its part better had it sanctified Him in a more positive way, but the fullfillment of His will is inevitable, for all of creation exists only for that purpose. This is the ultimate dimension of God's Oneness: it means that everything is inseparable from His control and guidance.

Sometimes mankind basks in the light of His mercy and the human mind is illuminated by the brilliance of comprehending Him. Other times we shudder in the chill of night and our perceptions are clouded by our failure to understand His ways. These are the spiritual days and nights of our existence. In either kind of experience we must find ways to strengthen our faith in Him as our God, our Creator, our all-powerful Guide; and we must proclaim our conviction that He is One and that any other claimants to power are impostors.

God's essence does not become enhanced by our acknowledgment of Him.

God's essence does not become enhanced by our acknowledgment of Him; the Name אֱלֹהִים, *God,* describes Him as the Ultimate Power, and as such He becomes no stronger by virtue of our recognition or weaker by virtue of our denial. But God wants something more. In His wisdom He decreed that His creatures should declare Him to be King. In Jewish thought, there is a difference between a מֹשֵׁל, *dictator,* and a מֶלֶךְ, *king.* The despot is not dependent on the good will of his subjects; he imposes his will whether or not it is welcome. But the 'King' acquires that title in its most meaningful sense only with the respect and consent of the governed. If his subjects accept his legitimacy he earns the Hebrew title מֶלֶךְ, *king,* otherwise, no matter how absolute his power, he is called a מֹשֵׁל, *dictator.* [This concept is discussed at length in the Overview to *Vayigash.*] God wants to be more than our Master; He wants to be our King and for this to happen we must accept His reign.

God wants to be more than our Master; He wants to be our King and for this to happen we must accept His reign.

All of this we accomplish when we recite the *Shema.* We proclaim our faith. We declare our knowledge — though our understanding may be far from perfect — that His will is done through every event, from the holy to the heinous. We accept God as our King — willingly, gladly, with a sense of privilege that He lowers Himself to let us serve Him; indeed, that He lets us be necessary to the accomplishment of His goals. Night and day we recite the *Shema,* symbolizing our acceptance of these ideals in every period and every condition of life. In the golden era of David and Solomon or on the racks of Torquemada's

Inquisition and under the swords of the Crusaders, Israel declares its faith and finds comfort in the knowledge that HASHEM is *our* God — for He revealed Himself to us and relies upon us to pierce the darkness of human perception with the light of His Oneness.

R' Akiva's Triumph

How easy it is to declare that God is King, Creator, and Guide of *others* — and how hard it is to accept His sovereignty over our*selves*. How easy to tell others that *their* travail is justified and that *they* must subject their urges and resources to His will — and how hard to admit that it was not a miscarriage of justice that we stubbed *our* toe or failed to gain riches and respect. How easy to preach that Israel in general has a demanding responsibility as the recipient of God's Torah and the bearer of his mission — but how hard for each son and daughter of Israel to live *his* own life, *her* own life, in accordance with that awareness.

God as King hardly had a subject who served Him better.

R' Akiva personified everything that is sublime in Israel. From ignoramus he made himself the teacher of Israel. In times of the most intense national chagrin and degradation, he inspired others to confidence and optimism. God as King hardly had a subject who served Him better. But R' Akiva's own heroic demonstration of Israel's courage in God's service left him the helpless prey of Turnus Rufus' torturers!

Dismay? No, R' Akiva was not dismayed. All his life he had prepared himself for the moment when even his life would be offered upon the altar of his King — the God whom *he* had made King. In the face of the blaspheming Turnus Rufus and in the presence of his grieving but inspired students, he taught his last and greatest lesson. Everything in life is God's gift and every event is a piece in the construction of His jigsaw puzzle. If R' Akiva's contribution had to be through the endurance of pain with the ecstatic conviction that even his suffering had meaning, then so be it.

A heavenly voice testified to his good fortune as the gates of the World to Come swung open to admit R' Akiva.

In his dying moments he proclaimed the *Shema* — and a heavenly voice testified to his good fortune as the gates of the World to Come swung open to admit R' Akiva.

Rabbi Nosson Scherman
Shevat 6, 5742

סדר קריאת שמע

◆§ Some essential laws pertaining to the recital of the Shema

The following has been culled from *Shulchan Aruch* and *Likkutei Mahariach*. Other laws have been inserted in their appropriate places in the commentary and as instructions within the Text.

- ☐ Before beginning the *Shema* one must bear in mind that he intends to fulfill the commandment of reciting the *Shema* twice daily.
- ☐ The first verse of *Shema* is the essential profession of our faith. It should be recited aloud in order to arouse one's full concentration on its meaning and significance.
- ☐ Some consider it preferable to recite the entire *Shema* aloud (except for the passage בָּרוּךְ שֵׁם) in order to arouse the concentration. However, at the minimum, the first verse should be said aloud, while the rest of *Shema* may be recited quietly, provided one hears what he is saying.
- ☐ Every word of the *Shema* must be recited with *kavannah* — concentration upon its meaning. All thoughts other than God's Unity must be shut out while the *Shema* is recited with concentration of heart and mind.
- ☐ While reciting the first verse, it is customary to cover the eyes with the right hand to avoid distraction and enhance the concentration.
- ☐ Although it is not the universal custom to chant the *Shema* with the cantillation melody used during the Synagogue Torah reading, it is laudable to do so unless one finds that such chanting interferes with his concentration. In any event, the punctuation must be followed so that phrases are grouped together properly in accordance with the syntax of each word-group and verse.
- ☐ Every word must be enunciated clearly and uttered with the correct grammatical emphasis. It is especially important to enunciate clearly and pause briefly between words ending and beginning with the same consonant, such as בְּכָל לְבַבְכֶם, וַאֲבַדְתֶּם מְהֵרָה, to avoid slurring, and between words one of which ends with a consonant and one of which begins with a silent letter [א or ע], such as וּרְאִיתֶם אתו, הַיּום עַל, אֲשֶׁר אָנֹכִי.
- ☐ The last word of the first verse, אֶחָד, must be pronounced with special emphasis [see commentary], while one meditates on God's sovereignty over the seven heavens and earth, and the four directions — east, south, west, and north.
- ☐ While reciting the three portions of the *Shema,* one may not communicate with someone else by winking or motioning with the lips or fingers.
- ☐ During morning services, the four *tzitzis* are to be gathered when one says the words וַהֲבִיאֵנוּ לְשָׁלוֹם, *Bring us in peace,* in the paragraph preceding the *Shema* in the siddur. From then on and throughout the *Shema,* the *tzitzis* are to be held — according to some customs, between the fourth finger and the little finger — against the heart.
- ☐ When reciting the third portion, וַיֹּאמֶר ה', *HASHEM said,* during morning services, one should also grasp the *tzitzis* with the right hand and look at them, until after he has said the words לְנֶאֱמָנִים וְנֶחֱמָדִים לָעַד in the אֱמֶת וְיַצִּיב prayer following *Shema*.

Immediately before reciting the *Shema* one must concentrate on his intention to fulfill the positive commandment of reciting the *Shema* twice daily.

When praying in private or without a minyan, add the following three-word formula

אֵל מֶלֶךְ נֶאֱמָן:

Before reciting the following verse, concentrate upon accepting God's absolute sovereignty. Then recite it aloud:

שְׁמַע יִשְׂרָאֵל יהוה אֱלֹהֵינוּ יהוה | אֶחָד:

After a short pause, the following verse is said in a whisper [except on Yom Kippur when it is recited aloud]:

בָּרוּךְ שֵׁם כְּבוֹד מַלְכוּתוֹ לְעוֹלָם וָעֶד.

◆§ The Shema/Preliminary Formula:

אֵל מֶלֶךְ נֶאֱמָן — *God, trustworthy King.* These three words are not part of the Biblical verses; they are added as an introductory formula in the liturgy when one recites *Shema* in the absence of a *minyan*. [When praying with a minyan this three-word formula is not recited; instead one listens to the *chazzan's* three-word repetition of the conclusion ה׳ אֱלֹהֵיכֶם אֱמֶת (see *comm.* below, p. 47).]

The reason for adding three words — at the beginning or the end — is as follows: The three paragraphs of the *Shema* contain a total of 245 words. The additional three words yield the total number of both the positive commandments and the organs in the human body. This expresses the concept that physical existence is indivisible from the spiritual obligation to obey the precepts of the Torah in their entirety.

The Sages accordingly maintain that "whoever recites the *Shema* with its 248 words in proper concentration will merit that the Holy One, Blessed is He, will watch over his every organ. — 'Watch over Mine,' said God, 'and I will watch over yours' " *(Midrash Tanchuma;* see *Daas Zekeinim).*

These words — the initials of which spell אָמֵן *(Shabbos* 19b) — were chosen to supply the three words needed for the total of 248 because they succinctly express the essence of our belief in God.

The *kavannah* [concentration of thought on the meaning of the words] one should have while reciting the formula is:

□ אֵל, *God* — You exist as the All-Powerful source of all mercy;

□ מֶלֶךְ, *King* — You rule, lead, and exercise supervision over all;

□ נֶאֱמָן, *trustworthy* — In dispensing reward and punishment, You are fair and scrupulous, apportioning no more suffering nor less good than one deserves *(Etz Yosef).*

According to *Rokeach* the *kavannah* is upon the initials אָמֵן, and upon the intimation of the words: אֵל, *God* — before Creation; מֶלֶךְ, *king* — over all of this world; נֶאֱמָן, *trustworthy* — to resurrect the dead at the time of Redemption.

◆§ The First Portion [*Deut.* 6:4-9]

In its Scriptural context: The first portion of *Shema* is in *Parshas Va'eschanan, Deuteronomy* 6:4-9. It was enunciated by Moses to the Israelites after he recounted the story of the Giving of the Ten Commandments, in the general context of Moses' eloquent appeal that the Jewish nation not forget what they had personally witnessed at the Revelation, and that they obey God's laws. Then he proceeded to declare the other foundation of the Torah: the Oneness of God and Israel's undivided love and loyalty to Him.

According to *Yerushalmi Berachos* 1:5 these following sections were chosen to form the daily reading of the *Shema* because their verses contain parallel allusions to the Ten Commandments. [See p. 63.]

Rambam notes that this passage is closely tied to the First Commandment — *I am HASHEM your God* — inasmuch as that commandment contains the principal of the unity

Immediately before reciting the *Shema* one must concentrate on his intention to fulfill the positive commandment of reciting the *Shema* twice daily.

When praying in private or without a minyan, add the following three-word formula

God, Trustworthy King.

Before reciting the following verse, concentrate upon accepting God's absolute sovereignty. Then recite it aloud:

Deuteronomy 6:4 **Hear, O Israel: HASHEM is [now] our God, HASHEM [will be] One.**

After a short pause, the following verse is said in a whisper [except on Yom Kippur when it is recited aloud]:

Pesachim 56a **Blessed be the Name of His glorious kingdom for all eternity.**

of God. In the *Shema,* Moses intended to elaborate on that Commandment and he began to do so soon after the Ten Commandments. This concept of God's absolute Unity is the essence of our faith, and whoever does not acknowledge it, denies the primary principle of our religion as if he worships idols.

◆§ The First Verse/The acceptance of God's absolute sovereignty

The recitation of *Shema* — especially its first verse — represents fulfillment of the paramount commandment of קַבָּלַת עוֹל מַלְכוּת שָׁמַיִם, *acceptance of God's absolute sovereignty.* For by declaring that God is One — Unique, and Indivisible — we thereby sublimate every facet of our personalities and possessions — our very lives — to His will.

4. שְׁמַע יִשְׂרָאֵל ה׳ אֱלֹהֵינוּ ה׳ אֶחָד — *Hear, O Israel: HASHEM is [now] our God, HASHEM [will be] One* [literally, *HASHEM is One; Alone; Unique*]. The translation follows *Rashi.* The Sages and commentators find many layers of meaning in this seminal verse — many of which will be cited below in the word-by-word exposition — but the consensus is that *Rashi's* interpretation is the minimum one must have in mind when reciting the passage since it takes into account every word, allowing for no superfluity.

As *Rashi* explains it, the phrase means "... *HASHEM,* Who now is only *our God* and not that of other peoples [i.e., Who, in this point in the history of the world is acknowledged as the true God only by Israel but not by all people of the earth] will in the future be [acknowledged by *all* as] *the One* [i.e., sole] *HASHEM.* Thus it is written [*Zephaniah* 3:9]: ... *For then I will turn to the peoples a pure language that they may all call upon the Name of HASHEM;* and it is further said [*Zechariah* 14:9]: *In that day* [of Ultimate Redemption] *shall HASHEM be One and His Name One."*

That is, God's unity is absolute even now, but the gentile nations do not acknowledge Him as One; only Israel does. In Messianic times, however, all the world will acknowledge that He is the sole God. Although the Sages derive the Biblical concept of God's Unity from our passage, if it enunciated only that — and did not express the additional idea that what only Israel acknowledges now will be acknowledged by all in the future — it would be sufficient to have said: *Hear O Israel our God is One,* or: *Hear O Israel: HASHEM is One (Mizrachi; cf. Gur Aryeh; Tzeidah LaDerech; Zikaron).*

Ibn Ezra explains the verse in *Zephaniah* cited by *Rashi: For then I will turn to the peoples a pure language,* i.e., the whole world will speak in the Holy Tongue — Hebrew — *that they may all call upon the Name of HASHEM ... In that day HASHEM shall be One and his Name One.* That is, God's Name will be One, for all will refer to Him unanimously as *HASHEM* [i.e., the Four-letter Name as it is written]. [See *Overview.*]

Among other interpretations of this primary passage are:

□ R' Saadiah Gaon: *Know, Israel, that HASHEM our God is the One God.*

□ Rashbam: ... *HASHEM alone is our God* and we have no other god with Him [comp. *II Chronicles* 13:10]; *HASHEM is One* — Him only do we serve.

□ Ralbag: *Perceive well, O congregation of Israel:* He Who is referred to as *'HASHEM' oversees us;* and though His Essence is beyond our meager comprehension, *HASHEM is One* — the Holy Being referred to by that Holy Name is One.

* * *

While reciting the *Shema,* one should concentrate on its parallels with the Ten Commandments [as listed on p. 63]. Since such prolonged concentration is difficult when one prays together with a congregation, at the very minimum one should concentrate on the first two Commandments alluded to in the first verse:

Hear O Israel, HASHEM is our God = I am HASHEM your God;

HASHEM is one = You shall not have any other gods.

These allusions are relatively easy to concentrate upon. It is known that these first two Commandments embrace all 613 *mitzvos,* since all of the positive commandments are implicit in *I am HASHEM your God,* while all the negative commandments are implicit in *You shall not have any other gods (Ba'er Hatev; Likkutei Mahariach).*

☙ Word-by-word exposition of the first verse:

□ **שְׁמַע — Hear.** Not simply *listen,* but consider well; concentrate, understand and absorb *(Sforno; Ralbag).*

The term also connotes *acceptance* as distinguished from האזן [from אזן, *ear*] which has the more literal connotation of inclining the ear to punctiliously listen [see *Rashi* to *Exodus* 15:26].

According to *Abudraham,* the term שְׁמַע implies testimony, as if each Israelite reciting the *Shema* tells his fellow: *"Listen! I believe that HASHEM our God is the One and only God in the world."* The letters ע and ד, which are written large in the Torah Scroll, form the word עד, *witness.* [See below: "The enlarged ע and ד."]

Abudraham also offers that the word שְׁמַע can be understood, homiletically, to form the initials of the steps by which one can learn to accept God's sovereignty: שְׂאוּ מָרוֹם עֵינֵיכֶם, *lift your eyes upward,* to realize that there is a purpose higher than your personal and physical needs and desires. When is the best time for this? שַׁחֲרִית מִנְחָה עַרְבִית, *at morning, afternoon, and evening prayers.* To whom? שַׁדַּי מֶלֶךְ עֶלְיוֹן, *to the Almighty, the exalted King.* If you do so, you will accept upon yourself עוֹל מַלְכוּת שָׁמַיִם, *the yoke of the Heavenly kingdom.* [This last phrase begins with the letters of שְׁמַע although they are in reverse order.]

The Talmudic Sages derive several laws from the use in our verse of the word שְׁמַע, *hear.* A sampling:

The *Shema* may be recited in any language ... for the Torah uses the expression *hear,* implying: בְּכָל לָשׁוֹן שֶׁאַתָּה שׁוֹמֵעַ, *In any language that you understand* [the verb שְׁמַע means both *hear* and *understand*] *(Berachos* 13a).

[The commentators explain that this applies only to one who does not understand Hebrew; one who understands Hebrew must read it in its original.]

Sefas Emes explains the connotation of the Talmudic dictum as follows: In every message that your ears absorb, *hear* in them: *HASHEM our God is the One God.* In everything perceive His greatness and Oneness; everything attests to Him.

R' Yose in the Talmud perceives a more literal connotation to *hear:* He who recites the *Shema* must do so audibly so he hears what he is reciting, for it says שְׁמַע, *hear,* which implies let your ear hear what you recite with your mouth *(Berachos* 15a).

That is, mental concentration on the *Shema* is not sufficient to fulfill the primary obligation [לְכַתְּחִלָּה]. If בְּדִיעֲבַד, *de facto,* one had recited the *Shema* inaudibly he has fulfilled his duty, but he must not do so regularly. [See also *v.* 6 below עַל לְבָבֶךָ, and *v.* 7 s.v. וְדִבַּרְתָּ בָּם.]

One who recites the *Shema* must direct his concentration on it since it says here שְׁמַע יִשְׂרָאֵל, *Hear O Israel,* and in another passage [*Deut.* 27:9] הַסְכֵּת וּשְׁמַע יִשְׂרָאֵל, *pay attention and hear, O Israel.* The similar expression shows that just as the latter 'hearing' must be accompanied by attention, so here it must be acompanied by attention *(Berachos* 16a).

□ **יִשְׂרָאֵל — Israel.** The term *Israel* — technically the spiritual name of the Patriarch Jacob [see *Gen.* 32:29, and *ArtScroll* comm. to 49:1] — is a collective reference to the lofty role of the Jewish nation as a whole.

Since we now declare our acceptance of God's sovereignty and acknowledgment of His Oneness, every member of Israel must join in comprehending that message *(R' Nosson Scherman).*

There is a Midrashic view cited in the Talmud, however, that *Israel* in our passage refers personally to Jacob himself, and that this passage, which the Torah now records in Moses' name, is a quotation of a statement of reassurance that Jacob's sons made to him on his deathbed before he granted them his final Patriarchal blessing. See footnote to בָּרוּךְ שֵׁם below.

☐ ה׳ — **HASHEM.** The Divinity is known to us by several Names, each of which reflects another of His different Aspects or Attributes as it is perceived in His conduct with mankind *(Sh'mos Rabbah* 3:6).

◂§ The Shem HaMeforash

The Four-Letter Name י־ה־ו־ה used here is known as the *Shem HaMeforash,* 'the clarified Name' or 'the separated Name.' In respect for its great sanctity, nowadays it is never pronounced as it is written. The name *Adonoy* [my lord] is substituted for it in prayer, while in common speech it is reverently pronounced הַשֵּׁם, *HASHEM* ['The Name' *par excellence*], and is usually abbreviated in printed Hebrew as ה׳ or יְיָ.

God referred to Himself by this Four Letter Name in His revelation to Moses, as we can find in *Exodus* 3:15: *'HASHEM' the God of your fathers ...* זֶה שְּׁמִי, *this is My Name* [לְעֹלָם] *forever, and this is My memorial for all generations.* As the Hebrew לְעֹלָם [*forever*] is spelled in the unvowelized Torah Scroll [לעלם instead of its usual spelling לעולם], it could be read לְעַלֵּם [*to conceal*] — *this is My name* **to be concealed.** In this the Rabbis found an allusion to the rule that this Name may not be read as it is written: its pronunciation is to be concealed, but another word — *Adonay* — is to be reverently substituted for it [see *Rashi ad loc.; Kiddushin* 71a; *Sh'mos Rabbah* 3:9].

Only in the Temple did the *Kohen Gadol* [High Priest], while ministering in the Temple on Yom Kippur, and the *Kohanim* [Priests], when blessing the masses [בִּרְכַּת כֹּהֲנִים] daily in the Temple courtyard, pronounce the Name as it is written. On Yom Kippur, the High Priest recited the *Shem HaMeforash* in his recitation of *Levit.* 16:30 during the confession of sins. When the priests and the people in the great hall heard him utter the *Shem HaMeforash,* they would prostrate themselves and glorify God, saying: בָּרוּךְ שֵׁם כְּבוֹד מַלְכוּתוֹ לְעוֹלָם וָעֶד, *Blessed be the Name of His glorious Kingdom for all eternity (Mishnah Yoma 6:27).*

After the death of Shimon HaTzaddik, successor to Ezra and High Priest of the Second Temple Era, certain Divine manifestations were no longer evident in the Temple, and the *Shem HaMeforash* was no longer uttered by the Kohanim in their blessings [See *Yoma* 39a; *Sotah* 13:8; see also ArtScroll *Bircas Kohanim* p. 36].

Outside of the Temple, however, pronunciation of this Name was prohibited from earliest times [cf. *Mishnah Berachos* 9:5; *Sotah* 7:6; *Tamid* 7:2 and commentaries]. Among those who are excluded from a share in the World to Come is "one who pronounces the Name according to its letters" *(Mishnah Sanhedrin* 10:1).

◂§ Meanings of the Name HASHEM

The Name *HASHEM* is used to depict God in His aspect as Dispenser of Divine mercy [מִדַּת הָרַחֲמִים]. This is derived in *Sifre* [*Deut.* 3:24]: 'Wherever God is referred to as *HASHEM* it designates His Attribute of Mercy, as it is written [*Exodus* 34:6]: ה׳ ה׳ אֵל רַחוּם, *HASHEM, HASHEM, merciful God.'* It is the "personal" Name of the Divinity in His relationship with the Jews, and denotes His utter transcendence and that he is the Source of all existence and continuity [see *Kuzari* 2:2; *Moreh Nevuchim* 1:61].

The spelling of the Name י־ה־ו־ה, is interpreted to connote הָיָה, הֹוֶה, וְיִהְיֶה, literally *He was, He is, and He will be;* it denotes the level where past, present, and future are merged and all are the same *(Tur Orach Chaim* 5). That is, God is Eternal and all time is united within Him. He exists eternally and His essence is unchangeable.

According to R' Yonah in *Sefer HaYirah,* when mentioning HASHEM'S Name throughout *Shema,* no special concentration [*kavannah*] is required except that one must bear in mind the simple meaning of the Name as it is pronounced [*Adonay*], which denotes Supreme Master over all. Exceptions are the two times when "HASHEM" occurs in the first passage of *Shema.* In those cases one must prolong pronunciation of the Names and concentrate on their meaning as they are spelled as well, which is הָיָה הֹוֶה וְיִהְיֶה, *He was, is, and will be,* as explained above.

◂§ The Name "Elohim"

☐ אֱלֹהֵינוּ — **Our God.** In contrast with *HASHEM,* אֱלֹהִים [*Elohim*] describes God in His *universal* aspect as Lord over all Creation. The word itself means All-Powerful — from אֵל, *power* — and is the Name used exclusively in the first chapter of *Genesis,* the account of creation, since it denotes Him Who has the power to produce all things (see *Ikkarim* 1:11).

It appears in the plural form [with the suffix ים] "as a matter of reverence, for every language has its reverent form of address [as in 'the plural of majesty'], but no idea of Divine plurality is to be inferred from this form, as evidenced by the fact that the verbs associated with it — for example בָּרָא, *created,* in *Gen.* 1:1 — are in singular" (*Ibn Ezra, Gen.* 1:1).

In essence, this Name depicts God in His aspect as Dispenser of Justice [מִדַּת הַדִּין] — Ruler, Director, Law-giver, and Judge of the World. [The latter translation is derived in *Sifre* to *Deut.* 3:24 (see above "*Meanings of the Name,*" which continues): "Wherever God is referred to as *Elohim* it designates His Attribute of Justice."]

Rambam notes that in other passages where Moses' speech to Israel is recorded, Moses normally used the second person and would say '*your* God,' as for example [*Deut.* 9:1-3]: *'Hear, O Israel, you are about to pass over the Jordan this day ... know, therefore, that HASHEM* **your** *God goes with you'*; and even in our very next verse: *'And You shall love HASHEM* **your** *God.'* In our passage, which is a declaration of God's unity, however, Moses changed his normal usage and said '**our** *God'* [thus including himself in this profession of our faith, for had he used the second person he might have appeared to have been excluding himself from this declaration *(R' Bachya; Racanati; Ma'or VaShemesh)*].

Haamek Davar cites *Rambam* and adds that, following the Midrashic tradition, another reason Moses used the second person was to cite *verbatim* the ancient formula ascribed to Jacob's sons, to give it [at God's command] the full force of Torah. "Similarly, there are many passages in Scripture that were well known before that particular prophet, who, under the guidance of the Prophetic Spirit, inscribed them in his book. In any event, the first two sections of *Shema* were already known in Israel before the people came to the plains of Moab [where Moses recorded them], for the people were already obligated in the *mitzvah* of *tefillin*" [which included these two sections].

◆§ Meanings of the Name "Elohim"

The primary explanation of *Elohim* are:

- A Name that, throughout Scriptures, signifies מָרוּת, *authority (Rashi* on *Deut.* 6:2);
- It denotes God as 'chief' *(Rambam);*
- It is a term signifying 'Proprietor' or 'Governor' of the world in broad terms; or in narrower terms, it designates a human judge (see *Kuzari* 4);
- It denotes God as the Eternal and Everlasting. Human judges are referred to as *Elohim* (in *Exodus* 22:8) because they judge 'in the image of God' *(Sforno);*
- It describes God as 'the Mighty One who wields authority over the beings Above and Below' *(Tur Orach Chaim* 5);
- It describes God as בַּעַל הַיְכוֹלֶת, *the Omnipotent,* the All-Powerful *(Shulchan Aruch* ibid.);
- In the plural form it signifies the many forces that are spread throughout Creation. All these forces emanate from the One God, and in Him are found the sources of all forces in complete unity *(Malbim);*
- It indicates the sum total of His attributes and powers united in Him (see *Overview).*

□ ה׳ אֶחָד — **HASHEM the One.** He is One in two essential senses: a) because there is no other God but He; b) because He is totally Unique in all existence, and hence beyond all comparison with anything else (*Akeidah; Rashbam).*

Though we perceive God in many roles — kind, angry, merciful, wise, judging, and so on — these are not different moods or attitudes as they would be in the multifaceted personality of a human being. Rather, all flow from a unified purpose and existence which is beyond our comprehension, but which we tend to understand only in terms of our limited perceptions.

Harav Gedaliah Schorr likened this concept to a ray of light seen through a prism. Though it is seen as a myriad of different colors, it is a single ray of light. So, too, God's many manifestations are truly one.

The entire concept that God is incorporeal — i.e., that He is Spirit and not matter — finds its root in our passage, which establishes this Divine unity. As *Rambam* writes in *Moreh Nevuchim* 2:1; "Nothing corporeal can be a unity, either because everything corporeal is divisible or because it is compound; that is to say, logically it can be separated into elements. Because something can be identified as a distinct and particular body only when a distinguishing element is added to its corporeal elemental substratum, it must include at least two elements. But it has been proven that the Absolute allows for no dualism whatever."

When saying the word אֶחָד, *One,* a person should draw out the second syllable a bit and emphasize the final consonant. The first syllable, אֶ, is not to be drawn out. While saying the א, which has the numerical value of one, one should think of the unity of God. While drawing out the ח (a letter with the numerical value of eight), one should bear in mind that God is Master of the earth and the seven heavens. While clearly enunciating the final ד (which has the numerical value of four), one should bear in mind that God is Master in all four directions, meaning everywhere *(Berachos* 13b; *Rokeach; Semak;* see *Shulchan Aruch).*

The Sages note that "whoever prolongs the word אֶחָד has his days and years prolonged" because he prolongs the word in order to concentrate more intensively on God's mastery over all aspects of existence *(Berachos* ibid.).

According to the Talmudic and Midrashic interpretation which attributes this verse to Jacob's children, this phrase implies: *"We are united in our common belief in God —* Just as there is only One [God] in your heart, so in our heart there is only One". [See *comm.* to בָּרוּךְ שֵׁם.]

◆§ The enlarged ע and ד

In Torah scrolls, the letters ע of שְׁמַע and ד of אֶחָד are written large. Together they form the word עֵד, *witness.* As the commentators explain, the inner implication of the enlarged letters is to allude to the thought that every Israelite, by pronouncing the *Shema,* becomes one of HASHEM'S witnesses, declaring His Unity to all the world *(Abudraham; Kol Bo; Rokeach).*

Sforno perceives that the enlarged ד, with the numerical value of four, draws attention to God's uniqueness. There are three lower forms of existence: that of earth with animal and vegetable life that are both subject to death and decomposition; that of the heavenly spheres; and that of the spiritual beings like angels. God is a 'fourth' form of existence, he is incomparably elevated and removed from any of the others. The enlarged ע [*ayin* means 'eye'] of שְׁמַע suggests that it is proper to open wide our eye and concentrate on these great and sublime matters.

Kabbalistically, the enlarged ד alludes to the additional verse — *Blessed be the Name of His glorious kingdom for all eternity* — that is added to the daily recital of the *Shema,* but which was not recorded in the Torah *(Rambam; R' Bachya).*

According to *R' Hirsch,* following *Baal HaTurim,* the practical reason for the enlarged ד is to distinguish ה' אֶחָד, *One God,* from the blasphemous reading ה' אַחֵר, *another God.* Conversely, we find that in *Exodus* 34:14 — *You shall not bow* לְאֵל אַחֵר, *to another god* — the ר in אַחֵר is written large, in order that one should not utter erroneously the blasphemy: *You shall not bow* לְאֵל אֶחָד, *to One God.* The ע in *Shema* is also enlarged, possibly to avoid an interchange with the letter א which would yield in the blasphemous reading: שְׁמָא יִשְׂרָאֵל, *perhaps, O Israel.* Together, the enlarged letters ע and ד, form the word עֵד, meaning *testimony* or *witness.* This expresses that whoever recites *Shema Yisrael* appoints himself as a witness to himself and to the world testifying to God's unity.

◆§ The response of Jacob and the angels

בָּרוּךְ שֵׁם כְּבוֹד מַלְכוּתוֹ לְעוֹלָם וָעֶד — *Blessed be the name of His glorious kingdom for all eternity* [or: *Blessed be the Name; His glorious kingdom is for all eternity*]. Having proclaimed God as our King, we thank Him for granting us the privilege of serving Him, Whose kingdom is eternal and unbounded *(Etz Yosef).*

This verse is not included in the Torah, but is of very ancient origin. It was recited in the Temple as a response (similar to our *Amen)* whenever HASHEM'S Four-Letter Name was uttered in a blessing [*Taanis* 16b], and on Yom Kippur when the *Kohen Gadol* mentioned HASHEM'S Name on Yom Kippur in the Temple [*Yoma* 35a]. According to *Bereishis Rabbah* §65 it formed the angels' response to Israel's recital of the *Shema* [see below].

The Sages give two reasons for saying this verse silently:

(a) According to tradition, at Jacob's deathbed his children affirmed their loyalty to God by proclaiming the verse *Shema.* Jacob responded with the words *Blessed be the Name, etc.* The Sages taught: Should we say these words in our prayers because Jacob said it? Yes. But, on the other hand, Moses did not transmit it to us, for it is not found in the Torah. Therefore, let us say it

One should pause briefly before beginning the next paragraph so as to make a distinction between the primary acceptance of God's Heavenly Kingdom, and acceptance of the commandments, which is the theme of the following, a theme he should bear in mind before beginning the paragraph:

ה וְאָהַבְתָּ אֵת יהוה אֱלֹהֶיךָ בְּכָל־לְבָבְךָ וּבְכָל־נַפְשְׁךָ

silently *(Pesachim* 56a).

(b) Moses heard this beautiful prayer from the angels, and taught it to Israel. We dare not say it aloud, because we are unworthy of using an angelic formula. On Yom Kippur, however, when Israel elevates itself to the sin-free level of angels, we may proclaim it loudly *(Devarim Rabbah* 2:36). [1]

☙ **Commandments of the first chapter:** *To love God; to think of the commandments; to instruct our children in the Torah; to recite God's word when retiring and arising; tefillin and mezuzah.*

While reciting the first verse of this section, one should concentrate upon fulfilling the positive commandment to love HASHEM, which is one of the 248 positive commandments.

The first verse of *Shema* refers to God as He proclaims Himself to the entire nation; therefore the first verse describes Him in the plural as אֱלֹהֵינוּ, **our** *God.* The following section — worded in the singular — turns to each individual and portrays God to him as **your** personal God; this emphasizes that each individual is the special object of God's love *(R' Hirsch).*

5. וְאָהַבְתָּ אֵת ה׳ אֱלֹהֶיךָ — *(And) you shall love HASHEM your God.* The meaning is: Fulfill His commandments out of love and not out of fear, for one who serves out of love is incomparably superior to one who serves out of fear. For in the case of one who serves his master out of fear, should the master trouble him excessively, he would leave him and go away *(Rashi).*

In another verse [*Deut.* 6:13), however, we read: *HASHEM your God, you shall* **fear.** We learn, accordingly, that we must conduct ourselves with the attributes of both fear and love: When we are tempted to indulge in something forbidden, *fear* of God will cause us to reject the sin; when we arduously fulfill a positive command even though there are grounds for exemption, we act out of *love (R' Meyuchas).*

As noted above, the name *HASHEM* represents His Attribute of Mercy, while *Elohim* [God] represents His Attribute of Strict Justice. The dual usage in this verse of *HASHEM* your *God,* implies: Whether He deals mercifully or strictly with you, in

1. The following treatment of the subject of the origins of *Shema* and the verse, *Blessed be the Name of His glorious kingdom for all eternity,* is taken from the footnote to the commentary of *Genesis* 49:1 in ArtScroll *Bereishis:*

In a discussion about the origins of the first verses of *Shema,* the Sages [*Pesachim* 56a] record the following tradition:

When Jacob wished to reveal the End of Days to his son, the *Shechinah* [Divine Presence] departed from him. Jacob grew frightened and mused: "Perhaps, Heaven forbid, there is someone unworthy among my children [lit., 'in my bed'], like Abraham who begot Ishmael, or like my father Isaac who begot Esau [and this is why the *Shechinah* left me when my children arrived]?"

Thereupon his sons reassured him: "שְׁמַע יִשְׂרָאֵל ה׳ אֱלֹהֵינוּ ה׳ אֶחָד, *Hear O Israel* [i.e. our father] — *HASHEM is our God, HASHEM is One!* Just as there is only One in your heart, so is there only One in our heart."

[Although it is normally forbidden to address one's father by name, in this case it was permitted since the name Israel denotes greatness and authority (see *Genesis* 32:29) and as such it was more of a title than a name. It was as if they said, "Listen Master."]

At that moment Jacob, in relief that God's reason for denying them knowledge of the future was not because they lacked faith in Him ח״ו even to the slightest degree, exclaimed: בָּרוּךְ שֵׁם כְּבוֹד מַלְכוּתוֹ לְעוֹלָם וָעֶד, *Blessed be the Name of His glorious kingdom for all eternity.* [*See Maharsha.*]

The Talmudic discussion continues: The Sages pondered, Shall we say it? [I.e., shall we include the phrase בָּרוּךְ שֵׁם, *blessed be the name,* etc., during our daily recitations of *Shema?*] Moses our teacher did not. [That is, Moses did not include that phrase in the chapter of the *Shema (Deut.* 6:4-9). If Jacob's response were said in the *Shema,* we would be inserting something not written in the Torah.] However, Jacob *did* say it. [Therefore, if we exclude it, we would be ignoring Jacob's response to the first declaration of the *Shema.*] Accordingly the Sages established that the phrase בָּרוּךְ שֵׁם, *Blessed be the Name* etc., be recited silently [to make it apparent that it is not part of the *Shema* as written in the Torah but that it was uttered by Jacob *(Mishnah Berurah* 61:30 s.v. בְּחַשַׁאי)].

One should pause briefly before beginning the next paragraph so as to make a distinction between the primary acceptance of God's Heavenly Kingdom, and acceptance of the commandments, which is the theme of the following, a theme he should bear in mind before beginning the paragraph:

Deuteronomy 6:5-9 [5] *You shall love HASHEM, your God, will all your heart and with all your soul and with all your resources.*

either case, and in all ways: Love Him *(Alshich).*

One should have in mind that his love of God is absolute — even to the point of sacrificing all his desires, life, and possessions for God's sake *(Orach Chaim* 61).

☙ Love of HASHEM

The obvious question arises: Since love is a matter of human emotion, how is it possible to legislate love when an individual cannot muster up such feeling? That God *does* demand this of us, however, proves that the ability to love is intrinsic to everyone. The duty devolves upon us to arouse this emotion and bring it from potentiality to reality. This, then, is the essence of this *mitzvah:* that we do anything necessary to remove the impediments and arouse our latent love of God *(Sfas Emes).*

According to *Rashi,* following *Sifre* [see next verse], the Torah itself tells us in the following verse how to achieve love of God: *Let these matters, which I command you today, be upon your heart* — for thereby you will arrive at a recognition of HASHEM and will cling to His ways.

As *Rambam* explains: How can the Torah legislate love? — By contemplating God's greatness, the intricacy of His creation, and His simultaneous concern for the welfare of each insignificant creature, one can condition himself to love his Creator *(Yesodei HaTorah* 2:1-2). Thus, according to *Rambam,* love of God arises from intellectual conviction and from contemplation of God's greatness and His commandments, His words and His deeds. Thus, though the emotion of love is beyond man's control, by contemplation and study — activities that *are* subject to his will — man can attain love of Him.

Rambam pursues this theme further in his *Sefer HaMitzvos,* where he explains that this commandment also embodies the obligation that we should call upon all mankind to serve God and have faith in Him as Abraham did. For, "just as you recount the praises of someone you love and call upon other people to love him too,

Indeed, the halachah, as codified in *Shulchan Aruch* [ibid.] is that when reciting the *Shema* throughout the year we whisper the phrase *Blessed be* etc.

The only time this phrase is said aloud is on Yom Kippur. This custom is based on an alternate version of the declaration's origin. As *Tur* writes in *Hilchos Yom Kippur* §619:

> It is the custom in Ashkenaz [i.e. Germany and the Eastern European countries] to recite בָּרוּךְ שֵׁם כְּבוֹד מַלְכוּתוֹ לְעוֹלָם וָעֶד in a loud voice on Yom Kippur. Support for this is in the Midrash, *Devarim Rabbah (Sidrah Va'eschanan),* where it is written that 'when Moses ascended to heaven he heard the Ministering Angels praising God, "Blessed be the name of His glorious kingdom for all eternity," and Moses brought this declaration back to Israel. This may be compared to a man who stole jewelry from the royal palace [i.e., Moses 'stole' the declaration of the angels, as it were], which he gave to his wife, telling her, "Do not wear these in public, but only in the house." '
>
> Therefore, concludes *Tur* citing the *Midrash,* "throughout the year we recite the declaration in a whisper, but on Yom Kippur when we are as pure as the Ministering Angels we recite it publicly [i.e. in a loud voice]."
>
> [Comp. also *Devarim Rabbah* 2:31, according to which 'Blessed be, etc.' was *Moses'* response at Sinai to HASHEM'S exhortation: *'Hear O Israel, I am HASHEM your God ...'* See also *Magen Avraham* 619 §8.]

R' Levi in *Devarim Rabbah* 2:35 also cites the view that Jacob's children reassured him of their faith by saying *Shema* as quoted above from *Pesachim* 56a. He remarks that when a Jew recites *Shema* nowadays, it is as if he says: 'Hear our father Israel: your command to our ancestors is still observed by us: HASHEM is our God, HASHEM is One!'

[Interestingly, in the Aramaic *Targum Yerushalmi* to our verse, Jacob's response to his sons' recitation of the *Shema* is given as יְהֵא שְׁמֵהּ רַבָּא מְבָרַךְ לְעָלַם וּלְעָלְמֵי עָלְמַיָּא, *'May His Great Name be blessed forever and ever.'* This response has been preserved as the primary response in the *Kaddish* prayer. See Overview to *ArtScroll Kaddish.*]

so it is that upon attaining true love of God and coming closer to a true understanding of His essence you will undoubtedly call upon the foolish and ignorant to seek a knowledge of the truth that you have already acquired."

In the words of the *Sifre:* [The commandment] *And you shall love HASHEM your God* implies that you should make Him beloved by man, as Abraham your father did. Just as Abraham, out of the strength of his convictions and of his great love for God, called upon mankind to believe in Him, so you are to love Him to the extent that you will call other men to Him.[1]

In his *Hilchos Teshuvah* [10:3,6], *Rambam* elaborates further on the emotional aspects of love of God:

What is the proper kind of love? It is that one should love HASHEM with such an exceedingly great and powerful love that his very soul be bound up in love of God. He will find himself constantly enraptured by it as if he were afflicted by the lovesickness of one who cannot clear his mind from passion for his beloved and he pines for her always, whether he sits or stands, whether he eats or drinks. Even greater than this should be the love of God in the hearts of those who love Him, enraptured by it always, as He commanded *with all your heart and with all your soul.* Solomon meant this allegorically when he said, *"For I am lovesick"* [*Song of Songs* 2, 5]. The whole *Song of Songs* is an allegory of man's love for God. [See Overview to ArtScroll *Shir HaShirim,* and *Hirhurei Teshuvah.*] It is well known and quite clear that love of the Holy One, Blessed is He, cannot become established in the human heart until man is so completely enraptured by it that he neglects everything else on earth, as He commanded: *With all your heart and with all your soul.* One can love HASHEM only in proportion to the measure of the knowledge one has gained of Him. According to the knowledge so the love, whether less or more. Therefore man should devote himself to understanding and learning the wisdom and analytical skills that make his Maker known to him in accordance with his capacities as we have explained ... [see also *Yesodei HaTorah* 2:1.]

בְּכָל לְבָבְךָ — *With all your heart.* In Scriptural terminology, the 'heart' symbolizes man's intellectual spirit *(Ibn Ezra).*

By bidding us to love HASHEM with all the powers of our heart, our verse includes all the powers of the body since they all originate in the heart. The sense of the entire passage is: Make the perception of God the aim of all your actions *(Rambam, Moreh Nevuchim* 1:59). [See above: *Love of HASHEM.*]

The Sages in the Mishnah [*Berachos* 9:5] and *Sifre* note that the verse uses the **לֵבָב** [with a double **ב**] for *heart* instead of the more familiar **לֵב**. From this they derive that we are bidden to love God with our 'double' heart. As *Rashi* explains: *With all your heart* — with both **יֵצֶר הַטּוֹב וְיֵצֶר הָרָע**, *the Good and Evil Inclinations.*

How can one love God with his inclination to do evil? — The true function of the Evil Inclination is to elevate man by providing him with a challenge to overcome.

Furthermore, even man's baser instincts — aspects of his Evil Inclination — must be

1. **Inspiring love by example**

The Talmud *(Yoma* 86a) perceives this obligation to love God in a broader sense. If one truly loves God, he will not be content to fulfill the commandments himself; he will act in such a way in all his daily activities with his fellow men that his actions will inspire others. Although our verse says only *And you shall love HASHEM your God,* the Sages expound that it means also that the Name of Heaven should become beloved through you [מִתְאַהֵב עַל יָדְךָ]. A Jew should study Scripture and Mishnah, and serve Torah scholars and deal graciously with his fellow creatures. Then his fellow creatures will say of him, 'Fortunate is his father who taught him Torah! Fortunate is his teacher who taught him Torah! Woe to those who do not study Torah! So and so who studies Torah — how pleasant is his behavior and how proper are his deeds. To him the verse applies: *And he said to me: You are My servant Israel, in whom I will be glorified' (Isaiah* 49:3).

However, if one studies Torah and Mishnah and serves Torah scholars, but is not honest in his dealings, does not converse pleasantly with people — what do people say of him? 'Woe to so and so who studies Torah! Woe to his father who taught him Torah! Pity his teacher who taught him Torah! So and so who studies Torah — see how corrupt are his deeds and how ugly his behavior! To him may the text be applied *(Ezek.* 36:20): *In that men said of them: These are HASHEM's people but they are departed from His land' (Yoma* 86a).

Similarly, *Sefer Chareidim* writes that included in the *mitzvah* of loving God is loving a Torah scholar who studies God's Word. The Talmud [*Shabbos* 23b] states that someone who loves Torah scholars will be blessed with children who are Torah scholars.

harnessed to serve God. All of man's earthly passions and ambitions must be made instruments in the service of God. Greed can be channeled to acquire money for charity; jealousy can goad one to greater efforts in his studies; hatred can be utilized to thwart God's enemies (*R' Yonah* to above Mishnah).

Alternately, *Rashi* interprets that expression *with all your heart* [the emphasis in this interpretation being on the word *all*] signifies: Your heart should not be at variance with God. [That is, do not be content merely to control your urges to sin. Instead, you should sublimate your urges to the point where your only desire is to love and serve God. You are to love Him with *all* your heart.]

Ramban cites the Midrashic opinion that *heart* figuratively refers to the power of desire. In the literal sense, however, he maintains that it denotes the rational soul — the intellect — 'since [in Scriptural terminology] the heart is the intellect's resting place.'

וּבְכָל נַפְשְׁךָ — *And with all your soul. Soul* figuratively refers to man's *emotions;* sometimes Scripture uses the term *liver* or *innards* as a metaphor for this concept. Specifically, *soul* in this context refers to man's *will* and *desires* [see this use in *Gen.* 23:8] and we are bidden to channel all our desires and emotions toward love of HASHEM (*Ibn Ezra; Alshich).*

Rashi, following the Talmudic Sages [*Berachos* 54a;61b; *Sifre*], interprets *soul* in its most literal sense as signifying life, and explains that our passage bids us to love God with total conviction and dedication — *With all your soul* — even if you must sacrifice your life for His sake [lit. *even if He takes your soul*].[1]

— "With every breath one breathes man is obligated to praise his Creator" (*Midrash).*

[In the vast majority of cases, however, the Torah *commands* Jews to put life ahead of the commandments. Thus, for example, work is done on the Sabbath where a life is at stake. The commandment to accept martyrdom for the sake of God applies only to the three cardinal sins — עֲבוֹדָה זָרָה, *idolatry;* גִּלּוּי עֲרָיוֹת, *forbidden sexual union;* and שְׁפִיכַת דָּמִים, *murder* — and to cases where commission of a sin would involve desecration of God's name. These principles are spelled out in *Sanhedrin* 74a and *Yoreh Deah* §157.]

Ramban notes the apparent superfluity in the word *'all'* in this phrase. Following the Midrashic interpretation that *your soul* refers to martyrdom, what is signified by this additional word; one cannot speak of *partial* martyrdom? He suggests, accordingly, that suffering, or the sacrifice of bodily organs, is referred to as 'part of the soul,' while death is termed 'with *all* your soul.'

וּבְכָל מְאֹדֶךָ — *And with all your resources.* The translation follows the Talmud [*Berachos* 54a and 61b] and *Rashi* on *Chumash:* It means *with all your money* [or: *property*]. This command is added because there are people whose wealth is dearer to them than their own lives. [Accordingly, we must love God no matter what material sacrifice our loyalty entails, and whenever we recite these words we must bear in mind our willingness to submit to this test (*Ibn Shu'ib).*]

The Talmudic passage reads: If it says *with all your soul,* why should it also say *with all your resources;* and if it says *with all your resources* why should it say *with all your soul?* — Should there be a man who values his life more than his money, it tells him, *with all your soul;* and should there be a man who values his money more than his life, it tells him *with all your resources.*

1. **R' Akiva's martyrdom while reciting the Shema**

The classical example of loving God with one's last drop of blood is the Talmudic Sage, R' Akiva. He longed for the time when his daily acceptance of the obligation to love God might be put to the test and confirmed by action; when he was called upon to give his life for God's sake, would he be equal to the challenge? The moment came when he was arrested for publicly violating the Roman decree forbidding the Jews to study and teach the Torah, and was sentenced to death by torture.

When he was taken out for execution, it was the time for the recital of the *Shema.* While the Roman executioner tore his flesh with iron combs, R' Akiva was reciting the *Shema,* accepting upon himself the kingship of Heaven.

"Our teacher," his weeping disciples said, "even to this point?"

"All my days," R' Akiva told them, "I have been troubled by the passage *with all your soul.* I interpret it, 'even if He takes your soul,' and I have always longed for the opportunity of fulfilling this. Now that I have the opportunity of loving God with my whole life, should I not rejoice?"

R' Akiva prolonged the word *echad* until he died.

A Divine voice was heard proclaiming, "Happy are you, Akiva, that your soul departed with the word *echad!* ..."

ו וּבְכָל־מְאֹדֶךָ: וְהָיוּ הַדְּבָרִים הָאֵלֶּה אֲשֶׁר אָנֹכִי מְצַוְּךָ
ז הַיּוֹם עַל־לְבָבֶךָ: וְשִׁנַּנְתָּם לְבָנֶיךָ וְדִבַּרְתָּ בָּם בְּשִׁבְתְּךָ

Alternatively, *Rashi* cites the interpretation [ibid. 61b] that מְאֹד is related to the word מִדָּה, *measure,* and the phrase means: *And with all your 'measures.'* That is, your love for God should be undiminished no matter what measure [i.e. treatment] He deals out to you — whether He treats you generously or not.

— Love God in times of bliss and happiness and in times of stress and misfortune. While we recite these words we must concentrate on our gracious acceptance of the treatment God subjects us to *(Ibn Shu'ib).*

It is from our passage that the Talmudic Sages [*Berachos* 54a] derive the dictum: "חַיָּיב אָדָם לְבָרֵךְ עַל־הָרָעָה כְּשֵׁם שֶׁמְּבָרֵךְ עַל הַטּוֹבָה, *It is incumbent on a man to bless God for the evil in the same way as for the good.*"[1]

Following the primary interpretation that the word מְאֹד refers to *wealth,* the *Vilna Gaon* used to render the passage homiletically: *You shall serve HASHEM ... even with all your possessions* — that is, even if you are very wealthy.

Ibn Ezra and *Ramban* interpret the term as deriving from מְאֹד, *much,* the passage meaning love Him *very, very much* — with all your intensity of feeling. *Ramban* cites the Rabbinic interpretation (quoted above) that it means *with all your resources,* since one's property is called מְאֹד, *abundance* ... and the *mitzvah* is to love Him "with all the abundance of your wealth."

The use of the term מְאֹד [*much*] to imply *resources* rather than more common terms, such as קִנְיָן, *possessions;* רְכוּשׁ, *wealth;* or כֶּסֶף, *money,* connotes that more than financial resources is meant. It refers to anything to which an individual might be closely attached. Even *that* must be sacrificed when love of God is at stake *(Chofetz Chaim).*

However, while we are bidden to forfeit all our resources rather than violate a prohibition of the Torah, we are not required to sacrifice more than a fifth of our resources in order to fulfill a positive commandment (see *Orach Chaim* §696).[2]

1. Two brothers, Rabbis Pinchas and Shmelka Horowitz, who later became very distinguished chassidic leaders, came to the Maggid (preacher) of Mezritch to inquire about the nature of Chassidic philosophy and teaching. During their discussion, they asked him to explain how it was possible to thank God equally for good and for bad. To that, the Maggid replied, 'Go to my Zussia, he will answer you.'

Rabbi Zussia of Anipoli was a disciple who spent most of his day in the Maggid's study hall. He was poverty-stricken, in constant pain from a variety of physical maladies, and his wife was a notorious shrew. Nevertheless, R' Zussia was famous for his unvarying good cheer. The two visiting brothers went to him and asked their question, telling him that the Maggid had directed them to him.

R' Zussia seemed dumbfounded. He said, 'That is a difficult question, but I cannot imagine why the Maggid sent you to me. Only someone who has experienced suffering and problems can answer such a question. I, thank God, have always had a good life with everything I need!'

Then the two rabbis understood what the Maggid meant. A person should always be so joyous that he accepts whatever God metes out to him with the same grateful acknowledgment.

2. This phrase *with all your resources* only occurs in this portion of *Shema,* which is addressed in singular to individuals. However, the second section, וְהָיָה, which is worded in plural to the community, omits this concept of sacrificing all community resources for God's sake. This is because the entire community's preservation of property and the means of earning a livelihood are matters of life and death, and as such are included in וּבְכָל נַפְשְׁכֶם, *and with all your souls* [p. 33 below] *(Rabbi of Kotzk).*

Rabbi Zalman Sorotzkin (Oznaim LaTorah) discusses this concept, explaining a basic difference between the entire community and its members. Even if an individual gives up all his resources and his means of a livelihood for the sake of God, he is not without hope because he can rely on the community to come to his assistance, as has happened countless times throughout Jewish history. When an individual is asked to serve God with all his *resources,* he knows that his *life* is not at stake; therefore he must be instructed further that, if need be, even his life should be forfeit if necessary. For an entire community to become destitute, however, is far more serious than a mere matter of economics. Without resources and a means of earning them — and without the community to help them — utter poverty can mean disease and starvation. Therefore, the second section's command that even a community must serve God with all his resources is tantamount to telling them that they must be ready even to give up their livelihood if need be. [See Second Portion p. 33 for additional reasons.]

[6]Let these matters which I command you this day, be upon your heart. [7] Teach them thoroughly to your children and speak of them while you sit in your home, while you walk

6. How are we to achieve the 'love' of God demanded of us in the previous verse? — The following verse tells us: *Let these words which I command you today be upon your heart* — for by constant absorption with the words of Torah, you will arrive at a recognition of God and will cling to His way *(Sifre; Rashi).*

Thus, this passage advocates diligent Torah-study, since that will lead to proper love of God *(Haamek Davar).* [See above: "Love of HASHEM."]

וְהָיוּ הַדְּבָרִים הָאֵלֶּה — *And let these matters* [lit. *and these words shall be*].

These words: either the words of this chapter, mandating love of God, or the *mitzvos* of the Torah in general (see *Mizrachi; Gur Aryeh; R' Hirsch; Haamek Davar.* See also *HaKsav V'HaKabbalah* who goes to great length to stress that the emphasis is on the *mitzvah* of loving God mandated in this chapter).

The Rabbis in the Talmud variously interpret that the expression וְהָיוּ, *and they shall be,* implies that 'they must remain as they are.' This teaches that one who recites the *Shema* fulfills his obligation only if the words are recited in the order in which they are written *(Berachos* 13a).

אֲשֶׁר אָנֹכִי מְצַוְּךָ הַיּוֹם — *Which I command you this day.* The word הַיּוֹם, *this day,* carries with it a sublime message beyond the literal connotation: Do not regard the Divine commands as old and obsolete; but regard them as eternally fresh, like a new royal proclamation reaching you this very day [which all cheerfully obey because it denotes that the monarch had but that very day expressed his will] *(Rashi; Sifre).*[1]

While reciting the *Shema,* one must be careful to pause between the word הַיּוֹם, *today,* and the following phrase עַל לְבָבֶךָ, *upon your heart,* so it not appear as if the verse implied: let it be upon your heart only *today* — but not other days *(Shulchan Aruch;* see *Pesachim* 56a).

עַל־לְבָבֶךָ — *Be upon your heart.* The intent of *upon your heart* is that these words should govern your heart, i.e., that you be in charge of your emotions and not *vice versa (R' Menachem Mendel of Kalish).*

— In the literal sense: You should always be prepared to fulfill these words *(R' Hoffmann).*

This is the method of attaining love of God. If one remains *always* conscious of the teachings of the Torah and of his obligations to God, he will inevitably come to love Him *(Sifre).*

— The teachings should figuratively *lay upon your heart* like a stone, and when, in a propitious moment of inspiration, the heart "opens" receptively, then these words will enter it directly *(R' Menachem Mendel of Kotzk).*

7. וְשִׁנַּנְתָּם לְבָנֶיךָ — [*And*] *teach them thoroughly to your children.*[2] Literally the verb signifies 'impress sharply.' The words of the Torah shall be 'sharp' [i.e. familiar] in your mouth, so that if a person asks you anything concerning them you will not stammer but will answer immediately *(Kiddushin* 30a; *Rashi).*

Rashi thereby maintains that וְשִׁנַּנְתָּם is derived

1. Everyone must view himself as if he were the only person in the universe; as if God's commands applied to him only; as if the Torah were the only Book he had; and as if that day were his last. In this way, one will certainly not waste a precious moment in his service to God and performance of *mitzvos.* This is the implication of our verse: "*And let these matters* — of This Torah, which is the only Book you possess, *which I command you* — you specifically, this day — only this day do you have the ability to heed My words for by the morrow you might no longer be alive" *(Chofetz Chaim).*

2. The *Chidushei HaRim* had thirteen children, all of whom died in his lifetime. He resolutely withstood all of these tragedies shedding hardly a tear, but would merely say, "HASHEM has given and HASHEM has taken away."

When his last child died, however, he could not maintain his composure, but wept bitterly and uncontrollably. One of his close chassidim asked him why on his earlier losses he was able to control his emotions whereas here he was unable to do so.

"I am weeping over one thing," the Rebbe said, "that henceforth I will be unable to fulfill the *mitzvah* of וְשִׁנַּנְתָּם לְבָנֶיךָ, *teach them thoroughly to your children.*"

ח בְּבֵיתֶ֫ךָ וּבְלֶכְתְּךָ֣ בַדֶּ֔רֶךְ וּֽבְשָׁכְבְּךָ֖ וּבְקוּמֶֽךָ׃ וּקְשַׁרְתָּ֥ם

from the verb שנן, *sharpen,* rather than from the verb שנה, *teach* [as in מִשְׁנָה]. [*Rashbam, Ibn Ezra* and other commentators concur.] The passage would accordingly be contextually rendered: *And you shall master them thoroughly for the sake of your children (Mizrachi; Tzeidah laDerech).*

Rashi continues that the word *children* refers [also] to students. Furthermore, just as the word *children* can be extended to denote *students,* so the term אָב [*father*] can be extended to denote a *teacher.*

The commentators explain that *Rashi* is drawn to this interpretation that *children* in our context refers to *students* because the obligation upon a father to teach Torah to his sons and grandsons was stated explicitly several verses earlier in the Torah [*Deut.* 4:9]. Thus, *Rashi* pursues the interpretation that this verse has the more general application that it is incumbent upon everyone to transmit Torah knowledge to disciples *(Maskil l'David).*

וְדִבַּרְתָּ בָּם — *And speak of them.* Your *principal* topic of conversation should be about them [i.e. the Words of Torah]: they should not be relegated to secondary importance *(Rashi).*

By constantly reviewing your Torah knowledge, you will not forget it. Memory is best preserved by a constant verbal repetition. Hence the precept that one should *speak* of the Divine commandments *(Sforno).*

They are to be a theme of living interest, early and late, at home and abroad. This does not exclude other talk entirely; rather, as *Rashi* stresses, we are exhorted that Torah topics form our *principal* conversation *(Gur Aryeh).*

[*Rashi's* interpretation follows one view in the Talmud *(Yoma* 19a); there is another view cited there, however, that this passage enjoins us not to engage in idle and loose talk.]

According to Talmud *Yerushalmi Sotah* 7:1 we derive from this verse — which is interpreted to imply: בְּכָל לָשׁוֹן שֶׁאַתָּה מְדַבֵּר, *in every language that you speak* — that the *Shema* may be recited in any language [(if one does not understand Hebrew) [see *Berachos* 13a cited in *comm.* to *Shema.* Cf. *Torah Temimah*].

בְּשִׁבְתְּךָ בְּבֵיתֶךָ וּבְלֶכְתְּךָ בַדֶּרֶךְ — *While you sit in your home, while you walk on the way.* — That is, during, [and in the manner of] your usual course of living [see below] *(Rashi).*

Even when one is pursuing his usual daily activities, and his mind is preoccupied with the business at hand, even then he should focus his thought on whatever Torah matters he can meditate upon at that moment *(Etz Yosef).*

◆§ The time for reading Shema

וּבְשָׁכְבְּךָ וּבְקוּמֶךָ — [*And*] *when you recline and when you arise.* [This passage is not merely figurative; it refers to the mandated reading of the *Shema* in the evening and in the morning.] *Rashi* explains that the reference to 'reclining and arising' is not to imply that the time of reciting *Shema* depends on an *individual's* personal habits — for example it does not apply to one who reclines [i.e., naps] in the middle of the day or who arises in the middle of the night. Rather, our verse refers to the *usual* manner of things. The requirement to recite *Shema* applies to the *customary* times of retiring and awakening.

[This passage is the subject of halachic controversy between the schools of Shammai and Hillel *(Berachos* 10b). According to the former, the words *recline* and *arise* are to be interpreted literally: in the evening one should recline while reciting the *Shema,* and in the morning one should stand. The disciples of Hillel disagree. They deduce from וּבְלֶכְתְּךָ בַדֶּרֶךְ, *and while you walk on the way,* that one reads *Shema* כְּדַרְכּוֹ, *in his natural manner,* whether walking, sitting, or standing. If so our phrase cannot place a requirement on reclining or standing; hence the phrase refers to the *time* when the *Shema* is to be recited — viz. in the evening when people *generally* recline and in the morning when people *generally* arise (see below). The *Halachah* follows the latter view, and *Rashi* accordingly bases his interpretation on it.]

The time for reciting the night-*Shema* is all night — from the time the stars become visible [צֵאת הַכּוֹכָבִים], until *daybreak* [עֲלוֹת הַשַּׁחַר]. However, the Sages ordained that it should be recited before midnight, lest someone fall asleep and forget to recite it. The time for reciting the day-*Shema* begins from the time there is enough daylight for someone to recognize a comrade from a distance of about four cubits [about eight feet] until a quarter of the daylight hours have passed.

on the way, when you recline and when you arise. [8] *Bind them as a sign upon your arm and they shall be tefillin*

◆§ The ritual

The ritual of the evening *Shema* consists of the three sections of the *Shema* preceded by two benedictions and followed by another two. Of the preliminary benedictions, the first refers to the Divine ordering of day and night, הַמַּעֲרִיב עֲרָבִים; and the second describes the love of God shown by the giving of the Torah, אַהֲבַת עוֹלָם. Of the benedictions following the *Shema*, the first is a proclamation of faith, אֱמֶת וֶאֱמוּנָה; and the second, a prayer for peaceful repose, הַשְׁכִּיבֵנוּ. The Evening Service continues with the *Amidah*, and *Aleinu*. [The benediction בָּרוּךְ ה׳ לְעוֹלָם was added in later times.] The *Shema* is also recited — with the addition of certain psalms and benedictions — before retiring to sleep [see pp. 48-62].

The morning *Shema* is preceded by two benedictions, and followed by one. These Benedictions are (1): Praise of God as the Creator of the light of day, יוֹצֵר אוֹר; (2) Praise of God as Giver of the Torah, אַהֲבָה רַבָּה; and (3) Praise of God as the Redeemer of Israel, גָּאַל יִשְׂרָאֵל. Immediately thereafter in the morning service comes the *Amidah*.

◆§ Tefillin

8. וּקְשַׁרְתָּם לְאוֹת עַל־יָדֶךָ — [*And you shall*] ***bind them*** [i.e., the words of this section along with the other sections mandated by Halachah] *as a sign upon your arm.*

[This is not merely figurative.] — It refers to the *tefillin* for the arm *(Rashi).*

[The term *tefillin* (commonly rendered with the Greek word, *phylacteries)* — singular *tefillah* — derives from the root פלל, having the connotation of *prayer* (Hebrew: *tefillah), judgment* [*Psalms* 106:30] and *testimony.* See *Tosafos Menachos* 34b s.v. לְטוֹטָפֹת; *Tur Orach Chaim* 25; *Shorashim* s.v. פלל; comm. to *Ezekiel* 24:17 s.v. פְּאֵרְךָ where *Targum Yonasan* interprets that word as טֹטְפָתָךְ. See below on טֹטָפֹת.]

The *mitzvah* 562 of *tefillin* had already been mentioned in *Exodus* 13:9, but here the Torah clarifies that the *tefillin* are to be *bound* on the arm and head *(Ramban).*

Tefillin contain four paragraphs: קַדֶּשׁ *(Exodus* 13:1-10); וְהָיָה כִּי יְבִיאֲךָ *(ibid.* 11-16); שְׁמַע *(Deut.* 4-8); וְהָיָה אִם שָׁמֹעַ *(ibid.* 11:13-21).

Ramban and *Chinuch* explain that these four sections were chosen in preference to all other passages of the Torah because they embrace the acceptance of Heavenly sovereignty, the precept of the Unity of God, the acceptance of His commandments with the acknowledgment that they involve reward and punishment, and the Exodus from Egypt — all fundamental doctrines of Judaism. Furthermore, the law of *tefillin* is mentioned in these four sections.

For the *tefillin* on the arm, the four paragraphs are written on one strip of parchment and housed in a single case, but for the *tefillin* of the head, the four paragraphs are written on separate pieces of parchment and placed into a case divided into four compartments. This is exegetically derived from the *singular* word **אוֹת**, *sign,* associated with the hand *tefillin,* and the *plural* טֹטָפֹת, [meaning *four* (see *Rashi* below)] associated with the head *tefillin.* The laws of the construction of *tefillin* were transmitted to Moses at Sinai הֲלָכָה לְמֹשֶׁה מִסִּינַי (see *Menachos* 34-36).

The commentators explain that *tefillin* is one of the commandments that are like emblems identifying us as God's servants. Just as royal officials wear uniforms and insignia that distinguish them from others and remind them constantly of their duty to the sovereign, so too the Jew is set apart by such insignia. Among them are circumcision in his flesh, *tefillin* on his head and arm, *tzitzis* on his garment, and *mezuzah* on his doorpost. They are constantly visible reminders, pointing his way wherever he goes and whatever he does, proclaiming that an Eye from which he cannot hide sees his every deed.

In ancient times *tefillin* were worn throughout the day; nowadays their use is generally confined to morning prayers.

◆§ Position of the hand-tefillin

The word יָד can be rendered either *arm* (including the hand) or *hand,* depending on the context [see *Arachin* 19b; *Tos. Menachos* 37a s.v. קבורת], although in common usage it has come to be used nearly always for *hand. Tosefta (Shabbos*

ט לְאוֹת עַל־יָדֶךָ וְהָיוּ לְטֹטָפֹת בֵּין עֵינֶיךָ: וּכְתַבְתָּם עַל־
מְזֻזוֹת בֵּיתֶךָ וּבִשְׁעָרֶיךָ:

9:15) proves from *Judges* 15:14 that the entire arm is called יָד (see also *Malbim* to *Mechilta, Bo* §110). In the case of *tefillin,* עַל יָדֶךָ must be rendered *upon your arm* — not *upon your hand* — since the Talmud [*Menachos ibid.* and *Sifre*] derives that the hand-*tefillin* must be bound on the inner biceps muscle — opposite the heart. [See comm. to parallel phrase in Second Portion, *v.* 18, s.v. וּקְשַׁרְתֶּם p. 38.] Thus, it is not "on the *hand*" but on the muscle of the *upper arm,* which controls the entire organ. This also conforms with the parallel text in *Exodus* 13:9 where the hand-*tefillin* are to be לְךָ לְאוֹת, *to you a sign,* i.e. a *personal* sign visible to the wearer alone [on the part of the arm usually covered by the sleeve] rather than on the *"hand"* — where it would be seen by all. The head-*tefillin,* however, are to be seen by all *(Menachos* ibid.). [See *B'chor Shor* below בֵּין עֵינֶיךָ.]

The *arm* on which the *tefillin* is to be put is the left one. The Sages expound this in two ways. First, when this commandment is given in *Exodus* 13:6, the word יָדְךָ is spelled יָדְכָה [=יַד כֵּהָה 'weak arm'] implying the left, which is the weaker of the two hands. The second derivation of this law is from the proximity to one another of two words: וּקְשַׁרְתָּם, *and you shall bind them* in our verse, and וּכְתַבְתָּם, *and you shall write them,* in the next verse. The Talmud, *Menachos* 37a, interprets: "Just as writing is with the right hand so the binding shall be done with the right." Since one must use his right hand to bind the hand-*tefillin,* it must be put on the left arm. [There is also an exposition in *Menachos* 366 based upon *Isaiah* 48:13, *Judges* 5:26, and *Psalms* 74:11 where *hand* clearly means left hand.]

According to both derivations, a left-handed person would put tefillin on his right hand, because his right arm is weaker and because he writes and binds with his left hand.

Inasmuch as *tefillin* are referred to as אוֹת, *sign* [see especially *Exodus* 13:16], the Sages derive that *tefillin* are not worn on Sabbaths and festivals, because these sacred days are themselves referred to as 'signs' between God and Israel. [See *Exod.* 31:13 and *comm.*] *(Eruvin* 96a; see *Torah Sheleimah).*

Shulchan Aruch cites the custom that while saying the words וּקְשַׁרְתָּם לְאוֹת עַל־יָדֶךָ [during *Shacharis* services], one should touch the *tefillin* of the arm, and while saying the words וְהָיוּ לְטֹטָפֹת בֵּין עֵינֶיךָ, touch the *tefillin* of the head. Some have the custom of kissing the fingers after touching the *tefillin.*

וְהָיוּ לְטֹטָפֹת בֵּין עֵינֶיךָ — *And they shall be* [for] *tefillin between your eyes.*

— A reference to the *tefillin* for the head *(Rashi).*

Position of the head-tefillin

The expression "**between** your eyes," as it is used in Scripture, refers to the front part of the skull, *above the center-point between the eyes.* This definition is derived from *Deuteronomy* 14:1, as explained below. Thus, the head-*tefillin* are to be placed between the hairline and the spot toward the upper part of the head where the skull of a baby is still tender. [See *Menachos* 37a,b.] That they are placed above the hairline is derived from another law that involves a comparison with *Deuteronomy* 14:1. There we are enjoined from excessive manifestations of mourning: *You shall not cut yourselves nor make a bald patch between your eyes for the dead.* Obviously, that verse does not mean literally *between your eyes,* for no hair grows there. Rather, both verses designate a place above the hairline on the anterior part of the skull — "the seat of the organ from which the eyes are controlled and the impressions of the thoughts they gather are received" *(R' Hirsch).*

"There is no doubt regarding the interpretation [that *upon your* **hand** and **between** *your eyes* refer respectively to the inner part of the upper arm against the heart, and to the anterior part of the skull] ... So have we received the tradition from our Rabbis, and so have our forefathers done. Whoever casts doubts upon this is like one who would question that the letter **א** is called *aleph* rather than *beth,* and they will in the future be summoned to render judgment" *(B'chor Shor).*

The *mitzvah* of *tefillin* is mentioned earlier in *Exodus,* in two almost identical passages: *Exodus* 13:9, *And it shall be as a "sign" for you upon your hand, and as a between your eyes.* 9 *And write them on the doorposts of your house and upon your gates.*

"memorial" between your eyes; and *ibid., v.* 16, *And it shall be as a "sign" for you upon your hand, and as "tefillin"* [Hebrew: *totafos* (see below)] *between your eyes.*

Ramban to *Exod.* ibid. explains that the expression *as a "memorial"* [לְזִכָּרוֹן] *between your eyes* implies that the head-*tefillin* are to be placed at the "seat of remembrance," high above the eyes at the beginning of the brain. The expression *"between* [בֵּין] the eyes" indicates that they are to be placed on the *middle* of the head not toward the side.

◆§ Hand-tefillin before head-tefillin

Since the hand-*tefillin* is mentioned first, the *halachah* is that the hand-*tefillin* must be put on before the head-*tefillin*. However, the head-*tefillin* is to be removed first, then the hand-*tefillin*. The latter law is derived from our passage, which is expounded *(Menachos* 36a) to imply that whenever the head-*tefillin* is worn, it must be worn in tandem with the hand-*tefillin*. In connection with the head-*tefillin*, our verse uses the plural expression וְהָיוּ, **they** *shall be.* This implies that whenever the head-*tefillin* are worn, *both tefillin* should be on the body. Consequently, it should be put on last and taken off first (see *Rashi ad loc.* and *Torah Temimah).*

◆§ Meaning of the word טֹטָפֹת

The etymology of the word טֹטָפֹת is obscure. It occurs in the Torah only here, in the parallel phrase in *Deut.* 13:18, and in *Exodus* 13:9 where the *mitzvah* of *tefillin* is first mentioned.

The translation of טֹטָפֹת as *tefillin* follows *Onkelos,* and *Rashi* to *Exod.* 13:16. *Rashi* quotes the Talmudic derivation [*Sanhedrin* 4b] that the word is a compound of the foreign words *tot* and *pas* — each being a numeral meaning *two*, the one in the language of Katpi [Caspian; Coptic(?)] and the other in the language of Afriki [a district of North Africa; Phrygian(?)]. He explains that *tefillin* are so called because the head-*tefillin* consists of four compartments.

Abarbanel suggests that the word may be derived from the old Egyptian word *tot* or *otat,* meaning brain, the organ above which the head-*tefillin* are placed *(Abarbanel).*

Onkelos renders the term as *tefillin* rather than the Aramaic equivalent, *totafos,* because *Onkelos* customarily preserves the familiar meaning of a term, in this case, *tefillin,* rather than the strict literal sense of the word. [That the Aramaic word for *tefillin* is *totafos* is evident from *Ezekiel* 24:17 where the Hebrew adjective for *tefillin,* פְּאֵר, *majesty,* is rendered in the *Targum* as טוֹטְפְתָךְ.] *Onkelos* acted similarly in *Leviticus* 23:40 where he does not translate the following terms literally but gives them their traditional *halachic* meaning: פְּרִי עֵץ הָדָר [fruit of a goodly tree]=*esrog;* כַּפֹּת תְּמָרִים [branches of palm trees]=*lulav;* עֲנַף עֵץ־עָבֹת [boughs of thick trees]=*hadasim;* עַרְבֵי נַחַל [brook willows]=*aravos (Marpei Lashon; Shaarei Aharon).*

In an alternative interpretation, *Rashi* [in *Exodus* ibid.] quotes the grammarian Menachem ben Saruk who derives the word from the root נטף, *to speak* [see *Ezekiel* 21:2; *Micah* 2:6]; hence *totafos* is something that inspires conversation, and is the equivalent of the parallel expression *memorial* in *Exodus* 13:9. That is, the head-*tefillin* will serve as a reminder of God's miracles, and inspire all who see it to speak about them.

Ramban maintains that in the literal sense the Sages [*Shabbos* 57a] understood the word טֹטָפֹת as denoting an ornament worn over the forehead extending from ear to ear, as they have ruled in the Mishnah [ibid.]: "A woman may not go out on the Sabbath with a *totefes* or head-bangles [i.e. frontlets]." He writes that since the Sages spoke and knew the language of Scripture, we can well accept their definition. [See also *Targum* to *II Samuel* 1:10.] That the Torah employs the plural term *totafos* rather than the singular *totefes* is because the head-*tefillin* contains several compartments. These compartments have the form and arrangement that we have received from our forebears, who in turn saw the prophets and ancient ones acting the same way, in a tradition dating back to Moses at Sinai ... *Tefillin* on the arm, next to the heart, symbolizes that all one's strength and passions are dedicated to God, while *tefillin* on the head symbolizes dedication to Him of the intellect.

This is one of the verses that parallels

one of the Ten Commandments: *You shall not covet your neighbor's house.* Our passage accordingly specifies בֵּיתֶךָ, *'your house,'* not your neighbor's house, implying that one should be content with his own lot and not be envious of his neighbor's. See p. 63.

9. The law of Mezuzah

וּכְתַבְתָּם עַל מְזֻזוֹת בֵּיתֶךָ וּבִשְׁעָרֶיךָ — *And write them on the doorposts of your house and upon* [lit. *in*] *your gates.* This commandment is fulfilled by affixing a *mezuzah*-scroll to each doorpost in Jewish houses. Literally, the word *mezuzah* means *doorpost* [see *Exodus* 12:7, 22, 23; and 21:6]. Although this passage would seem to require that one should write the words directly on the doorpost, the Sages in *Menachos* 34a teach that they are to be written on a scroll. This is derived by means of a *gezeirah shavah* (see footnote above) from the fact that the verb כתב, *write,* is used also in connection with the law of a bill of divorce [*Deut.* 24:1], where the writing must be done on a scroll [cf. *Tosafos*]; similarly in the case of *mezuzah,* the writing must be done on a scroll in the prescribed manner and affixed to the doorpost. According to another view there in the Talmud this teaching is derived from the word וּכְתַבְתָּם, *and you shall write them,* which alludes to a כְּתִיבָה תַּמָּה, *perfectly distinct writing.* That is, the Hebrew וּכְתַבְתָּם is interpreted as though it were two words וּכְתַב תָּם, *write perfectly,* and this can be accomplished only when writing with ink upon a scroll, for, as the commentators explain, any writing with ink directly upon a doorpost of wood, brick, or stone would be imperfect and indistinct.

Thus, although the word *mezuzah* means doorpost in Scriptural Hebrew, in popular usage it has come to refer to the *scroll,* rather than to the doorpost itself.

The *mezuzah* contains the first two sections of *Shema:* שְׁמַע and וְהָיָה אִם שָׁמֹעַ written in the manner of letters of the Torah scroll, traditionally in 22 lines. Both of these sections contain references to the law of *mezuzah* in their final verses. On the back of the parchment the Name שַׁדַּי (*"Almighty,"* but also, according to *Kol Bo,* the initial letters of שׁוֹמֵר דַּלְתוֹת יִשְׂרָאֵל, *Guardian of the doors of Israel)* is written, and the parchment is inserted into its case so that the word is visible through an aperture in the case.

At the bottom of the blank side, the letters כוזו במוכסז כוזו are also written, which, according to the Kabbalistic alphabetical system in which every letter alludes the preceding one, reads: ה' אלהינו ה', *HASHEM, our God, HASHEM.* The rolled up parchment is affixed to the right-hand doorpost of every room, house, or gate, in the top third of the doorpost and slanting inward. It is customary to touch the *mezuzah* reverently and kiss the fingers that touched it whenever entering or leaving a house.

When one enters the house, he touches the *mezuzah* to remind himself that he is treading upon consecrated ground; when he leaves, he touches it to commit his house to the protection of God to Whom it is dedicated *(R' Hirsch, Choreb;* see *Yoreh Deah* 285).

That the *mezuzah* is affixed to the upper third of the doorpost is derived in the Talmud [*Menachos* 33a] from the proximity of the phrases וּקְשַׁרְתָּם ... וּכְתַבְתָּם, *and you shall bind them ... and you shall write them.* Just as the binding of the *tefillin* is 'high up' [on the arm, and toward the top of the head], so must the 'writing' be placed high up, on the top third of the doorpost.

That the *mezuzah* is to be affixed to the *right* doorpost is derived in the Talmud [*ibid.* 34a] from the expression *'on the doorposts* בֵּיתֶךָ *of your house'* which is interpreted to imply בִּיאָתְךָ, *as you enter,* i.e., on the right side, since one steps into a house with his right foot first. Another Sage in the Talmud derives it from *II Kings* 12:10, which reads ... *on the right side as one comes into the house of HASHEM.*

Another exegesis derived from this phrase is that *'your' house* refers to the one who lives there; thus, the responsibility for affixing a *mezuzah* to a dwelling rests with the tenant, rather than the landlord.

Basing himself on some early Midrashim that are at variance with the Masoretic text, and according to which the word מְזֻזוֹת in our passage is spelled 'defectively' without the ו [see *Minchas Shay* to *Exodus* 12:7], *Rashi* comments: The word is spelled מזזת [which in the unvowelized Torah can be read as if it were in the singular מְזֻזַת]. This indicates that it is necessary to affix only one *mezuzah* to a doorpost. [Cf. *Menachos* 34a; *Sifsei Chachomim;* and *HaKsav V'Hakabalah.*]

☙ Purpose of Mezuzah

The *mezuzah* is a symbol that all of man's possessions belong to God Who, in His graciousness, granted them to us, and that it is prohibited for one to enjoy them until he offers thanks and blessing to their

Giver. Since man's primary possession is his home, God commanded that a *mezuzah* be attached to the various doorposts, so that every time one enters and leaves a room one will recall God to Whom all property belongs, and realize that all is His, and man should not glory in his own wealth since all is Divinely bestowed *(Iyun Tefillah).*

Furthermore, throughout Talmudic, Kabbalistic and Rabbinic literature we find many references to the fact that the sacred words of the *mezuzah* have a mystical protective power to ward off evil from the home on which it is affixed and its occupants.[1]

Aruch HaShulchan cautions, however, that this aspect of the *mezuzah* should not form a person's primary intention in fulfilling the precept. Rather one must fulfill it because it is God's Will, and the reward will inevitably follow.

Finally, as *Ramban* writes in his conclusion to the laws of *mezuzah* [6:13]: A person should be scrupulous regarding the precept of the *mezuzah;* for it is an eternal obligation binding upon everyone. Whenever one enters or leaves a home, he will encounter the Declaration of the Unity of the Name of the Holy One, Blessed is He, and will recall the love due Him, and will be aroused from his slumber and his preoccupation with transitory vanities. He will realize that nothing endures forever except for knowledge of the Rock of the Universe. Then he will return at once to his proper senses and he will walk the paths of the righteous. Our early Sages said [*Menachos* 33a]: "Whoever has *tefillin* on his head and arm, *tzitzis* on his garment, and a *mezuzah* on his door is assured not to sin, for he has many to remind him — angels that rescue him from sinning, as it is said *(Psalms* 34:8): *The angel of HASHEM encamps round those that fear Him, and delivers them."*

The term וּבִשְׁעָרֶיךָ, *and upon your gates,* extends the obligation of affixing a *mezuzah* to the gates of courtyards, provinces, and cities *(Rashi; Yoma* 10a).

Based on the term *'and* **in** *your gates,' Haamek Davar* suggests that on public gateways it is proper to chisel out an area on the post for the *mezuzah,* so that it can be recessed. While it is permitted to mount a *mezuzah* on the surface, nevertheless it is advisable to recess it. Inside a home, where cleanliness is assured, it is better for the *mezuzah* to be visible; however, on public gates, where cleanliness cannot be guaranteed, it is best for the *mezuzah* to be recessed and concealed.

◆§ The Second Portion [*Deut.* 11:13-21].

Acceptance of the Commandments. *The reward for the fulfillment of the* mitzvos; *the punishment for their transgression; reiteration of the contents of the first portion.*

Regarding the sequence of the portions of the *Shema,* the *Mishnah* [*Berachos* 13a] states: "Why was the section of שְׁמַע placed before that of וְהָיָה אִם שָׁמֹעַ? — So that one should first accept upon himself עוֹל מַלְכוּת שָׁמַיִם, *God's absolute sovereignty* [by proclaiming His unity], and then accept upon himself the עוֹל הַמִּצְוֹת, *the yoke of the commandments"* [by the passage: *If you shall hearken diligently to all My commandments*].

Most of this section is in the plural inasmuch as it speaks of the performance of the commandments, which is preferably done in public. The Sages have said [*Yalkut Beha'alosecha*] "One cannot compare communal performance to private performance." [See *Rashi* to *v.* 13 below.]

In the Scriptural context: In the Biblical verses preceding this message [*Deut.* 11:10*ff*], Moses continues his farewell exhortation to the Jewish people to heed God's commands

1. Talmud [*Avodah Zarah* 11a] relates a story of Onkelos, a Roman noble who converted to Judaism. His relative, the Roman Emperor, sent a succession of troops to arrest him for his conversion, but Onkelos succeeded in convincing all to convert. Finally, the emperor sent a company with strict orders not to allow Onkelos to engage them in conversation.

The ploy succeeded but, as they were escorting Onkelos out of the house, he looked at the *mezuzah* on his doorpost, placed his hand upon it, and said: "I will tell you what this is. The universal custom is for a human king to sit inside a room with his servants guarding him from the outside. With the Holy One, Blessed is He, however, His servants are inside a room and He guards them from the outside [by means of the *mezuzah*], *as it is said* [*Psalms* 121:8]: *HASHEM will guard your leaving and your entering henceforth and forevermore."* When the Roman soldiers heard that, they too converted, and the emperor stopped his attempts to arrest Onkelos.

One should bear in mind before reciting the next paragraph that he is about to declare his belief in the principle of reward and punishment.

יג **וְהָיָה** אִם־שָׁמֹעַ תִּשְׁמְעוּ אֶל־מִצְוֹתַי אֲשֶׁר אָנֹכִי
מְצַוֶּה אֶתְכֶם הַיּוֹם לְאַהֲבָה אֶת־יְהוָה
יד אֱלֹהֵיכֶם וּלְעָבְדוֹ בְּכָל־לְבַבְכֶם וּבְכָל־נַפְשְׁכֶם: וְנָתַתִּי

lest they suffer the consequences of disobedience. As *Rashi* and *Ramban* explain the passage, Moses informed them that *Eretz Yisrael,* which they would soon be entering, was different from Egypt inasmuch as *Eretz Yisrael's* fertility was dependent directly upon the bounty of rain from heaven, while Egypt was irrigated regularly by the overflow of the Nile. *Eretz Yisrael's* rain would be withheld or granted according to Israel's faithfulness to God, for His special attention is directed to that land, and He gives it rain only if His Torah is obeyed.

13. וְהָיָה — *And it will come to pass.* In the verses preceding this one in the Torah [*Deut.* 11:1-12], Israel is promised a blessed, prosperous life in *Eretz Yisrael,* a land "which drinks water of the rain of heaven" [ibid. *v.* 11]. *Rashi* writes that this condition is dependent upon our behavior, and the opening word in passage, וְהָיָה, *and it will come to pass* [*v.* 13], refers back to the description in *v.* 11 of *Eretz Yisrael's* dependence on God for rain, and implies that the foregoing blessings will be fulfilled — וְהָיָה, *And it will come to pass* — on the condition that you hearken to God's commandments ... for, if you do — [v. 14]: *then I will provide rain for your land,* etc.

אִם שָׁמֹעַ תִּשְׁמְעוּ אֶל מִצְוֹתַי — *If you continually hearken* [lit. *if hearken you will hearken;* in Scriptural style, the compound infinitive serves to emphasize the verb] *to My commandments.* [Moses now speaks in the name of God.]

The use of the compound verb implies *continuity in observance:* If you hearken to what you have already studied you will hearken to new subjects as well. [As *Me'am Loez* explains, if someone involves himself diligently in mastering and remembering what he has learned, his understanding will increase and he will inevitably go on to increase his knowledge. The same holds true for the performance of commandments — if someone applies himself to them conscientiously, he will find himself going on to newer and greater accomplishments.] Conversely, the idiom אִם שָׁכֹחַ תִּשְׁכַּח, *if you continually forget* [*Deut.* 8:19] means: If you have begun to forget, ultimately you will forget it all. Compare the passage in *Megillas Setarim* [some versions read "in the Megillah," and "Megillas Chassidim"; the exact reference, however, is unknown]: "If you forsake Me one day, I will forsake you two days" *(Rashi).*

Yerushalmi Berachos 9:5 illustrates the last quoted concept as follows: If two people part from each other — one going east and the other west, at the end of one day they will be two days distance from one another. [Thus, we are enjoined in this passage of *Shema* to continually hearken to the *mitzvos;* to neglect them — even for a short while — results in an unbridgeable gap.]

אֲשֶׁר אָנֹכִי מְצַוֶּה אֶתְכֶם — *Which I command you.* They must be fulfilled not because reason dictates it, but because *I* command you; *mitzvos* must be performed because they represent God's will *(Me'am Loez).*

הַיּוֹם — *This day.* That is, as if I commanded them to you this day. [Thus, though the Torah was given thousands of years ago, we should fulfill its precepts as enthusiastically as if we had received them only today.] The *mitzvos* should always be fresh to you as though you heard them today for the very first time *(Rashi; Sifre).*

Similarly, we must always fulfill the *mitzvos* as if their fulfillment were possible only הַיּוֹם, *that very day,* and if we were to wait for the morrow we might forfeit the opportunity. Man must never put off the performance of a *mitzvah* for the next day since we are but mortals and cannot be assured of still being alive tomorrow *(Divrei Shlomo).*[1]

1. An additional interpretation of this passage is that we must perceive the reward for Torah observance as being earned on the basis of performing to our capacity, rather than by the *quantitative* accomplishments we achieve. Thus, if one person does his best *qualitatively* according to his own

One should bear in mind before eciting the next paragraph that he is about to declare his belief in the principle of reward and punishment.

Deuteronomy 11:13-21

13 And it will come to pass — if you continually hearken
to My commandments which I command you this
day, to love HASHEM, your God, and to serve Him, with
all your heart and with all your soul — 14 then I will

לְאַהֲבָה אֶת ה׳ אֱלֹהֵיכֶם — *To love HASHEM, your God.* Do not perform *mitzvos* for an ulterior motive such as status or profit. Do them out of love for God, and eventually the honor will come *(Rashi).*

וּלְעָבְדוֹ בְּכָל לְבַבְכֶם וּבְכָל נַפְשְׁכֶם — *And to serve him, with all your heart and with all your soul.* The verse commands us to "serve" God with all our "heart." The word serve usually implies a deed. What is "service of the heart"? — service of the heart is prayer *(Taanis 29; Rashi). Rambam* in *Hilchos Tefillah* 1:1 (see *Kessef Mishnah)* and *Semag, Asin* §19 accordingly infer from our passage the requirement to serve God daily with prayer.

While praying one must devote his *total* concentration to God, and allow no stray thought to enter his mind. The Rabbis inferred from this passage that "prayer without concentration [כַּוָּנָה] is like a body without a soul" *(Chovos Halevavos Shaar HaNefesh* 3).

Why does the Torah repeat *with all your heart and with all your soul* when this had already been mentioned in the first portion of *Shema?* — Because that admonition was addressed to the people as individuals [the entire first section of *Shema* is worded in the singular], while this was an admonition addressed [in plural] to the entire community *(Rashi).*

Maskil l'David explains that *Rashi's* differentiation between an individual and a community is intended to explain why this portion — directed to the community — omits the requirement that God be served *with all your resources,* a requirement that *does* appear in the first portion of *Shema.* In the phrase וּבְכָל מְאֹדֶךָ in the first portion, *Rashi* noted that the requirement to love God with all one's resources was mandated to individuals because there are some people whose resources are dearer to them than their own lives [see comm. p. 23.] However, such a perverted idea could not apply to a community as a whole, which could not place greater value to its treasury than its very survival.[1]

ability, but a more gifted person accomplishes more while expending much less effort, the first is more worthy of reward. We must never become frustrated that we cannot possibly achieve *total* fulfillment of the *mitzvos,* nor hope to master the entire realm of Torah knowledge. Our reward comes from our day-to-day effort, as the Sages said [*Pirkei Avos* 2:21]: "It is not up to you to complete the work, yet you are not free to desist from it." The good that God wants to see accomplished on earth is not meant for any *individual* to complete. No one has the right to argue, "what I can do is but so little," and sit back idly. Even if our utmost effort yields only a fraction of what must be accomplished, our reward will be great nevertheless because we have contributed what is expected of us.

The Midrash cites a parable: Someone engaged a group of day laborers to fill a great well with water — a futile task. The fools among them said, "I'll *never* complete this task; it's futile!" But the wise ones among them said, "Look. I'm being paid daily for my labor; what do I care how deep the well is? To the contrary, I should be grateful that it's so deep; I'm assured of a job for a long time!"

The Holy One, Blessed is He,said similarly to mankind, "Study and observe *mitzvos* daily, and you will be paid your reward on that basis. I will not castigate you for not having learnt more than you were able to."

1. One of the disciples of the *Chiddushei HaRim* misused public funds. The rebbe admonished him severely for his conduct, even going so far as to call him a "murderer."

When the rebbe's intimates asked him why he had called this man a "murderer" when he was charged only with robbery, the rebbe answered, "In the second portion of Shema the term מְאֹד, *resources,* does not appear because that portion is addressed to the community as a whole and public resources are included in the phrase *all your soul.* Such public monies are sanctified for charitable needs, saving lives, supporting widows and orphans — whoever dares tamper with such holy funds may truly be termed a murderer."

מְטַר־אַרְצְכֶם בְּעִתּוֹ יוֹרֶה וּמַלְקוֹשׁ וְאָסַפְתָּ דְגָנֶךָ
טו וְתִירֹשְׁךָ וְיִצְהָרֶךָ: וְנָתַתִּי עֵשֶׂב בְּשָׂדְךָ לִבְהֶמְתֶּךָ וְאָכַלְתָּ

[For another explanation of why *all your resources* is mentioned only in connection with individuals, see comm. to first section.]

R' Hirsch suggests that מְאֹדְכֶם, *with all your resources,* is not needed in the context of this verse already implied in וּלְעָבְדוֹ, *and to serve him.* The requirement to serve God demands implicitly that one devote all his energies and means to accomplish God's will; if he withholds his resources from this mission, he is limiting his service of God. When our verse speaks of *heart* and *soul,* it refers to the *manner* in which God is to be served — energetically, cheerfully, and unrestrainedly.

14. The reward for compliance

"When you do what you are obligated to do, I, in turn, will do what I am committed to do [and repay your loyalty]" *(Sifre; Rashi)* ...

Here again, Moses speaks in the first-person, as he did in the first verse of this portion, because he speaks in the name of God and apparently cites His words:

וְנָתַתִּי מְטַר אַרְצְכֶם בְּעִתּוֹ — *Then I will provide rain for your land in its proper time.* — So *Eretz Yisrael* can truly be described as a land "which drinks water of the rain of heaven" [see *Rashi v.* 13].

The blessing of rain is given priority because everything else depends upon precipitation in its proper season: physical health, good harvests, and fruitful cattle *(Rambam* to *Levit.* 26:4).

Then I will provide — "I" [God], Myself will provide you with these blessings — not through the agency of an angel or emissary *(Sifre).*

Each rainfall will be an act of God's direct Providence, and not *solely* the result of meteorological laws of nature. Although the laws of nature, too, are His creation, the *primary* cause of rain is not predetermined, but remains God's providential care *(R' Hirsch).*

Rashi — citing *Sifre* — explains that *in its proper time* refers to convenient times, such as nighttime — especially Sabbath eves — when people are usually at home and would not be inconvenienced by rain. [See *Taanis* 23a where Wednesday evening is also mentioned in this context; cf. *Mizrachi.*]

Rashi is drawn to this Midrashic interpretation rather than the seemingly obvious interpretation that *proper time* refers to the most propitious times for agriculture, since such an advantageous schedule of rainfall is implied in the promise *'I will provide rain for your land.'* If rain were to fall out of season, it would do the land no good and could surely not be considered a blessing. *In its proper time,* therefore, must suggest the deeper connotation that *Rashi* elicits from the Midrash *(Mizrachi).*

The Hebrew term used in our verse for rain, מָטָר, denotes the kind of rain that is a gift of God and a symbol of Divine favor. There is also a 'natural' rain that forms as a result of the vapor ascending to the clouds from the earth. Such rain is called גֶּשֶׁם and comes randomly; it may or may not be propitious *(Malbim* to *Gen.* 2:5).

יוֹרֶה וּמַלְקוֹשׁ — *The early and late rains.* יוֹרֶה, *early rain,* is rain that falls in *Eretz Yisrael* in the planting season [*Cheshvan* — October and November] and drenches [מַרְוֶה] the soil; מַלְקוֹשׁ, *late rain* [from the root לקש which means *late, retarded* [see *Onkelos, Genesis* 30:42)] is the spring showers [in *Nissan* — March and April] that fall before the harvest and ripen the grain on the stalk *(Rashi; Taanis* 6a).

Another reason for the name יוֹרֶה for *early rain* is given in the Talmud, *Taanis* 6a: These rains [announcing as they do, the impending winter season] 'instruct' [from ירה, *teach*] people to plaster their roofs, to gather in their fruit, and attend to their [winter] needs.

Ibn Ezra similarly explains that יורה refers to the *early rains* — since rain in that season *portends* [יורה] a propitious year.

According to *Sifre* יורה is derived from ירה [arrows] since it falls torrentially, penetrating the soil like an arrow.

Eretz Yisrael's fertility was dependent on the regular start of these periods of rain, especially the first rain. The lack of rain in Cheshvan was regarded as a sign of Divine displeasure and portended great natural calamity. Such droughts would bring about the imposition of public fasts [תַּעֲנִית צִבּוּר] of increasing severity, as recorded in *Taanis* 6a and 15a [see ArtScroll Mishnah, *Taanis* with *Yad Avraham* commentary].

וְאָסַפְתָּ דְגָנֶךָ וְתִירֹשְׁךָ וְיִצְהָרֶךָ — *That you may gather in your grain, your wine, and your oil.* The emphasis is on וְאָסַפְתָּ: *You,* and

provide rain for your land in its proper time, the early and late rains, that you may gather in your grain, your wine, and your oil. [15] *I will provide grass in your field for your cattle and you will eat and be satisfied.* [16] *Beware lest your*

not your enemies, will gather in the produce *(Rashi)*.

— This and the next verse change to the second-person *singular* to emphasize that each *individual* Jew will benefit from the nation's compliance with God's Torah *(R' Bachya)*.

The translation of תִּירשׁ as *wine* follows *Onkelos*. Although in the Torah the terms יַיִן and תִּירשׁ are synonymous, the *Talmud* notes that in common usage there is a distinction between תִּירשׁ, which referred to a sweeter, less fermented wine, and יַיִן which referred to fully aged wine (see *Rashi* to *Nedarim* 76b). Apparently, however, even תִּירשׁ would be intoxicating when consumed in sufficient quantity (see *Sanhedrin* 70b).

יִצְהָר [from the root צהר, *light*] refers to pure olive oil used for kindling lamps *(Etz Yosef)*.

As noted on p. 63, the *Shema* parallels the Ten Commandments. *Yerushalmi Berachos* 1:5 explains that our verse parallels the commandment: You shall not steal — וְאָסַפְתָּ דְגָנֶךָ, *that you may gather in* **your** *grain*, and not your neighbor's grain.

Oznaim LaTorah suggests that this is why our verse is in singular. Were it in plural the parallel exegesis prohibiting stealing could not have been elicited.

According to *Acharis Shalom*, the passage is in singular to allude to the fact that crops will be so abundant that each individual will be totally occupied in gathering his own produce.[1]

15. וְנָתַתִּי עֵשֶׂב בְּשָׂדְךָ לִבְהֶמְתֶּךָ *[And] I will provide grass [or: herbage] in your field for your cattle.* The blessing is that you will find pasturage for your cattle in your own fields, and will not have to lead them a long distance away to graze *(Rashi* from *Sifre)*.

In an alternate interpretation from *Sifre, Rashi* explains that the passage means that grain will grow so profusely that one will be able to constantly cut his grain for fodder throughout the rainy season when it grows; and by discontinuing his cutting for a mere thirty days before the harvest, his field will yield as large a crop as if he had not been cutting for the cattle.

וְאָכַלְתָּ וְשָׂבָעְתָּ — *And you will eat and be satisfied.* This refers to *your grain, your wine, and your oil* in the preceding verse *(Ibn Ezra)*.

This is a new blessing [not to be understood as being in consequence of God's giving grass in the fields for the cattle. Rather, it is a blessing to man himself.] It implies that a blessing will be on the bread within the stomach, meaning that one will feel sated with what he eats *(Rashi)*.

[As *Rashi* comments in *Levit.* 25:19 and 26:35, this blessing means that one need not eat much in order to be full. Rather the idea is that he will find satisfaction in the food he eats. The food itself, as it were, will be blessed (see *Ramban*).]

According to *Ramban*, this phrase modifies the previous phrases: you will eat *your grain, wine, and oil*, as well as the offspring of the thriving cattle, for when *I will provide grass — you will be satisfied.*

From the fact that the Torah here speaks *first* of pasture for the cattle, and only *then* continues: *and you will eat and be satisfied*, the Sages deduce that one must first feed his animals before partaking of his own

1. In *Berachos* 35b, R' Yishmael understands this verse to mean that despite the Jew's paramount obligation to engage in the study of Torah, he must not rely on miracles for his livelihood. Thus, *You may gather in your grain* is telling us to engage also in work and commerce when necessary. R' Shimon bar Yochai disagrees: 'If a man plows at plowing time, sows at sowing time, harvests at harvest time, threshes at threshing time, and winnows at winnow time, what will become of Torah [study]? Rather, when Jews are *perfectly* righteous, God sees to it that their needs are provided by others; when they are only relatively righteous [see *Tos.* s.v. כאן] they will be forced to see to their own livelihoods.

Abaye observed that those who attempted to follow R' Shimon's course of relying on miracles did not succeed. *Maharsha* explains that R' Shimon never intended his advice except for people with the highest degree of righteousness. For such people, it is indeed more important that they dedicate themselves totally to service of God.

Nevertheless the *Halachah* is clear *(Rambam, Hil. Talmud Torah* 3:6-7; *Yoreh De'ah* 241:1) that the preferred course is that one should give his Torah studies priority to whatever degree possible.

וְשָׂבָעְתָּ: הִשָּׁמְרוּ לָכֶם פֶּן־יִפְתֶּה לְבַבְכֶם וְסַרְתֶּם טז
וַעֲבַדְתֶּם אֱלֹהִים אֲחֵרִים וְהִשְׁתַּחֲוִיתֶם לָהֶם: וְחָרָה יז
אַף־יהוה בָּכֶם וְעָצַר אֶת־הַשָּׁמַיִם וְלֹא־יִהְיֶה מָטָר
וְהָאֲדָמָה לֹא תִתֵּן אֶת־יְבוּלָהּ וַאֲבַדְתֶּם מְהֵרָה מֵעַל
הָאָרֶץ הַטֹּבָה אֲשֶׁר יהוה נֹתֵן לָכֶם: וְשַׂמְתֶּם אֶת־דְּבָרַי יח
אֵלֶּה עַל־לְבַבְכֶם וְעַל־נַפְשְׁכֶם וּקְשַׁרְתֶּם אֹתָם לְאוֹת

meal. [The *halachah,* however, is that this stricture applies only to food. Concerning drink, however, man takes precedence as we derive from *Genesis* 24:14 where Rebecca offers drink to Eliezer before his camels *(Magen Avraham* to *Shulchan Aruch O. Ch.* 167:18. See footnote to ArtScroll *Bereishis ad loc.* p. 911. See also *HaGaon R' Moshe Feinstein, Igros Moshe, Orach Chaim II,* responsa 52).]

16. Warning against violating the Torah

As in *Deut.* 8:11, after the words, *Eat and be satisfied,* a warning note is sounded — *'Beware!'* Satiety induces forgetfulness of God, for prosperity is the greatest challenge to piety.

הִשָּׁמְרוּ לָכֶם פֶּן יִפְתֶּה לְבַבְכֶם — *Beware lest your heart be seduced.* — When you have eaten and are full, beware that you do not rebel against God, for in time of prosperity one needs particularly to be on guard against disloyalty to God, as indicated in *Deut.* 8:12-14, where first it says: *Lest you will have eaten your fill ... and your herds and flocks are multiplied,* and then: *and your heart will grow haughty and you will forget your God (Rashi).*

Cf. also *Deut.* 32:15 וַיִּשְׁמַן יְשֻׁרוּן וַיִּבְעָט, *When Jeshurun grew fat, it kicked (Dover Shalom).*

Lest your heart be seduced, into attributing the blessings you enjoy to 'other gods' *(Ibn Caspi).*

Chizkuni interprets this verb not as *seduce* — in which case, he suggests, the context would demand the reflexive יְפוּתֶּה — but from the cognate root פתי, foolishness. He renders: *Lest your heart become foolish.*

וְסַרְתֶּם וַעֲבַדְתֶּם אֱלֹהִים אֲחֵרִים וְהִשְׁתַּחֲוִיתֶם לָהֶם — *And you turn astray and serve the gods of others and bow to them. And you turn astray* — from the Torah — *and serve the gods of others,* for if man neglects the Torah he begins a course that will end in idolatry *(Rashi).*

The phrase אֱלֹהִים אֲחֵרִים, literally, *other gods,* [cannot be taken in the sense that there are indeed other Divinities with godly powers. Rather, it] means *gods of others:* they are not gods but others worship them as such. Alternatively, it refers to gods that are 'other' [i.e., alien] to those who worship them; one calls upon them and they do not respond; consequently they became like 'strangers' to him *(Rashi* here and in *Exodus* 20:3).

17. וְחָרָה אַף־ה׳ בָּכֶם — *Then the wrath of HASHEM will blaze against you.* The expression חָרָה אַף denotes outwardly displayed, flared up anger. The expression is idiomatic and metaphorically refers to *flaring nostrils. Rashi* in *Exodus* 15:8 explains that this term is used to describe *fierce anger* since, when one is angry, the nostrils flare up and become 'hot.' Conversely, when one's anger subsides one is described as נִתְקָרְרָה דַעְתּוֹ, *his mind becomes cooled.*

Of course, when speaking of God, this expression cannot be taken literally since God is incorporeal. Such usage — where physical or emotional attributes are ascribed to God — is termed ''anthropomorphism'' and ''anthropopathism'' respectively. ''The Torah speaks in the language of men,'' and such expressions figuratively depict these emotions from the human vantage point.

וְעָצַר אֶת הַשָּׁמַיִם וְלֹא יִהְיֶה מָטָר — *He will restrain the heaven so there will be no rain.* [Rain, as noted, is a gift of God. In times of His wrath, he withholds it.]

This verse is preceded by a reference to idolatry. We derive from this that as a result of the sin of idolatry, rain is withheld *(Yerushalmi, Taanis* 3:3).

וְהָאֲדָמָה לֹא תִתֵּן אֶת יְבוּלָהּ — *And the soil will not yield its produce.* — It will not even yield what you have brought [Hebrew cognate verb מוֹבִיל, from root יבל] to it; your harvest will not even equal the

heart be seduced and you turn astray and serve the gods
of others and bow to them. 17 *Then the wrath of HASHEM*
will blaze against you. He will restrain the heaven so there
will be no rain and the soil will not yield its produce. And
you will swiftly be banished from the goodly land which
HASHEM gives you. 18 *Place these words of Mine upon*
your heart and upon your soul; bind them for a sign upon

quantity of seed you planted in it. See *Haggai* 1:6 *(Rashi).*

[Comp. *Rashi* on Leviticus 26:40: *And your land will not yield its produce* (יְבוּלָהּ): — Even what you brought (מוּבִיל) to it at planting time.]

וַאֲבַדְתֶּם מְהֵרָה מֵעַל הָאָרֶץ הַטֹּבָה — *And you will swiftly be banished from* [*upon*] *the goodly land.* First will come famine. If that does not bring repentance, exile will follow *(Vilna Gaon).*

The word **וַאֲבַדְתֶּם**, from the root **אבד**, is usually rendered *perish*. In this case, however, *Rashi* — following *Sifre* — maintains that *perishing* from the land is not what the context implies, nor that death would be the consequence of the lack of rain and its attendant famine. [For had **אבד** the implication of *perish*, the passage should have read **וַאֲבַדְתֶּם עַל הָאָרֶץ**, not **מֵעַל** *(Torah Temimah).*] Rather, the verse now introduces an *additional* calamity with which God would punish them — exile from the land. Furthermore, mention of *the goodly* land suggests that their sin of idolatry was due to the abundance of good which the Land had given them, indicating that we are not dealing here with a famine. Instead, this calamity results from a *prosperity* that dulls awareness of God; as *Rashi* writes above, satiety induces forgetfulness of God, and as noted above, the *good land* will provide that satiety. [*Chizkuni* and *Radak* also interpret this passage in the sense of exile. (Comp. *Isaiah* 27:13 where **הָאוֹבְדִים** also means *exiles).*]

Sforno, however, subscribes to the view that **וַאֲבַדְתֶּם** is to be interpreted *You shall perish* — from the famine mentioned in the previous passage, which will be more severe than death by the sword.

The meaning of **מְהֵרָה**, *swiftly* is: You will be given no probationary period. But, should you ask, why was the generation of the Flood granted a 120 year probationary period before God brought the Flood on them [see *Rashi* to *Genesis* 6:4]? — The answer is: The generation of the Flood had no one from whom to learn, while you *do* have examples from whom to learn *(Rashi; Sifre).*

אֲשֶׁר ה׳ נֹתֵן לָכֶם — *Which HASHEM gives you.* I.e., will give you. [Although the land had not yet been given to Israel, Moses uses the present tense, *gives,* because God's assurance to do something is no less real than a historical fact.]

18. Tefillin, Torah-study, and mezuzah/ The observance of mitzvos in Exile

וְשַׂמְתֶּם אֶת־דְּבָרַי אֵלֶּה עַל לְבַבְכֶם וְעַל נַפְשְׁכֶם — *Place these words of Mine upon your heart and upon your soul.* It is contextually unclear why the commandments of *tefillin* and *mezuzah,* mentioned further in this verse, are reiterated here after the threat of exile from the Land. *Rashi,* following *Sifre* [as explained by *Rambam;* see below], interprets that this verse stresses the necessity for Torah observance even in Exile [lest one think that observance of the *mitzvos* applies only in *Eretz Yisrael*].

In *Rashi's* words: *And place these words of Mine,* etc.: Even after you have been exiled, make yourselves distinctive [from the residents of the gentile nations among whom you will be dispersed] by means of My precepts: Don *tefillin,* attach *mezuzos* to your doorposts, so that they will not be novelties to you when you return [to *Eretz Yisrael* where their performance has a degree of holiness far beyond that attainable elsewhere *(R' Bachya;* see *Ramban* below)]. Similarly, Scripture records in *Jeremiah* 31:21 [where Jeremiah addressed the following prophecy to the Israelites who were about to go into the Babylonian exile]: *"Set up distinguishing marks for yourselves"* [that is, retain your distinctiveness in exile through the commandments].

עַל־יֶדְכֶם וְהָיוּ לְטוֹטָפֹת בֵּין עֵינֵיכֶם: וְלִמַּדְתֶּם אֹתָם יט
אֶת־בְּנֵיכֶם לְדַבֵּר בָּם בְּשִׁבְתְּךָ בְּבֵיתֶךָ וּבְלֶכְתְּךָ בַדֶּרֶךְ
וּבְשָׁכְבְּךָ וּבְקוּמֶךָ: וּכְתַבְתָּם עַל־מְזוּזוֹת בֵּיתֶךָ כ
וּבִשְׁעָרֶיךָ: לְמַעַן יִרְבּוּ יְמֵיכֶם וִימֵי בְנֵיכֶם עַל הָאֲדָמָה כא

Thus, *Ramban* explains, from the Midrashic expositions cited by *Rashi* — wherein the *mitzvos* of *tefillin*, Torah study, and *mezuzah* are reiterated in this context of exile — we derive that these commandments — and others like them — are personal obligations [חוֹבַת הַגּוּף], in contrast to commandments that apply only to the land [חוֹבַת קַרְקַע]. Personal commandments are binding everywhere, and we are obligated to observe them even in Exile, whereas we are exempt in Exile from commandments which apply to the land (חוֹבַת הַקַּרְקַע] such as heave-offerings and tithes, since land-related commandments apply only in *Eretz Yisrael*. [See *Ramban* to *Leviticus* 18:28 for his elaboration on the qualitative superiority of *mitzvah*-performance in *Eretz Yisrael. See also R' Nosson Scherman's Overview* to *Lech-Lecha* in ArtScroll *Bereishis*.]

Others, such as *Ibn Ezra*, who follow the non-Midrashic sense of the verse, do not perceive this as referring to *mitzvah*-observance in Exile, but as a summary and exhortation of how Israel is to *avoid* the disasters foreboded in the previous verses. They would render: *Thus, you shall place these words of Mine*, etc. — so you will not be exiled — but *prolong your days in your land* (*v.* 21).

Sforno renders: *Place ... upon your heart* — to meditate thereon; *and upon your soul* — to fulfill them willingly.

☙ Tefillin

וּקְשַׁרְתֶּם אֹתָם לְאוֹת עַל־יֶדְכֶם — [*And*] *bind them for a sign upon your arm.* [See comm. to parallel phrase in first section, p. 26].

From the continuity in this verse of the word וּקְשַׁרְתֶּם, *bind them*, with the word in the preceding passage, עַל לְבַבְכֶם, *upon your heart*, the Sages in the Talmud [*Menachos* 37b] derive that *tefillin* are to be worn high up on the arm opposite the heart.

The symbolism of the positions of both *tefillin* are clearly stated in the prayer customarily recited daily before *tefillin* are donned: "He has commanded us to lay the *tefillin* on the arm as a memorial of His outstretched arm; and that it should be opposite the heart, to subjugate thereby the desires and designs of our heart to His service, blessed is His Name; and upon the head opposite the brain, so that the soul, which is in my brain, along with my other senses and faculties, may all be subjugated to His service, blessed is His Name.

וְהָיוּ לְטוֹטָפֹת בֵּין עֵינֵיכֶם — *And they shall be* [for] *tefillin between your eyes.* [See comm. to parallel phrase in the First Portion p. 28.]

☙ Torah-study

וְלִמַּדְתֶּם אֹתָם אֶת־בְּנֵיכֶם — [*And you shall*] *teach them to your children.*[1] Accustom your children to *mitzvos* (*Sforno*).

The word אתם is pronounced אֹתָם, *them*, referring to the words of Torah which you are to teach your children. But it can also be pronounced אַתֶּם, *you*, as if to say וְלִמַּדְתֶּם אַתֶּם, *you are to study* [Torah]. Do not content yourself with making sure your children study. Unless you set a proper *personal* example for them, why should they heed your urgings that *they* study? (*Chofetz Chaim*).[2]

1. The chassidic master, R' Simcha Bunam of P'schis'cha, said of someone who urged his children to study although he studied very little himself: "We can assume that his children will not become scholars, because their father did not set an example. But at least we can be sure that they will urge *their* children to study."

2. In discussing public education of children, the Talmud [*Bava Basra* 21a] records the following: The name of R' Yehoshua ben Gamla is to be recalled for the good, for were it not for him the Torah would have been forgotten in Israel. At first, if a child had a father, his father taught him, and if he had no father he did not learn at all. They were guided by the verse, *Teach them to your children*, emphasizing that everyone should teach his own children.

They then made an ordinance that teachers be appointed in Jerusalem; in this they were guided by

your arm and they shall be tefillin between your eyes.
19 *Teach them to your children, to discuss them while you*
sit in your home, while you walk on the way, when you
recline and when you arise. 20 *And write them on the*
doorposts of your house and upon your gates. 21 *In order*
to prolong your days and the days of your children upon

The Talmud hometically propounds that the word וְלִמַּדְתֶּם [*and you shall teach them*] can be read as if vowelized וּלְמַד תַּם [study perfectly]. This means that one's study [לִמּוּד] must be enunciated faultlessly [תַּם]. One must make a pause between similar sounds [רֶוַח בֵּין הַדְּבֵקִים]. That is, if the last letter of a word is the same as the first letter of the next, care must be taken not to slur them together, or they will sound like one long word. Examples of such words in the *Shema,* between which one must be careful to pause and enunciate clearly, are: עַל לְבָבֶךָ; עַל לְבַבְכֶם; בְּכָל לְבָבְךָ; בְּכָל לְבַבְכֶם; עֵשֶׂב בְּשָׂדְךָ; וַאֲבַדְתֶּם מְהֵרָה; הַכָּנָף פְּתִיל; אֶתְכֶם מֵאֶרֶץ *(Berachos* 15b).

לְדַבֵּר בָּם — *To discuss them.* Constantly *(Sforno)* ...

From the time a child can speak, his father should teach him the verse תּוֹרָה צִוָּה לָנוּ משֶׁה מוֹרָשָׁה קְהִלַּת יַעֲקֹב, *Moses commanded us the Torah as a possession of the congregation of Jacob* [*Deut.* 33:4], so that Torah study is the foundation upon which he is taught to speak. Also, the father should accustom the child to the Hebrew language and Torah *(Rashi; Succah* 42a).

בְּשִׁבְתְּךָ בְּבֵיתֶךָ וּבְלֶכְתְּךָ בַדֶּרֶךְ ... — *While you sit in your home,* [and] *while you walk on the way.* In giving the command to educate children, the verse speaks in the plural [וְלִמַּדְתֶּם]: this alludes to a communal responsibility to arrange for the education of children. Then it reverts to the singular, *while you sit* [בְּשִׁבְתְּךָ]: this teaches that the individual parent is not absolved from his personal duty to teach his own child *(Iyun Tefillah).*

The verse is homiletically interpreted: *while dwelling at your home* — in *Eretz Yisrael, while walking on the way* — in Exile; *while you recline* — when you are in degraded circumstances *and while you arise* — when you are on the ascendant.

וּכְתַבְתָּם עַל מְזוּזוֹת בֵּיתֶךָ וּבִשְׁעָרֶיךָ — *And write them on the doorposts of your house and upon* [lit. *in*] *your gates.* [See comm. to parallel phrase end of first section.]

[Although many *siddurim* set verse 21 as a new paragraph, leading some to believe that there are *four* paragraphs in the *Shema,* the verse is part of the chapter which begins וְהָיָה and no special separation sets it off in the Torah.]

21. לְמַעַן יִרְבּוּ יְמֵיכֶם וִימֵי בְנֵיכֶם — *In order to prolong your days and the days of your children.* If you fulfill the aforesaid *mitzvos* [*love of God; Torah-study; tefillin; mezuzah*] even in Exile, you will return to *Eretz Yisrael* and enjoy longevity there (following *Rashi* and *Rambam* in *v.* 18). Alternatively, while you are in *Eretz Yisrael* you should fulfill the aforesaid *mitzvos* properly — and *place these words of Mine upon your heart* — so that it will not become necessary to exile you in the first place (the latter follows *Ibn Ezra).*

This passage is conditional: *If* you will fulfill the Torah *then your days ... will be prolonged,* but if not the opposite will happen *(Rashi; Sifre).*

This verse parallels the Commandment *"Honor your father and your mother so your days will be prolonged ... "*

עַל הָאֲדָמָה — *Upon the ground.* I.e., the life-sustaining sacred soil of *Eretz Yisrael (Alshich)* ...

the verse [*Isaiah* 2:3]: *For from Zion shall the Torah go forth.* Even so, however, if a child had a father, the father would take him up to Jerusalem and have him taught there; and if not the child would not go there to learn.

They ordained, therefore, that teachers should be appointed in each province and the boys should enter the schools at the age of sixteen or seventeen. But this was problematic, for if the teacher punished them they used to rebel and leave the school.

Ultimately, R' Yehoshua ben Gamla came and ordained that teachers of *young* children should be appointed in each and every town, and that children should enter school at the age of six or seven.

אֲשֶׁר נִשְׁבַּע יהוה לַאֲבֹתֵיכֶם לָתֵת לָהֶם כִּימֵי הַשָּׁמַיִם עַל־הָאָרֶץ:

Before reciting this last portion of Shema one must have in his mind that he is about to fulfill the commandment of declaring that God took us out of Egypt.

לז-לח **וַיֹּאמֶר** יהוה אֶל־מֹשֶׁה לֵּאמֹר: דַּבֵּר אֶל־בְּנֵי יִשְׂרָאֵל וְאָמַרְתָּ אֲלֵהֶם וְעָשׂוּ לָהֶם צִיצִת

אֲשֶׁר נִשְׁבַּע ה׳ לַאֲבֹתֵיכֶם לָתֵת לָהֶם — *That HASHEM has sworn to your ancestors to give* [*it*] *to them.* The passage specifies that God has sworn to give it לָהֶם, *to them* — the ancestors — not לָכֶם, *to you.* From this [i.e. the fact that the Land was still to be given to the ancestors who had already long-since died — the implication being that they will resurrect in order to receive the Land], the Midrash derives an allusion to תְּחִיַּת הַמֵּתִים, *Resurrection of the Dead,* in the Torah *(Rashi; Sifre).*

The Doctrine of Resurrection of the Dead, i.e. that following the Messianic Redemption all the dead will be revived to once again lead normal lives [see R' Saadiah Gaon *Emunos V'Deos* ch. 7], is one of the essential beliefs of Judaism, and *Rambam* lists it among the primary tenets of the Faith. This ancient Doctrine finds *explicit* expression in many Scriptural references, such as in Hannah's prayer [*I Samuel* 2:6]: *"HASHEM causes death and gives life, casts down into the grave and raises up"*; cf. also *Isaiah* 26:19; *Psalms* 16:9; more explicitly, *Daniel* 12:2: *Many of those who sleep in the dusty earth shall awaken, these for everlasting life and these for shame* ... [see ArtScroll commentary there].

All of the above references are from the Books of Scripture known as Prophets and Writings; *Rashi* accordingly cites *Sifre* that our verse provides one of the rare allusions to this Doctrine in the Torah itself.

כִּימֵי הַשָּׁמַיִם עַל הָאָרֶץ — *Like the days of the heaven on the earth.* [The idiom means 'forever,' since the heavens will remain in place as long as the universe endures.] This refers to the quality of life. If you obey the Torah, your transitory life on earth will be as worthwhile as the true, heavenly life *(HaKsav V'HaKabbalah).*

Just as the heaven brings abundance to earth — through the sun, moon, rain, and so on — so your righteous lives will be a source of benefit to everything on earth *(Ksav Sofer).*

☙ The Third Portion [*Numbers* 15:37-41]

The Talmud [*Berachos* 12b] lists five commandments to be found in this portion: 1). The law of *tzitzis* [*v.* 38]; 2). Remembrance of the Exodus [*v.* 41]; 3). The requirement to remember all the commandments and to beware of heresy (see *Maharsha*) [*v.* 39]; 4). Avoidance of sinful thoughts [*v.* 39]; 5). Avoidance of idolatrous thoughts [*v.* 39].

"Why does the section of וְהָיָה אִם שָׁמֹעַ precede that of וַיֹּאמֶר ה׳? — Because the former section [dealing as it does with all the *mitzvos*] is applicable to both the day and the night, whereas the latter section [which deals primarily with *tzitzis*] is applicable only to the day" [since the wearing of *tzitzis* is not obligatory at night] *(Berachos* 13a).

Later, the Talmud offers an additional reason for the sequence: The section of שְׁמַע precedes וְהָיָה אִם שָׁמֹעַ, because the former mentions *learning* [וְדִבַּרְתָּ בָּם], *teaching* [וְשִׁנַּנְתָּם לְבָנֶיךָ], and *doing* [the *mitzvos* of love of God, *tefillin* and *mezuzah*]; and the section of וְהָיָה אִם שָׁמֹעַ precedes וַיֹּאמֶר ה׳ because the former mentions both *teaching* and *doing* whereas the latter mentions *doing* only.

In the Scriptural context: This section is the closing paragraph of *Parshas Sh'lach* which deals primarily with the incident of the Spies. Immediately preceding it is the story of the intentional Sabbath-violator who incurred the death penalty for his transgression.

Purpose of the Mitzvah of Tzitzis. *Ramban* maintains that God commanded the *mitzvah* of *tzitzis* after the incident of the Sabbath violation to emphasize that by means of the *mitzvah* of *tzitzis* the Jews will remember all the commandments, including the Sabbath. [See *Rashi* citing *R' Moshe HaDarshan* on *v.* 41.]

According to the *Yalkut,* after the incident of the violation Moses told God that these people had violated the Sabbath because the commandments were still new to them and

the ground that HASHEM has sworn to your ancestors to give them, like the days of the heaven on the earth.

Before reciting this last portion of Shema one must have in his mind that he is about to fulfill the commandment of declaring that God took us out of Egypt.

Numbers 15:37-41

37 And HASHEM said to Moses, saying: 38 Speak to the Children of Israel and say to them that they are to

not sufficiently ingrained in their minds. During the weekdays, the Jews have a physical 'sign' — *tefillin* — to remind them of the *mitzvos* and the covenant with God that distinguish them from the gentiles; on Sabbath, however, there is no special distinctive symbol. In response God mandated that *tzitzis* be worn — even on the Sabbath — to serve as a *constant* reminder of all the commandments.

The Midrash observes that every moment and activity in a Jew's life is charged and regulated with some sort of commandment. Even when he wraps himself in a garment, God legislated that it be fringed with *tzitzis*.

Furthermore, the Sages invested the precept of *tzitzis* with exalted symbolism. *Tzitzis* is regarded as a reminder to the Jew to observe the *mitzvos*, its function being similar to that of the *mezuzah* on the doorposts and to the *tefillin* on the arm and head. The Talmud [*Menachos* 44a] tells of a person who was saved from sensual sin because he wore *tzitzis*.

Its inclusion in the Shema. The reason this portion was designated as part of the twice-daily recitation of *Shema* is because it recalls the Exodus from Egypt, an event that a Jew is commanded to remember *all the days of your life* [see *Deut.* 16:3]. *'All'* is an inclusive word implying something in addition to whatever is stated explicitly. The Sages expound that it teaches the additional obligation to recall the Exodus in the evening as well as the morning.

Although other portions of the Torah mention the Exodus, only this one was selected for inclusion in the *Shema* because, as noted above, it contains a total of five commandments, not only mention of the Exodus *(Berachos* 12b).

According to Talmud *Yerushalmi*, this section was chosen for inclusion in the daily recital of the *Shema* because of its parallel references to the Ten Commandments [see *Tosafos, Berachos* 12b, s.v. בִּקְשׁוּ: see also p. 63].

37. וַיֹּאמֶר ה׳ אֶל מֹשֶׁה לֵּאמֹר — *And HASHEM said to Moses, saying.*[1] The superfluous expression *saying* — literally *to say* — throughout the Torah has the connotation of *to say,* i.e. transmit, to all future generations (לֵאמֹר לְדוֹרוֹת); it also implies that the statement it introduces was transmitted in a clear unambiguous manner. In the case of the transmission of a *mitzvah*, as in our passage, the word *to say* connotes that the relatively brief recorded text was accompanied by elaboration and specifications of the meaning and performance of the *mitzvah* in תּוֹרָה שֶׁבְּעַל פֶּה, *Oral Law* transmitted to Moses at Sinai, and then handed down from generation to generation *(HaKsav V'Hakabbalah;* see *Ramban* beginning of *Leviticus; Iyun Tefillah).*

38. דַּבֵּר אֶל בְּנֵי יִשְׂרָאֵל וְאָמַרְתָּ אֲלֵהֶם — *Speak to the Children* [lit. *sons*] *of Israel and say to them.* There is a rule in Biblical interpretation that wherever both terms דַּבֵּר, *speak*, and וְאָמַרְתָּ, *say*, occur in one passage, the former term means: *introduce*

1. The expression וַיֹּאמֶר ה׳, *HASHEM said*, has a more conciliatory connotation than the common וַיְדַבֵּר ה׳, *HASHEM spoke.* This reflects the Midrashic interpretation [mentioned in the prefatory comment above] that following the incident of the Sabbath violation recorded in the Torah immediately preceding this verse, Moses was distressed and said to God, "During the weekdays the Jews wear *tefillin* and remember the commandments; what shall they wear on Sabbath to serve as a reminder?"

"I will command them to wear *tzitzis* [which shall apply even on the Sabbath]," God answered, "and this shall remind them of the commandments always." Thus, since God wished to conciliate Moses and respond to his wishes, the term וַיֹּאמֶר is used to introduce this *mitzvah (Or HaChaim).*

According to *Harav Moshe Feinstein* שליט״א, the more conciliatory term אמר is used to introduce this *mitzvah,* because *tzitzis* are not obligatory in the same absolute sense as are other *mitzvos.* According to the Scriptural *halachah,* only when one wears a four-cornered garment does the

עַל־כַּנְפֵי בִגְדֵיהֶם לְדֹרֹתָם וְנָתְנוּ עַל־צִיצִת הַכָּנָף פְּתִיל
לט תְּכֵלֶת: וְהָיָה לָכֶם לְצִיצִת וּרְאִיתֶם אֹתוֹ וּזְכַרְתֶּם אֶת־

the topic in general, and the latter means: *elaborate upon it.* In the context of this *mitzvah,* this elaboration consists of the number of threads, the manner of tying the knots, etc., all of which are not specified in the Torah, but which we know from the tradition handed down generation to generation from Moses at Sinai. Thus, only the general outline of the mitzvah was recorded in the Torah, but detailed laws, which Moses taught to Israel, remained as the Oral Law *(R' Bachya; Etz Yosef).*

The Rabbis [*Pesikta Zutresa,* see *Hagahos Maimonis*] derive from the specification בְּנֵי יִשְׂרָאֵל, lit. the *'sons' of Israel,* that women are exempt from this commandment; see below, p. 45. Cf. *Tosafos Gittin* §5b and *Torah Temimah* §106.

Furthermore, in the Talmud [*Menachos* 42a], from the phrase *Children of Israel* the law is codified that only a Jew can make *tzitzis;* if a gentile makes *tzitzis* for a Jew they are invalid.

וְעָשׂוּ לָהֶם צִיצִת — *That they are to* [lit. *and they shall*] *make themselves* [lit. *to them*] *tassels.* [Hebrew: *tzitzis.*]

Rashi offers two reasons why these tassels are called *tzitzis:* a) because of the threads that hang down from it, the term **צִיצִת** meaning *curls* or *locks,* as in *Ezekiel* 7:3; b) because the command associated with them is that: *You shall look upon it* [*v.* 39], and the word **צִיצִית**, according to this interpretation, is derived from the verb **צִיץ**, *gaze,* as in *Song of Songs* 2:9, and the noun denotes "an object to be gazed at."

☙ Not an absolute command

This verse is not an absolute command, for as noted below, the Torah obligates one to attach *tzitzis* only if he is wearing a four-cornered garment. Rather, the command is conditional, as if to say: If you own a four-cornered garment and wish to wear it, then be aware that you must *first make yourselves tassels (HaKsav V'Hakabalah).*

According to accepted *halachah, tzitzis* is a חוֹבַת גַּבְרָא, *incumbent on the person,* and not חוֹבַת טַלִּית, *incumbent on the garment.* That is, the duty is only incumbent when a four-cornered garment is worn, but כְּלִי מוּנָח בְּקוּפְסָא, *a garment in the closet,* need not have *tzitzis.*

As *R' Hirsch* emphasizes in this connection, though the Torah does not require that a four-cornered garment be worn, the Torah assumes that we will wear such a garment and expects us to impose this duty on ourselves, as indeed we do. See below.

From the emphasis on the word וְעָשׂוּ, *they are to make,* the Rabbis expound the Law that the *tzitzis* must be specially made for the purpose. The threads used for *tzitzis* must be spun with the expressed intention that they are being made for *tzitzis.* ... Furthermore, previously wound and tied *tzitzis* that are later sewn onto a garment are not valid *(Rambam* 1:11-12; see *Menachos* 42a-b).

Additionally, the superfluous word לָהֶם, *to them,* is interpreted to denote that the *tzitzis* must be of material that belongs to the owner; if one steals thread and makes *tzitzis* from it, it is invalid *(Succah* 9a; *Orach Chaim* 1:6).

עַל כַּנְפֵי בִגְדֵיהֶם לְדֹרֹתָם — *On the corners of their garments, throughout their generations.* Technically the obligation of this *mitzvah* applies only if one is wearing a garment of four or more corners, in which case he must affix *tzitzis* to four of them [*Menachos* 43b; *Orach Chaim* §17 and §24]. When such four-cornered garments, such as four-cornered cloaks, went out of style, a typical wardrobe no longer included a garment that required *tzitzis* [see *Orach Chaim* 10:18]. Then the Rabbis exegetically extended the *mitzvah* and ruled that one *should* wear a four-cornered garment in order to make it possible to fulfill the *mitzvah* לְדֹרֹתָם, *throughout all generations.* [See *Sefer HaChinuch.*]

Accordingly, the *mitzvah* is now fulfilled by means of a *tallis katan* ['small tallis'] or *arba kanfos* [*'four corners'*] — a rectangular four-cornered undergarment (for adults about 18-24 inches wide by about four feet long; for children,

obligation to attach *tzitzis* to each of the corners apply, but it is only by Rabbinic mandate that one *must* wear such a garment in order to affix *tzitzis* to it. [See *comm.* to *v.* 38 s.v. וְעָשׂוּ] *(R' A. Fishelis, Kol Ram).*

make themselves tassels on the corners of their garments, throughout their generations. And they are to place upon the tassels of each corner a thread of t'cheiles. 39 *And it shall constitute tassels for you, that you may see it and*

proportionately smaller) — with an aperture in the center to let it pass over the head — which is worn all day. In addition, a full-sized *tallis* is worn during morning prayers. To the four corners of such garments are fashioned the *tzitzis.* As is the case with other *mitzvos*, the donning of such garments requires an appropriate benediction. [See *Orach Chaim* §8.]

The word לְדֹרֹתָם, *throughout their generations*, emphasizes that the precept of *tzitzis* — which serves as a remembrance of all the *mitzvos* — applies to *all* generations, even to a wholly righteous one which might think it does not require such symbolic reminders and might think itself exempt from this commandment *(Or HaChaim).*

Or HaChaim observes further that the word לְדֹרֹתָם, *throughout their generations*, occurs after the command of the *white* threads, not of the *t'cheiles* threads, because in effect only the white threads would be in use for all generations, not the *t'cheiles* [see below]. *(Chasam Sofer* comments similarly.)

From the expression 'on the corners,' the Talmud [*Menachos* 42a] derives that the *tzitzis* must be inserted some distance — at least three finger-breadths — from the corner so that they can *hang over* the corners. It is invalid if the *tzitzis* were attached at the actual corners. This follows the halachic pratice codified in *Shulchan Aruch.*

The commentators stress that in order to properly fulfill this aspect of the *mitzvah*, the *tzitzis* should be affixed so they are knotted across the vertical part of the garment, so the *tzitzis* will hang *on* the corners, which would not be the case if they were knotted so they hang straight down. [See *Torah Temimah; Shulchan Aruch* 11:15.]

The word כנף, *corner*, also means *wing.* Homiletically, therefore, the wearing of *tzitzis* on the *corners* of garments is a reminder of how God redeemed the Israelites from Egypt "bearing them on eagle's wings" [*Exodus* 19:4] (*Rashi v.* 41 citing *R' Moshe HaDarshan).*

וְנָתְנוּ עַל צִיצִת הַכָּנָף פְּתִיל תְּכֵלֶת — *And they are to place upon the tassels of each* [lit. of the] *corner a thread* [lit. *a twist* (see *Rashi* to *Deut.* 32:5)] of t'cheiles.

That is, **among** the tassels of each corner there is to be entwined a single thread of *t'cheiles.* In this context, עַל, *upon*, denotes *with*, as in *Levit.* 25:31 **עַל שְׂדֵה הָאָרֶץ with** *the fields of the country (Chizkuni).*

◆§ T'cheiles

T'cheiles refers to wool died with the bluish color of a rare species of fish known as the *chilazon* (see *Rashi* here and to *Exodus* 25:4).

The exact identity of the *chilazon* is unknown. It is assumed to be a boneless invertebrate, of the snail family, which was so rare that it surfaced but once in seventy years [*Menachos* 44a; see *Rashi* in *Sanhedrin* 91a and *Megillah* 6a]. According to *Megillah* 6a, the *chilazon* was found in the waters of the territory of Zebulun, whose descendants engaged in its traffic [see *Rashi* to *Genesis* 49:34 *(ArtScroll* ed. p. 2158)].

The color of *t'cheiles* itself is the subject of various opinions, ranging from sky-blue *(Rambam)* to the color of the nighttime sky *(R' Moshe HaDarshan* cited by *Rashi* to *Numbers* 15:41) to a greenish-blue *(Rashi* to our verse [and *Ibn Ezra* to *Exodus* 25:4] who renders ירק. It is not clear if *Rashi* means 'greenish' blue, i.e. aquamarine, but the Talmud compares the color of *t'cheiles* to the sea; see below).

Rambam [*Hil. Tzitzis* 2:1] writes that wherever *t'cheiles* thread is mentioned in the Torah, it refers to wool dyed blue [azure], the color of the clear bright sky. The color must retain its luster and be resistant to fading. [See *Rambam* there for a description of the process by which the blue threads were dyed.]

As noted, even in Talmudic times it was scarce. For many centuries,the identity of the *chilazon* has been unknown. Therefore our *tzitzis* do not contain the *t'cheiles* thread.

Nevertheless, the *mitzvah* of *tzitzis* — i.e. the white threads without the addition of the *t'cheiles* threads — remains binding

כָּל־מִצְוֺת יהוה וַעֲשִׂיתֶם אֹתָם וְלֹא תָתוּרוּ אַחֲרֵי
לְבַבְכֶם וְאַחֲרֵי עֵינֵיכֶם אֲשֶׁר־אַתֶּם זֹנִים אַחֲרֵיהֶם:
מ לְמַעַן תִּזְכְּרוּ וַעֲשִׂיתֶם אֶת־כָּל־מִצְוֺתָי וִהְיִיתֶם קְדֹשִׁים

even in the absence of *t'cheiles* (*Menachos* 38a). [See *Or HaChaim* cited above on לְדרֹתָם.]

The number of *t'cheiles* strands, and the manner in which the *t'cheiles* was wrapped and knotted with the white strands are also the subject of controversy among the Talmudic commentators and halachic codifiers [see *Rashi* and *Tosafos*, *Menachos* 38a]. For a description of the knotting and winding with the *t'cheiles* see *Rambam* 1:6-7, and R' G. Ch. Leiner (the 'Radziner'): *Psil T'cheiles* in *S'funei T'munei Chol* p. 113*ff*.

☙ Manner of Knotting

Nowadays, when only white threads are used, each tassel consists of one very long and three shorter white threads which are passed through the holes in the four corners of the garment and folded so as to make eight strands. They are then fastened with a double knot. The long thread, known as the *shamash* [lit. *attendant*], is wound around the other threads 7, 8, 11, and 13 times respectively [the total, 39, being the numerical equivalent of ה' אחד, *HASHEM is One* (cf. *Bais Yosef* §11)]. After each prescribed number of windings, a double knot is tied. Each tassel, therefore, will consist of a knot, 7 turns, a knot, 8 turns, a knot, 11 turns, a knot, 13 turns, a knot, and 8 free-hanging threads. Thus, each *tzitzis* consists of 13 elements — 5 double knots and 8 threads (see *Rashi* below s.v. וּרְאִיתֶם).

R' Hirsch notes that as fringes of the garment [צִיצִת הַכָּנָף] they are presumed to be מִין כָּנָף, similar to the garment in color. Since garments were predominantly white, *tzitzis* are referred to in general terms as לָבָן, *'white.'* But the color is entirely immaterial; they are called white only in the sense that they are not *t'cheiles* (*Menachos* 38a). *Rambam* interprets similarly.

39. וְהָיָה לָכֶם לְצִיצִת — *And it shall constitute tassels for you.* According to *Rashba* [following the second view in *Rashi* on the word צִיצִת]: 'It shall constitute *an object of gazing* for you.'

— The singular [וְהָיָה, *and* it *shall constitute*, and צִיצִת (the plural would be צִיצִיּוֹת)] indicates that *collectively*, the white and *t'cheiles* threads *together* constitute the single *mitzvah* of *tzitzis*. Furthermore, since the fulfillment of the *mitzvah* requires the presence of all *four* tassels — the tying of only three tassels is not even a partial *mitzvah* in the absence of the fourth — all four constitute together the one *mitzvah* of *tzitzis*, rather than four separate *mitzvos* (*Menachos* 28a; *Rambam Hilchos Tzitzis* 1:5).

וּרְאִיתֶם אֹתוֹ וּזְכַרְתֶּם ... וַעֲשִׂיתֶם אֹתָם — *That you may* [lit. *and you shall*] *see it* [i.e. the *tzitzis*, all four, as noted, being considered one *mitzvah* or: according to *Rambam*: that you may see the *t'cheiles*] *and remember all the commandments of HASHEM and perform them.*

The phrase *and you shall see it* indicates that the *tzitzis* must be visible (*Ibn Ezra*).

[This is one of the sources of the custom to wear the *tzitzis* visibly outside of one's garments. However, the simple connotation of *Ibn Ezra's* comment is that the *mitzvah* of *tzitzis* applies only to daytime. See below.]

While reciting these words in the morning, one should hold the lower portion of the *tzitzis* in his right hand while still grasping the higher, knotted, part of the *tzitzis* in his left hand, look at them, and then pass them over his eyes. Customs vary, but many kiss the *tzitzis* as mentioned, in order to display a love for the *mitzvah* (see *Beis Yosef* and *Orach Chaim* 24:5).

The Sages and commentators variously interpret exactly how the *tzitzis* would invoke this 'remembrance' of all HASHEM's *mitzvos*.

Rashi cites *Tanchuma* that the word *tzitzis* [spelled 'full' with both *yuds* as it is pronounced (see *Ramban; Daas Zekeinim; Mizrachi; Gur Aryeh*)] has a numerical value of 600 [צ=90; י=10; צ=90; י=10; ת=400], and each corner contains 13 elements, i.e., 5 knots and 8 threads for a total of 613 — the number of Scriptural commandments. [Thus, as the Sages remarked שְׁקוּלָה צִיצִת כְּנֶגֶד כָּל הַמִּצְוֹת,

remember all the commandments of HASHEM and perform them; and not explore after your heart and after your eyes after which you go astray. 40 *So that you may remember and perform all My commandments; then you*

The *mitzvah* of *tzitzis* is equal to all the other *mitzvos*."]

According to *Ramban*, it is the *t'cheiles* strand that will invoke this recollection of the sum total of the *mitzvos*. For, as the Talmud notes [*Menachos* 43b], *t'cheiles* is reminiscent of the sea, which is reminiscent of the sky, which is reminiscent of God's Throne of Glory which, as noted in *Ezekiel* 1:26, had the appearance of a sapphire stone. Hence, the sight of the *tzitzis* serves as a reminder of one's duties to God. [*Ramban* also records a Kabbalistic reason for the remembrance invoked by the *t'cheiles*.]

The Talmud [*Menachos* 43b] also mentions that *tzitzis* are like an insignia that identifies one as the King's servant, and reminds him of his obligation to loyally abide by the King's commands. For in effect, one should not rely on remembrance alone; man requires something tangible with which to stimulate the remembrance and observance. As the Sages observed, "Seeing leads to remembering, and remembering leads to performance."

The emphasis is on וַעֲשִׂיתֶם אֹתָם, *perform them*, since to remember without action is a useless intellectual exercise *(R' Nosson Scherman)*.

⌘ Several laws are derived from the expression וּרְאִיתֶם אֹתוֹ, and you shall see it. *A sampling:*

□ Women are exempt; blind men are obligated

The phrase *you shall see it* intimates that the *mitzvah* applies to daytime only which is the "time for seeing" [שְׁעַת רְאִיָּה]. Thus, since *tzitzis* is a מִצְוַת עֲשֵׂה שֶׁהַזְּמַן גְּרָמָא, *"a positive precept dependent on a fixed time,"* women are exempt from it, for women are exempt from time-related precepts *(Rambam, Hil. Tzitzis* 3:7; see *Menachos* 43a; *Shulchan Aruch* 17:1).

Although *seeing* is crucial to this *mitzvah*, four-cornered garments worn by a blind man must have *tzitzis*. The 'seeing' referred to in our verse merely designates daytime as the time of seeing in general, even if a particular individual is deprived of his sight (see *Menachos* 43a).

□ The time for reading Shema

From the phrase *you shall see it*, the Sages derive the time when it is permitted to begin reading the *Shema* in the morning. Since the portion of *tzitzis* is read with *Shema*, it may be presumed that both begin at the same time. The Sages [in *Berachos* 9a] accordingly expound that one may recite the *Shema* in the morning from the time that there is enough daylight to distinguish between *t'cheiles* and white, i.e. the various threads of the *tzitzis* *(Menachos* 43a; cf. *Yerushalmi Berachos* 1:2).

□ Seeing the Divine Presence

Homiletically, the word אֹתוֹ is perceived by analogy from *Deut.* 6:13 to refer to God, and our passage accordingly implies that by virtue of the merit of scrupulous observance of the mitzvah of *tzitzis* one becomes worthy of וּרְאִיתֶם אֹתוֹ, 'seeing *Him*,' i.e., receiving the Divine Presence *(Menachos* 43b).

וְלֹא תָתוּרוּ אַחֲרֵי לְבַבְכֶם וְאַחֲרֵי עֵינֵיכֶם — *And not explore after your heart and after your eyes.* The heart and the eyes are 'spies' for the body, its agents of sin — the eye sees, then the heart craves, then the body sins *(Rashi)*.

The 'heart' [the Biblical metaphor representing the intellect] leads one to heretical thoughts, while one's 'eyes' lead him to crave immorality *(Berachos* 12b).

As noted on p. 63 the passages of *Shema* contain allusions to the Ten Commandments. Our passage parallels the Commandment לֹא תִנְאָף, *You shall not commit adultery.*

אֲשֶׁר־אַתֶּם זֹנִים אַחֲרֵיהֶם — *After which you go astray. 'Going astray'* is an allusion to leaving God's service in favor of idols [see וַיִּזְנוּ in *Judges* 8:33] *(Berachos* 12b).

40. לְמַעַן תִּזְכְּרוּ וַעֲשִׂיתֶם אֶת־כָּל־מִצְוֹתָי — *So that you may remember and perform all My commandments.* The previous verse spoke of remembering God and His commandments, which would be evoked by looking at the *tzitzis*. But this verse informs us that the ultimate *purpose* of this

מא לֵאלֹהֵיכֶם: אֲנִי יְהוָה אֱלֹהֵיכֶם אֲשֶׁר הוֹצֵאתִי אֶתְכֶם מֵאֶרֶץ מִצְרַיִם לִהְיוֹת לָכֶם לֵאלֹהִים אֲנִי יְהוָה אֱלֹהֵיכֶם: אֱמֶת:

is to reach the point where we do not need external reminders, but that we *ourselves* keep God's commandments constantly in mind and fulfill them *(R' Hirsch).*

According to the Talmudic opinion noted on p. 63 that passages of *Shema* contain allusions to the Ten Commandments, our passage parallels the Command, זָכוֹר אֶת יוֹם הַשַּׁבָּת, *Remember the Sabbath day.* The Sabbath is equal in importance to all the *mitzvos* of the Torah just as *tzitzis* remind us of all the *mitzvos (Yerushalmi Berachos* 1:5).

Shulchan Aruch cautions that while reciting the *Shema,* one be particularly careful to enunciate the ז of תִּזְכְּרוּ, *you may remember,* so it not sound like תִּשְׂכְּרוּ, *you may hire, or* תִּשְׁקְרוּ, *you may falsify.* Similarly, we should enunciate carefully the ז in וּזְכַרְתֶּם.

וִהְיִיתֶם קְדשִׁים לֵאלֹהֵיכֶם — *Then you will be holy to your God.* [I.e., as a result of remembering and performing all God's *mitzvos,* you will rise up to a level of being 'holy' to God.]

קָדשׁ, *holy,* in its most literal sense, denotes dedication to a specific noble purpose (R' Hirsch).

According to *Rashi* in *Leviticus* 30:2 [following the dictum in *Yerushalmi Yevamos* 2:4] the term 'holy' applies to one who abstains from illicit sexual relationships [an absolution that is fostered by the proper observance of *tzitzis.* The Talmud records several instances where people were saved at the last moment from illicit unions by the sight of their *tzitzis*]. *Rashi* notes that wherever the Torah gives a warning to guard against immorality, it mentions 'holiness' in that context.

Ramban there, however, bases himself on other sources and maintains that the concept of 'holiness' has a more general application. It intimates practicing temperance and moderation even in permissible matters, such as eating, playing, and enjoying. The Torah does not forbid such pleasures, but the 'holy' person does not indulge himself to the point of becoming gluttonously addicted to such activites. If he oversteps the bounds of moderation such a person could become a נָבָל בִּרְשׁוּת הַתּוֹרָה, *a sordid person with the Torah's* [*technical*] *permission.* God therefore cautions us to be 'holy' — i.e. to avoid excesses and practice moderation.

41. אֲנִי ה׳ אֱלֹהֵיכֶם — *I am HASHEM, your God.* [As noted in the *comm.* to the first verse of *Shema,* HASHEM denotes God in His Aspect as Dispenser of Mercy, while *Elohim* [God] describes His Aspect as Dispenser of Justice.]

Rashi accordingly perceives the contextual implication of our passage to be: *I am HASHEM* — faithful to dispense reward [for your compliance]; *your God* — certain to mete out punishment [for violation of the commandments]. No act goes unnoticed.

אֲשֶׁר הוֹצֵאתִי אֶתְכֶם מֵאֶרֶץ מִצְרַיִם לִהְיוֹת לָכֶם לֵאלֹהִים — *Who has removed you from the land of Egypt to be a God to you.* It was for that reason that I removed you from Egypt — that you accept My decrees [i.e., that I be your God] *(Rashi).*

By redeeming the Jews from Egyptian slavery, God placed them under His special Providential care. Their continued existence is thus guaranteed by God *(Sforno).*

While reciting this passage of the *Shema* one should intend to fulfill the *mitzvah* of

will be holy to your God. [41] *I am HASHEM, your God, Who has removed you from the land of Egypt to be a God to you. I am HASHEM your God. True.*

remembering the Exodus from Egypt *(Arizal).*

Why is the Exodus from Egypt mentioned in connection with the *tzitzis?* — It intimates: "Just as in Egypt I distinguished between one who was genuinely a firstborn and one who was not, I will also seek out and punish one who deceitfully attaches a blue-dyed woolen thread to his garment and pretends it is genuine *t'cheiles*" *(Rashi; Bava Metzia* 61b).

אֲנִי ה׳ אֱלֹהֵיכֶם ... — *I am HASHEM your God* ... Why is this phrase repeated from above? — The earlier phrase implied, as noted above, that God will reward compliance and punish violation, which might be construed erroneously to imply that one might choose never to accept God's sovereignty upon himself and thereby avoid reward or punishment. To negate this, God now reiterated it in absolute terms: My sovereignty is based not upon your compliance or acceptance of Me, but rather, *I am HASHEM your God* — even against your will. [Comp. *Ezekiel* 20:23] *(Rashi* based on *Sifre;* cf. *Menachos* 44a; *Mizrachi; Be'er Yitzchak; Yalkut Yehudah; Sforno;* see also *Shabbos* 88a).

Kabbalistically, the repetition implies that HASHEM is our God in This World and in the Future World; or just as He manifested Himself as our God during the Egyptian Exodus, so will He do at the final Redemption when He gathers in the Exiles *(R' Bachya; Sifre).*

⁂ אֱמֶת — **True.** The word אֱמֶת, which is the beginning word of the next paragraph of prayers in the *Siddur,* does not occur in the Torah, and it is not said when chanting this portion in the Torah. It is appended to the recitation of the *Shema* to complete the total number of 248 words, including the prefatory formula אֵל מֶלֶךְ נֶאֱמָן, or the three word repetition of ה׳ אֱלֹהֵיכֶם אֱמֶת by the *chazzan.* [See prefatory *comm.* and *comm.* to אֵל מֶלֶךְ נֶאֱמָן]. It is read as a three word declaraton ה׳ אֱלֹהֵיכֶם אֱמֶת, *HASHEM your God, is true.* The law of not interrupting between the last words of *Shema* and אֱמֶת, *true,* is of ancient origin and its reason, as stated in the Talmud [*Berachos* 14a], is so that we may declare, as did the prophet [*Jeremiah* 10:10]: וַה׳ אֱלֹהִים אֱמֶת.

It would seem from this Talmudic law that the phrase is considered like one verse of *Shema* which one might not fragmentize with interruptions. It is curious, however, why if the law is so well rooted, the word אֱמֶת does not appear in the Torah at the end of this verse?

Presumably, it would appear that there was a tradition known by our Sages through the Oral Law that the word אֱמֶת was to have been included in the Torah in this verse — as it is included in Jeremiah's prophecy. However, it was omitted because the very next verse in the Torah [*Numbers* 15:1] introduces the revolt of Korach, and it is well-known that אֱמֶת, *truth,* is stifled by controversy. Thus, the word is not written in the Torah in this place, but may be said to "hover in the air." The Sages, however, introduced its recital during the *Shema* reading, and it has the force of a verse in which one may not make interruptions *(R' Mordechai Y. L. Zaks* cited in *Itturei Torah* and *Sefer Haparshiyos).*

קריאת שמע על המטה

רִבּוֹנוֹ שֶׁל עוֹלָם, הֲרֵינִי מוֹחֵל לְכָל־מִי שֶׁהִכְעִיס וְהִקְנִיט אוֹתִי, אוֹ שֶׁחָטָא כְנֶגְדִּי — בֵּין בְּגוּפִי, בֵּין בְּמָמוֹנִי, בֵּין בִּכְבוֹדִי, בֵּין בְּכָל־אֲשֶׁר לִי, בֵּין בְּאוֹנֶס, בֵּין בְּרָצוֹן, בֵּין בְּשׁוֹגֵג, בֵּין בְּמֵזִיד; בֵּין בְּדִבּוּר, בֵּין בְּמַעֲשֶׂה, בֵּין בְּמַחֲשָׁבָה, בֵּין בְּהִרְהוּר; בֵּין בְּגִלְגּוּל זֶה, בֵּין בְּגִלְגּוּל אַחֵר — לְכָל־בַּר יִשְׂרָאֵל, וְלֹא יֵעָנֵשׁ שׁוּם אָדָם בְּסִבָּתִי. יְהִי רָצוֹן מִלְּפָנֶיךָ יהוה אֱלֹהַי וֵאלֹהֵי אֲבוֹתַי, שֶׁלֹּא אֶחֱטָא עוֹד (וְלֹא אֶחֱזוֹר בָּהֶם, וְלֹא אָשׁוּב עוֹד לְהַכְעִיסְךָ, וְלֹא אֶעֱשֶׂה הָרַע בְּעֵינֶיךָ). וּמַה־שֶּׁחָטָאתִי לְפָנֶיךָ מְחוֹק בְּרַחֲמֶיךָ הָרַבִּים, אֲבָל לֹא עַל־יְדֵי יִסּוּרִים וָחֳלָיִים רָעִים. יִהְיוּ לְרָצוֹן אִמְרֵי־פִי וְהֶגְיוֹן לִבִּי לְפָנֶיךָ, יהוה צוּרִי וְגוֹאֲלִי.

בָּרוּךְ אַתָּה יהוה אֱלֹהֵינוּ, מֶלֶךְ הָעוֹלָם, הַמַּפִּיל חֶבְלֵי שֵׁנָה עַל־עֵינָי, וּתְנוּמָה עַל־עַפְעַפָּי (וּמֵאִיר לְאִישׁוֹן בַּת־עָיִן). וִיהִי רָצוֹן מִלְּפָנֶיךָ יהוה אֱלֹהַי וֵאלֹהֵי אֲבוֹתַי, שֶׁתַּשְׁכִּיבֵנִי לְשָׁלוֹם וְתַעֲמִידֵנִי (לְחַיִּים טוֹבִים וּ)לְשָׁלוֹם. (וְתֵן

קְרִיאַת שְׁמַע עַל הַמִּטָּה / The Bedtime Shema

The recital of the *Shema* immediately before retiring is perceived as a שְׁמִירָה, protection, against the dangers of the night *(Shulchan Aruch; Shelah; Zohar).*

"R' Yehoshua ben Levi says: Though one has recited the *Shema* in the synagogue [in the *Maariv* service] it is a *mitzvah* to recite it again upon his bed" *(Berachos* 4b).

R' Yitzchak observed: If one recites the *Shema* upon his bed, it is as though he held a two-edged sword in his hand [to protect him against the evils of the night] ... we derive this from *Psalms* 149:5-6: *Let the righteous exult in glory, let them sing for joy upon their beds,* and then it is written: *Let the praises of God be in their mouth, and a two-edged sword in their hand (Berachos* 5a).

The essence of this *Shema* is the *HaMapil* benediction and the first section of *Shema.* The recital of the other psalms and verses are of ancient origin — many of the sources can be traced to the Talmud and earliest halachic treatises [such as *Kol Bo*] *(Eliyah Rabbah).*

Women, too, have the custom of being scrupulous to recite the *Shema* before retiring, because of the protective benefits it offers *(ibid.; Pri Megadim).*

Prefatory supplication: forgiveness of others and prayer for God's forgiveness and protection

Before retiring for the evening it is proper for one to examine his deeds of that day; should one discover an ill-deed he should pray for forgiveness and undertake to correct his ways. It is also proper for one to forgive those who wronged him. In merit of this one will attain long life *(Mishnah Berurah* 239:1:9).

Accordingly, many recite this prayer before beginning the *Shema.*

בֵּין בְּגִלְגּוּל זֶה בֵּין בְּגִלְגּוּל אַחֵר — *Whether in this life or another life* [lit., *this transmigration or another transmigration*].

This term *gilgul* refers to the doctrine of גִּלְגּוּל נְשָׁמוֹת, *transmigration of souls,* one of the most mystical doctrines in Kabbalistic literature. In very simple terms it refers to the reincarnation of certain souls for a second period of physical life on earth — in the case of the wicked to correct certain evil deeds, or in the case of the righteous to allow 'sparks' of his soul to enlighten subsequent generations. This concept also finds expression in the doctrine of *yibum* — levirate marriage, in which a childless widow marries a brother

◆§ The Bedtime Shema

Master of the Universe, I hereby forgive anyone who angered or antagonized me or who sinned against me, whether against my body, my property, my honor or against anything of mine; whether [he did so] accidentally, willfully, carelessly, or purposely; whether through speech, deed, thought, or notion; whether in this life or another life° — [I forgive] every Jew. May no man be punished because of me. May it be Your will, HASHEM, my God and the God of my forefathers, that I may sin no more (nor repeat them, and may I not revert to angering You, and may I not do what is evil in Your eyes). Whatever sins I have done before You, may You blot out in Your abundant mercy, but not through suffering or bad illnesses.
Psalms *May the expressions of my mouth and the thoughts of my heart find favor*
19:15 *before You, HASHEM, my Rock and my Redeemer.*

Blessed are You, HASHEM, our God, King of the universe, Who casts the bonds of sleep upon my eyes and slumber upon my eyelids° (and Who illuminates the apple of the eye). May it be Your will, HASHEM, my God and the God of my forefathers, that You lay me down to sleep in peace° and raise me erect (for good life and) in peace.

of her deceased husband. As a result of such a union, the soul of the dead brother would become reincarnated in the child born of the levirate union. See *Ramban* to *Genesis* 38:8. [See also *Or Some'ach, Hil. Teshuvah* 5 s.v. וְיָדַעְתִּי.]

◆§ הַמַּפִּיל / HaMapil

This benediction is of ancient origin. Its text is a version of the one recorded in *Berachos* 60b. The words in parentheses are added in most *Nusach Sfard* siddurim.

There is a difference of opinion regarding the sequence of the prayers. The printed versions in most prayerbooks — which we follow in this volume — has the *'HaMapil'* benediction first and then the *Shema*. This follows the order recorded by *Rambam Hilchos Tefillah* 7:1. According to *Shulchan Aruch (Orach Chaim* 239:1) (apparently following the Talmud, *Berachos* 60b) it is better to begin by reciting the *Shema* and conclude with the *HaMapil* benediction. Since *HaMapil* refers directly to the onset of slumber it should be recited as close as possible to the moment of sleep.

Some say *HaMapil* after *Shema* and then recite the additional psalms and verses, while others recite *HaMapil* at the very end. The latter seems to be the more prevalent custom *(Mishneh Berurah* 239:1:23; *Aruch HaShulchan)*.

It is not proper to eat, drink, or talk after reciting the *HaMapil* benediction; one should go to sleep immediately thereafter. In case one is unable to fall asleep immediately one should repeat the passages of the *Shema* and Psalms until sleep overtakes him *(Derech HaChaim; Aruch HaShulchan)*.

הַמַּפִּיל חֶבְלֵי שֵׁנָה עַל עֵינַי וּתְנוּמָה עַל עַפְעַפָּי — *Who casts the bonds of sleep upon my eyes and slumber upon my eyelids.* This directly corresponds to the benediction recited in the morning: הַמַּעֲבִיר חֶבְלֵי שֵׁנָה מֵעֵינַי וּתְנוּמָה מֵעַפְעַפָּי, *Who removes the bonds of sleep from my eyes, and slumber from my eyelids.* There we thank God for returning us to active living; here we thank Him for the gift of sleep *(World of Prayer)*.

The expression *bonds of sleep* figuratively depicts the whole body as being securely chained in sleep. Others render חֶבְלֵי שֵׁנָה as 'portion' of sleep [see *Deut.* 32:9; *Chizkuni; Abudraham*].

This benediction and the corresponding one of the morning are expressed in first-person singular, because they are concerned with *personal* well-being [comp., however, *Magen Avraham* 46:4] *(R' Hirsch)*.

(וּמֵאִיר לְאִישׁוֹן בַּת־עָיִן — *And Who illuminates the apple of the eye.* See comm. below s.v. הַמֵּאִיר, *Who illuminates.)*

שֶׁתַּשְׁכִּיבֵנִי לְשָׁלוֹם ... וְאַל יְבַהֲלוּנִי רַעְיוֹנַי — *That You lay me down to sleep in peace ... may my ideas ... not confound me.*

The benediction refers first to protection

חֶלְקִי בְּתוֹרָתֶךָ, וְתַרְגִּילֵנִי לִדְבַר מִצְוָה, וְאַל תַּרְגִּילֵנִי לִדְבַר עֲבֵרָה: וְאַל תְּבִיאֵנִי לִידֵי חֵטְא, וְלֹא לִידֵי נִסָּיוֹן, וְלֹא לִידֵי בִזָּיוֹן. וְיִשְׁלוֹט בִּי יֵצֶר הַטּוֹב, וְאַל יִשְׁלוֹט בִּי יֵצֶר הָרָע. וְתַצִּילֵנִי מִשָּׂטָן וּמִפֶּגַע רָע, וּמֵחֳלָיִים רָעִים.) וְאַל יְבַהֲלוּנִי רַעְיוֹנַי, וַחֲלוֹמוֹת רָעִים, וְהַרְהוֹרִים רָעִים. וּתְהִי מִטָּתִי שְׁלֵמָה לְפָנֶיךָ. וְהָאֵר עֵינַי פֶּן אִישַׁן הַמָּוֶת. כִּי־אַתָּה הַמֵּאִיר לְאִישׁוֹן בַּת עָיִן. בָּרוּךְ אַתָּה יהוה, הַמֵּאִיר לָעוֹלָם כֻּלּוֹ בִּכְבוֹדוֹ.

אֵל מֶלֶךְ נֶאֱמָן:

שְׁמַע יִשְׂרָאֵל יהוָה אֱלֹהֵינוּ יהוָה | אֶחָד:

בָּרוּךְ שֵׁם כְּבוֹד מַלְכוּתוֹ לְעוֹלָם וָעֶד.

וְאָהַבְתָּ אֵת יהוָה אֱלֹהֶיךָ בְּכָל־לְבָבְךָ וּבְכָל־נַפְשְׁךָ וּבְכָל־מְאֹדֶךָ: וְהָיוּ הַדְּבָרִים הָאֵלֶּה אֲשֶׁר אָנֹכִי מְצַוְּךָ הַיּוֹם עַל־לְבָבֶךָ: וְשִׁנַּנְתָּם לְבָנֶיךָ וְדִבַּרְתָּ בָּם בְּשִׁבְתְּךָ בְּבֵיתֶךָ וּבְלֶכְתְּךָ בַדֶּרֶךְ וּבְשָׁכְבְּךָ וּבְקוּמֶךָ: וּקְשַׁרְתָּם לְאוֹת עַל־יָדֶךָ וְהָיוּ לְטֹטָפֹת בֵּין עֵינֶיךָ: וּכְתַבְתָּם עַל־מְזֻזוֹת בֵּיתֶךָ וּבִשְׁעָרֶיךָ:

וִיהִי נֹעַם אֲדֹנָי אֱלֹהֵינוּ עָלֵינוּ, וּמַעֲשֵׂה יָדֵינוּ כּוֹנְנָה עָלֵינוּ, וּמַעֲשֵׂה יָדֵינוּ כּוֹנְנֵהוּ.

from physical danger — שֶׁתַּשְׁכִּיבֵנִי לְשָׁלוֹם — and next to thoughts menacing our peace of mind and soul — וְאַל יְבַהֲלוּנִי גו׳. We pray that the ideas and fantasies [רַעְיוֹנוֹת] that we nurse in our wakeful hours not produce disturbing nightmares or immoral dreams. Such dreams menace the purity of our thoughts and feelings even during our waking *(World of Prayer)*.

וּתְהִי מִטָּתִי שְׁלֵמָה — *May my offspring be perfect* [lit. *may my (conjugal) bed be perfect*]. The expression is of Talmudic origin [*Pesachim* 56] and implies: Let all my children be perfect. This expression originally applied to the Patriarch Jacob whose progeny were all righteous, unlike Abraham and Isaac, each of whom produced a wicked son — Ishmael and Esau respectively. See *Rashi* to *Genesis* 47:31.

וְהָאֵר עֵינַי פֶּן אִישַׁן הַמָּוֶת — *And may You illuminate my eyes lest I die in sleep.* See *Psalm* 13:4, and the dictum in the Talmud 57b that "sleep is one-sixtieth of death." The idea is that when asleep we are in a state related to death and utter darkness, but God guards our souls, as it were. We now beseech Him to return us to a state of vigorous and sparkling light on the morrow lest we sleep the sleep of death.

הַמֵּאִיר לְאִישׁוֹן בַּת עָיִן — *Who illuminates the apple of the eye.* The terms אִישׁוֹן and בַּת עָיִן are essentially synonymous denoting the pupil of the eye; idiomatically called the "apple" of the eye. The expression is borrowed from Psalms 17:8, שָׁמְרֵנִי כְּאִישׁוֹן בַּת־עָיִן, *guard me as the apple of Your eye.* [See ArtScroll *comm.*]

The idea is that when one craves sleep the pupils of his eyes are figuratively darkened; when one has slept and is fully rested, his eyes are 'brightened' *(Abudraham)*.

◆§ The Shema

[For all full phrase-by-phrase commentary see pages 14-31.]

The halachic practice is that one who

(Grant my share in Your Torah and accustom me toward good deeds but do not accustom me toward bad deeds. Do not deliver me to sin nor to challenge nor to humiliation. Cause the good inclination to dominate me but do not let the evil inclination dominate me. Rescue me from impediment, from evil attack, and from bad illnesses.) May my ideas, bad dreams, and bad notions not confound me;° may my offspring be perfect° before You, and may You illuminate my eyes lest I die in sleep [for it is You who illuminates the apple of the eye]. Blessed are You HASHEM, Who illuminates the entire world with His glory.

God, Trustworthy King

Deuteronomy 6:4

Hear, O Israel: HASHEM is [now] our God, HASHEM [will be] One.

Pesachim 56a *Blessed be the Name of His glorious kingdom for all eternity.*

Deuteronomy 6:5-9 *You shall love HASHEM, your God, with all your heart and with all your soul and with all your resources. Let these matters, which I command you today, be upon your heart. Teach them thoroughly to your children and speak of them while you sit in your home, while you walk on the way, when you recline and when you arise. Bind them as a sign upon your arm and they shall be tefillin between your eyes. And write them on the doorposts of your house and upon your gates.*

Psalms 90:17 *May the pleasantness of my Lord, our God, be upon us° — may He establish our handiwork for us;° our handiwork may He establish.*

had recited the evening *Shema* in the *Maariv* service in its proper time [i.e. after the stars were out] now recites only the first portion of *Shema;* one who recited the *Maariv* service before nightfall [i.e., before it is quite dark] should recite all three portions of *Shema.* According to some authorities, all three portions of *Shema* should be repeated every night before retiring whether or not *Maariv* was recited in its ideal time since the 248 words of the entire *Shema* have a beneficial effect in protecting one's organs [see comm. on page 14]. However, since the Talmud *(Berachos* 60b) mentions only the first section, that suffices [except in the case of early *Maariv* as noted above, when all three portions must be recited] *(Aruch HaShulchan, Orach Chaim* 239; see *Abudraham; Rashi Berachos* 2a).

וִיהִי נֹעַם ... ישֵׁב בְּסֵתֶר / Psalms 90:17 — 91.

The recital of this psalm, as well as *Psalm* 3, before retiring is mentioned in the Talmud (*Shevuos* 15b). This psalm is described by the Talmud *(Shavuos* 15b) as שִׁיר שֶׁל פְּגָעִים, *Song Against Evil Occurrences,* or שִׁיר שֶׁל נְגָעִים, *Song Against Plagues.* It is a plea for protection from all harmful forces and influences. [See also *Rambam, Hil. Avodas Cochavim* 11:12.]

The verse וִיהִי נֹעַם, *May the pleasantness,* is the closing sentence of Psalm 90 which begins תְּפִלָּה לְמשֶׁה, *A prayer of Moses.* It was composed by Moses when the Tabernacle was completed. In the final verse he offered a short plea that our service of God be pleasing to Him and its effects be permanent, a fitting

יֹשֵׁב בְּסֵתֶר עֶלְיוֹן, בְּצֵל שַׁדַּי יִתְלוֹנָן. אֹמַר לַיהוה, מַחְסִי וּמְצוּדָתִי, אֱלֹהַי אֶבְטַח־בּוֹ. כִּי הוּא יַצִּילְךָ מִפַּח יָקוּשׁ, מִדֶּבֶר הַוּוֹת. בְּאֶבְרָתוֹ יָסֶךְ לָךְ, וְתַחַת־כְּנָפָיו תֶּחְסֶה, צִנָּה וְסֹחֵרָה אֲמִתּוֹ. לֹא־תִירָא מִפַּחַד לָיְלָה, מֵחֵץ יָעוּף יוֹמָם. מִדֶּבֶר בָּאֹפֶל יַהֲלֹךְ, מִקֶּטֶב יָשׁוּד צָהֳרָיִם. יִפֹּל מִצִּדְּךָ אֶלֶף, וּרְבָבָה מִימִינֶךָ, אֵלֶיךָ לֹא יִגָּשׁ. רַק בְּעֵינֶיךָ תַבִּיט, וְשִׁלֻּמַת רְשָׁעִים תִּרְאֶה. כִּי־אַתָּה יהוה מַחְסִי, עֶלְיוֹן שַׂמְתָּ מְעוֹנֶךָ. לֹא תְאֻנֶּה אֵלֶיךָ רָעָה, וְנֶגַע לֹא־יִקְרַב בְּאָהֳלֶךָ. כִּי מַלְאָכָיו יְצַוֶּה־לָּךְ, לִשְׁמָרְךָ בְּכָל־דְּרָכֶיךָ. עַל־כַּפַּיִם יִשָּׂאוּנְךָ, פֶּן־תִּגֹּף בָּאֶבֶן רַגְלֶךָ. עַל־שַׁחַל וָפֶתֶן תִּדְרֹךְ, תִּרְמֹס כְּפִיר וְתַנִּין. כִּי בִי חָשַׁק וַאֲפַלְּטֵהוּ, אֲשַׂגְּבֵהוּ, כִּי־יָדַע שְׁמִי. יִקְרָאֵנִי וְאֶעֱנֵהוּ, עִמּוֹ־אָנֹכִי בְצָרָה, אֲחַלְּצֵהוּ וַאֲכַבְּדֵהוּ. אֹרֶךְ יָמִים אַשְׂבִּיעֵהוּ, וְאַרְאֵהוּ בִּישׁוּעָתִי. אֹרֶךְ יָמִים אַשְׂבִּיעֵהוּ, וְאַרְאֵהוּ בִּישׁוּעָתִי.

יהוה מָה־רַבּוּ צָרָי, רַבִּים קָמִים עָלָי. רַבִּים אֹמְרִים לְנַפְשִׁי, אֵין יְשׁוּעָתָה לּוֹ בֵאלֹהִים סֶלָה. וְאַתָּה יהוה מָגֵן

prayer for recital before retiring.

Psalm 91, another one of the Psalms attributed to Moses, forms a comprehensive prayer for safeguarding us from all perils. Accordingly, it is an appropriate prayer before retiring, especially because of *v.* 5: *You shall not fear the terror of night.*

[The comments to the *Psalms* that follow have been gleaned primarily from the ArtScroll *Tehillim,* by Rabbi Avrohom Chaim Feuer. Refer to that work for a full commentary to the various psalms.]

וִיהִי נֹעַם ה׳ אֱלֹהֵינוּ — *May the pleasantness of my Lord, our God.* The term נֹעַם, *pleasantness,* refers to the bliss someone feels when he has done something that achieved its purpose. When man has this feeling of accomplishment, he is not alone — God, too, feels satisfaction that His will has been done *(Malbim).*

וּמַעֲשֵׂה יָדֵינוּ כּוֹנְנָה עָלֵינוּ — *May He establish our handiwork for us.* In any material activity, a craftsman shapes his creation, but remains dependent on it, in a sense. Architects and builders can erect a structure, but it rests on the earth, not on them, and *they* must depend on *it* for shelter. In the spiritual world, the opposite is true. One's Torah study develops in his own mind and his performance of a *mitzvah* has as much spiritual content as he puts into it. We pray now that our deeds be worthy of God's pleasure and that he 'establish' them as being significant *(Malbim).*

יֹשֵׁב בְּסֵתֶר / Psalm 91

יֹשֵׁב בְּסֵתֶר עֶלְיוֹן — *Whoever sits in the refuge* [lit. *hidden or secret place*] *of the Most High.* The person who scorns conventional forms of protection and seeks only the refuge provided by the Most High will find his faith rewarded. He will be enveloped by God's providence so that he can continue to seek holiness and wisdom without fear of those who would seek to harm him: *He shall dwell in the shadow of the Almighty (Rashi).*

אֹמַר לַה׳ מַחְסִי וּמְצוּדָתִי — *I will say of HASHEM; He is my refuge and my fortress.* The devout man who *dwells in the secret place of the Most High* declares publicly that God is his *refuge* from all physical dangers, and his *fortress,* protecting him from all human enemies *(Radak; Sforno).*

לֹא תִירָא מִפַּחַד לָיְלָה — *You shall not fear the terror of night.* If you put your faith in God, fear will be banished from your heart *(Rashi).*

וְנֶגַע לֹא יִקְרַב בְּאָהֳלֶךָ — *Nor will any plague come near your tent.* The Talmud *(Sanhedrin* 103a) perceives this as a

Psalm 91 Whoever sits in the refuge of the Most High° — he shall dwell in the shadow of the Almighty. I will say of HASHEM; He is my refuge and my fortress,° my God — I will trust in Him. That He will deliver you from the ensnaring trap and from devastating pestilence. With His pinion He will cover you, and beneath His wings you will be protected; His truth will be a shield and armor. You shall not fear the terror of night,° nor the arrow that flies by day; nor the pestilence that walks in gloom, nor the destroyer who lays waste at noon. A thousand will fall at your side and a myriad at your right hand, but to you it shall not approach. You will merely peer with your eyes and you will see the retribution of the wicked. Because 'You, HASHEM, are my refuge,' You have made the Most High Your dwelling place. No evil will befall you, nor will any plague come near your tent.° He will charge His angels for you, to protect you in all your ways.° They will carry you on their palms,° lest you strike your foot against a stone. You will tread upon the lion and the viper, you will trample the young lion and the serpent. For he has yearned for Me and I will deliver him; I will elevate him because he knows My Name. He will call upon Me and I will answer him, I am with him in distress, I will release him and I will honor him I will satisfy him with long life and show him My salvation. I will satisfy him with long life and show him My salvation.°

Psalms 3:2-9 HASHEM, how many are my tormentors!° The great rise up against me! The great say of my soul, 'There is no salvation for him from God.' Selah!° But you HASHEM are a shield for me — for my soul, and

blessing for domestic bliss [for *tent* signifies 'household']. 'May you raise worthy children and students who will not shame you by acting improperly in public.'

לִשְׁמָרְךָ בְּכָל דְּרָכֶיךָ — *To protect you in all your ways.* The Talmud *(Chagigah* 16a) teaches that these angels are not merely guardians, but witnesses as well. They observe every action and they are destined to testify for or against the man under their protection when he comes before the heavenly tribunal after death.

עַל כַּפַּיִם יִשָּׂאוּנְךָ — *They will carry you on [their] palms.* The angels created by the *mitzvos* that you perform with your *palms* [i.e., giving charity and doing acts of kindness) will raise you above all dangers that lurk in your path *(Zera Yaakov).*

וְאַרְאֵהוּ בִּישׁוּעָתִי — *And [I will] show him My salvation.* He will live to personally witness the salvation I will bring about at the advent of the Messiah, at the time of the revival of the dead, and at the salvation of the World to Come *(Radak).*

Indeed, it is not God who needs salvation, but Israel; yet God calls Israel's victory *'My salvation'* to emphasize that Israel's salvation is His as well *(Midrash Shocher Tov).* It is God's desire to display His Presence in this world, but if there were no Israel, no community of faith, then there would be no place for God to reveal His glory and no one to appreciate Him. Therefore, God, Himself, is the beneficiary of Israel's salvation *(Tehillos Hashem).*

There are Kabbalistic reasons for repeating the last verse. See *Likutei Mahariach.*

ה׳ מָה רַבּוּ צָרָי / Psalm 3

This psalm was composed by David, as its first verse states, " ... *When he [David] fled from Absalom his son,"* as he perceived through Divine inspiration that his salvation was forthcoming. Verse 6 — *I lay down and slept; yet I awoke, for HASHEM supports me* — makes this psalm especially appropriate for the night.

A full appreciation of this psalm is impossible without knowing the historical background of Absalom's revolt. See *II Samuel* chapters 15-19 for the full details.

בַּעֲדִי, כְּבוֹדִי וּמֵרִים רֹאשִׁי. קוֹלִי אֶל־יהוה אֶקְרָא, וַיַּעֲנֵנִי מֵהַר קָדְשׁוֹ סֶלָה. אֲנִי שָׁכַבְתִּי וָאִישָׁנָה, הֱקִיצוֹתִי, כִּי יהוה יִסְמְכֵנִי. לֹא־אִירָא מֵרִבְבוֹת עָם, אֲשֶׁר סָבִיב שָׁתוּ עָלָי. קוּמָה יהוה, הוֹשִׁיעֵנִי אֱלֹהַי, כִּי הִכִּיתָ אֶת־כָּל־אֹיְבַי לֶחִי, שִׁנֵּי רְשָׁעִים שִׁבַּרְתָּ. לַיהוה הַיְשׁוּעָה, עַל־עַמְּךָ בִרְכָתֶךָ סֶּלָה.

הַשְׁכִּיבֵנוּ יהוה אֱלֹהֵינוּ לְשָׁלוֹם, וְהַעֲמִידֵנוּ מַלְכֵּנוּ לְחַיִּים (טוֹבִים וּלְשָׁלוֹם). וּפְרוֹשׂ עָלֵינוּ סֻכַּת שְׁלוֹמֶךָ. וְתַקְּנֵנוּ בְּעֵצָה טוֹבָה מִלְּפָנֶיךָ. וְהוֹשִׁיעֵנוּ (מְהֵרָה) לְמַעַן שְׁמֶךָ. וְהָגֵן בַּעֲדֵנוּ, וְהָסֵר מֵעָלֵינוּ אוֹיֵב דֶּבֶר וְחֶרֶב וְרָעָב וְיָגוֹן. וְהָסֵר שָׂטָן מִלְּפָנֵינוּ וּמֵאַחֲרֵינוּ. וּבְצֵל כְּנָפֶיךָ תַּסְתִּירֵנוּ. כִּי אֵל שׁוֹמְרֵנוּ וּמַצִּילֵנוּ אָתָּה, כִּי אֵל מֶלֶךְ חַנּוּן וְרַחוּם אָתָּה. וּשְׁמוֹר צֵאתֵנוּ וּבוֹאֵנוּ לְחַיִּים וּלְשָׁלוֹם, מֵעַתָּה וְעַד עוֹלָם.

בָּרוּךְ יהוה בַּיּוֹם, בָּרוּךְ יהוה בַּלָּיְלָה, בָּרוּךְ יהוה בְּשָׁכְבֵנוּ, בָּרוּךְ יהוה בְּקוּמֵנוּ. כִּי בְיָדְךָ נַפְשׁוֹת הַחַיִּים וְהַמֵּתִים. אֲשֶׁר בְּיָדוֹ נֶפֶשׁ כָּל־חָי, וְרוּחַ כָּל־בְּשַׂר־אִישׁ. בְּיָדְךָ אַפְקִיד רוּחִי, פָּדִיתָה אוֹתִי, יהוה אֵל אֱמֶת. אֱלֹהֵינוּ שֶׁבַּשָּׁמַיִם, יַחֵד שִׁמְךָ וְקַיֵּם מַלְכוּתְךָ תָּמִיד, וּמְלוֹךְ עָלֵינוּ לְעוֹלָם וָעֶד.

סֶלָה — *Selah.* This word is one of the most difficult in Scripture. *Targum* and *Metzudas Zion* render it *'forever'*, thus we read here *'there is no salvation ... forever,'* a view that is supported by the Talmud *(Eruvin* 54a).

Ibn Ezra maintains that the word סֶלָה is always a reaffirmation of a preceding statement, i.e. 'all of the aforementioned is *true and certain.' Ibn Ezra* and *Radak* offer an alternate meaning that *'selah'* is a musical instruction addressed to the singers of the psalm. It indicates special emphasis and a raising of the voice.

קוֹלִי אֶל ה׳ אֶקְרָא וַיַּעֲנֵנִי — *With my voice I call out to HASHEM, and he answers* [lit. *'would* or *did answer'*] *me.*

Ibn Ezra connects this verse to the preceding one. David sees God as his shield because he knows that to win he need not even enter into battle; rather, he assures his victory by calling out sincerely to God.

וַיַּעֲנֵנִי — *And he answers me* [lit. *'He did answer me'*]. The word literally is in past tense. David had so much confidence in God's response that whenever he prayed he was sure that his wish would be fulfilled. It was as if God had *already* answered his request *(Radak).*

אֲנִי שָׁכַבְתִּי וָאִישָׁנָה — *I lay down and* [I] *slept.* In the darkest hour of his despair, David was numb with fear, so he retreated into senseless sleep *(Rashi).*

הֱקִיצוֹתִי— *Yet I awoke!* From my worries I awoke triumphantly, filled with confidence that God would support me *(Rashi).*

קוּמָה ה׳ הוֹשִׁיעֵנִי אֱלֹהַי — *Rise up, HASHEM, save me, my God!* Because I have unshakeable faith in You, it is only proper that You save me *(Metzudos).*

עַל עַמְּךָ בִרְכָתֶךָ — *Upon Your people is* [i.e. their duty is] *Your blessing.* I.e., to bless You and to offer thanks for Your salvation *(Rashi).* [God derives strength, so to speak, from the blessings and prayers of man. Man's appreciation of God's control of human events influences His guidance of the universe.]

◆§ הַשְׁכִּיבֵנוּ / Hashkiveinu

This prayer from the *Maariv* service describes God as our Savior from the

to raise up my pride. With my voice I call out to HASHEM, and He answers me° from His holy mountain. Selah. I lay down and slept;° yet I awoke,° for HASHEM supports me. I fear not the myriad people deployed against me from every side. Rise up, HASHEM, save me, My God!° For You struck all of my enemies on the cheek, You broke the teeth of the wicked. Salvation is HASHEM's, upon Your people is Your blessing.° Selah.

Siddur Maariv *Lay us down to sleep in peace,° HASHEM, our God; raise us erect, our King, to (good) life (and peace), and spread over us° the shelter of Your peace. Set us aright with good counsel from before Your presence, and save us (speedily) for Your Name's sake. Shield us, remove from us foe, plague, sword, famine, and woe; and remove spiritual impediment from before us and behind us° and shelter us in the shadow of Your wings — for God Who protects us and rescues us are You, for God Who is the merciful and compassionate King are You. Safeguard our going and coming — for life and peace, from now to eternity.*

Siddur Maariv *Blessed is HASHEM by day,° blessed is HASHEM by night. Blessed is HASHEM when we retire, blessed is HASHEM when we arise — for*
Job 12:10 *in Your hand are the souls of the living and the dead: The One in whose hand is the soul of all the living and the spirit of all human*
Psalms 31:6 *flesh. In Your hand I entrust my spirit,° You redeemed me HASHEM, O God of truth. Our God Who is in heaven, reveal the Oneness of Your Name, establish Your kingdom forever, and reign over us for all eternity.*

dangers and afflictions associated with the terrors of night, literally and figuratively *(Seder HaYom)*.

הַשְׁכִּיבֵנוּ ... לְשָׁלוֹם — *Lay us down to sleep in peace.* The purpose of sleep is to allow the body to rejuvenate itself, the better to serve God the next day *(R' Hirsch)*.

וּפְרוֹשׂ עָלֵינוּ — *And spread over us.* At night the commandment of *tzitzis* does not apply, so we are denuded of the *mitzvah* that envelops us in the daytime. In its absence, we ask God to 'spread a protective blessing of peace over us' *(Midrash Tehillim* 86:1).

וְתַקְּנֵנוּ בְּעֵצָה טוֹבָה — *Set us aright with good counsel.* Help us plan well at night for the activity of the next day, and let the relaxation of the night give us a clearer perspective for the deliberations of the day *(R' Hirsch)*.

מִלְּפָנֵינוּ וּמֵאַחֲרֵינוּ — *From before us and behind us.* Protect us from spiritual harm in the future [*before us*] and from the consequences of what has already occurred [*behind us*] *(R' Hirsch)*.

When we plan for the future, the Evil Inclination has endless arguments to convince us that sin is advantageous and virtue is archaic. When we seek to repent our misdeeds of the past, he argues that 'everyone' did the same thing and it is too late to cry over spilt milk *(Siach Yitzchak)*.

בָּרוּךְ ה׳ בַּיּוֹם / Additional verses

These passages which concentrate on human praise and supplication are essentially repeated from the *Maariv* service. The Talmud [*Berachos* 4a; see *Tosafos*] describes them as גְּאוּלָּה אֲרִיכְתָּא, extensions of the preceding blessing of redemption. The full prayer beginning בָּרוּךְ ה׳ לְעוֹלָם contains eighteen Divine Names, to parallel the eighteen benedictions in *Shemoneh Esrei.* The verses proclaim the incomparable glory, love, and justice of God, and pray for the recognition of Divine Unity by all peoples.

בְּיָדְךָ אַפְקִיד רוּחִי ... — *In Your hand I entrust my spirit* ... [*Psalms* 31:6]. The Talmud *(Berachos* 5a) puts this verse in the category of פְּסוּקֵי דְרַחֲמֵי, *verses of Divine Mercy.*

יִרְאוּ עֵינֵינוּ, וְיִשְׂמַח לִבֵּנוּ, וְתָגֵל נַפְשֵׁנוּ בִּישׁוּעָתְךָ בֶּאֱמֶת, בֶּאֱמֹר לְצִיּוֹן מָלַךְ אֱלֹהָיִךְ. יהוה מֶלֶךְ, יהוה מָלָךְ, יהוה יִמְלֹךְ לְעֹלָם וָעֶד. כִּי הַמַּלְכוּת שֶׁלְּךָ הִיא, וּלְעוֹלְמֵי עַד תִּמְלוֹךְ בְּכָבוֹד, כִּי אֵין לָנוּ מֶלֶךְ אֶלָּא אָתָּה.

הַמַּלְאָךְ הַגֹּאֵל אֹתִי מִכָּל־רָע יְבָרֵךְ אֶת־הַנְּעָרִים, וְיִקָּרֵא בָהֶם שְׁמִי וְשֵׁם אֲבֹתַי אַבְרָהָם וְיִצְחָק, וְיִדְגּוּ לָרֹב בְּקֶרֶב הָאָרֶץ.

וַיֹּאמֶר, אִם־שָׁמוֹעַ תִּשְׁמַע לְקוֹל יהוה אֱלֹהֶיךָ, וְהַיָּשָׁר בְּעֵינָיו תַּעֲשֶׂה, וְהַאֲזַנְתָּ לְמִצְוֹתָיו, וְשָׁמַרְתָּ כָּל־חֻקָּיו, כָּל־הַמַּחֲלָה אֲשֶׁר־שַׂמְתִּי בְמִצְרַיִם לֹא־אָשִׂים עָלֶיךָ, כִּי אֲנִי יהוה רֹפְאֶךָ.

וַיֹּאמֶר יהוה אֶל־הַשָּׂטָן, יִגְעַר יהוה בְּךָ הַשָּׂטָן, וְיִגְעַר יהוה בְּךָ הַבֹּחֵר בִּירוּשָׁלָיִם, הֲלוֹא זֶה אוּד מֻצָּל מֵאֵשׁ.

הִנֵּה מִטָּתוֹ שֶׁלִּשְׁלֹמֹה, שִׁשִּׁים גִּבֹּרִים סָבִיב לָהּ, מִגִּבֹּרֵי יִשְׂרָאֵל. כֻּלָּם אֲחֻזֵי חֶרֶב, מְלֻמְּדֵי מִלְחָמָה, אִישׁ חַרְבּוֹ

The *Zohar* comments: Every night when we go to sleep we entrust ourselves to God. Although our debt to God is great, He does not hold back the soul as payment. He is אֱמֶת, *true*, to His role as Guardian of souls, and returns them in the morning (*Ketzos HaChoshen* 4:1).

יִרְאוּ עֵינֵינוּ / Yir'u Eineinu

This collection of prayers is also borrowed from the *Maariv* service. It expresses the hope of the speedy establishment of HASHEM's kingdom.

הַמַּלְאָךְ / The angel

The following passages are a collection of Scriptural verses discussing God's "mercy." This first verse, *May the angel who redeems*, etc. was Jacob's blessing to his grandsons Ephraim and Manasseh [*Genesis* 48:16].

The prayer is directed not to the angel, who has no power except as an agent of God, but to God Who dispatched the angel. The sense is: *May it be pleasing to You that the angel whom you have always dispatched to redeem me from all evil shall bless the lads.* [For a full exposition of this verse, see ArtScroll *Genesis* 48:16.]

וְיִקָּרֵא בָהֶם שְׁמִי וכו' — *And may my name be declared upon them, and the names of my forefathers Abraham and Isaac.* May they constantly strive to such heights that they will be worthy to have their names coupled with those of the Patriarchs *(R' Avraham b. HaRambam).*

Haamek Davar comments that the invocation of the three Patriarchs was intended to invoke God's blessing in three areas: military security, livelihood, and internal peace and harmony.

וְיִדְגּוּ לָרֹב בְּקֶרֶב הָאָרֶץ — *And may they proliferate abundantly like fish within the land.*

Like fish — which are fruitful and which multiply, and which the Evil Eye cannot affect [since fish live in an element apart, in calm and unseen depths. Mankind, inhabitants of another element, remain unaware of this aquatic existence, and so do not cast an evil eye upon them. And in any event, the Evil Eye has no effect over what is hidden from sight (see *Berachos* 20a)]. So will Joseph's descendants multiply and be unharmed by the Evil Eye *(Rashi).* As *R' Hirsch* explains in his *Siddur* (p. 726), just as fish enjoy a quiet but contented and cheerful life beyond the conception of human beings, so Jews who live in the sphere assigned them by God will have a degree of serenity and happiness far beyond the comprehension

Siddur Maariv *May our eyes see,° our heart be glad, and our soul exult in Your true salvation — when Zion is told, 'your God has reigned!' HASHEM reigns, HASHEM has reigned, HASHEM will reign for all eternity. For the kingdom is Yours and You will reign for all eternity in glory for we have no king except for You!*

Genesis 48:16 *May the angel° who redeems me from all evil bless the lads, and may my name be declared upon them, and the names of my forefathers Abraham and Isaac,° and may they proliferate abundantly like fish° within the land.*

Exodus 15:26 *He said, 'If you diligently heed° the voice of HASHEM, your God, and do what is proper in His eyes, and you listen closely to His commandments and observe His decrees° — the entire malady that I inflicted upon Egypt° I will not inflict upon you, for I am HASHEM your Healer.'°*

Zechariah 3:2 *HASHEM said to the Satan,° 'HASHEM shall denounce you, O Satan, and HASHEM, Who selects Jerusalem, shall denounce you again. This is indeed a firebrand rescued from flames.'*

Song of Songs 3:7-8 *Behold! The couch of Shlomo! Sixty mighty ones round about it, of the mighty ones of Israel. All gripping the sword, learned in*

of those around them.

וַיֹּאמֶר אִם שָׁמוֹעַ תִּשְׁמַע / He said, 'If you diligently heed.'

This passage, from *Exodus* 15:26, was the Divine exhortation that Moses imparted to the Jewish nation when it began its arduous journey through the wilderness after being freed from Egyptian slavery. This verse forms the basis for the Talmudic statement [*Berachos* 5a] that Torah-study, no less than the reading of the *Shema*, wards off danger *(World of Prayer).*

חֻקָּיו — *His decrees.* These are the commandments which take the form of royal decrees with no reason assigned for their performance *(Rashi).*

כָּל הַמַּחֲלָה אֲשֶׁר שַׂמְתִּי בְמִצְרַיִם — *The entire malady that I inflicted upon Egypt.* I.e., the plagues. If the Jews remain loyal, they will be spared physical affliction *(Ramban).*

אֲנִי ה׳ רֹפְאֶךָ — *I am HASHEM your Healer.* From ills from which no physician can cure you *(Ibn Ezra).* [That is, God is the Primary Healer.]

— I instruct you that My Commandments will protect you from disease, like a physician who warns against eating something which would cause an illness *(Rashi).*

The clause is contingent: *If you will diligently* heed, I will not bring diseases upon you; but if you do not *heed,* I will. Nevertheless — *I am HASHEM Who heals you* [the diseases will not be incurable, as were those that God brought upon Egypt *(Torah Temimah)*] *(Talmud Sanhedrin* 101a).

וַיֹּאמֶר ה׳ אֶל הַשָּׂטָן / And HASHEM said to the Satan

This passage occurs in *Zechariah* 3:2 where the Prophet is shown a vision of *Joshua the High Priest standing before an angel of God, and the Satan* [accusing angel] *was standing at his right to accuse him.* The Satan accused Joshua of being too permissive with his sinful children, and of hindering the rebuilding of the Temple. Thereupon God — "Who chose Jerusalem" — rebuked Satan, reminding him that Joshua was like a *firebrand plucked out of the fire.* That is, Joshua had been Divinely vindicated inasmuch as he had been miraculously spared from the fires of Nebuchadnezzar. On a national level, the metaphor applies to the Jews as a whole. They, too, are like firebrands plucked from fire, for they had suffered from the fires of exile and endured it. They now merit redemption, not further accusation.

הִנֵּה מִטָּתוֹ / Behold! The couch

This passage from *Song of Songs* (3:7-8; see *Commentary* in the *ArtScroll* edition

עַל־יְרֵכוֹ מִפַּחַד בַּלֵּילוֹת.

יְבָרֶכְךָ יהוה וְיִשְׁמְרֶךָ. יָאֵר יהוה פָּנָיו אֵלֶיךָ, וִיחֻנֶּךָּ. יִשָּׂא יהוה פָּנָיו אֵלֶיךָ, וְיָשֵׂם לְךָ שָׁלוֹם.

הִנֵּה לֹא־יָנוּם וְלֹא יִישָׁן, שׁוֹמֵר יִשְׂרָאֵל.

לִישׁוּעָתְךָ קִוִּיתִי יהוה. קִוִּיתִי יהוה לִישׁוּעָתְךָ. יהוה לִישׁוּעָתְךָ קִוִּיתִי.

בְּשֵׁם יהוה אֱלֹהֵי יִשְׂרָאֵל, מִימִינִי מִיכָאֵל, וּמִשְּׂמֹאלִי גַּבְרִיאֵל, וּמִלְּפָנַי אוּרִיאֵל, וּמֵאֲחוֹרַי רְפָאֵל, וְעַל־רֹאשִׁי שְׁכִינַת אֵל.

שִׁיר הַמַּעֲלוֹת, אַשְׁרֵי כָּל־יְרֵא יהוה, הַהֹלֵךְ בִּדְרָכָיו. יְגִיעַ כַּפֶּיךָ כִּי תֹאכֵל, אַשְׁרֶיךָ וְטוֹב לָךְ. אֶשְׁתְּךָ

for the full literal and allegorical interpretation) refers allegorically to the Jewish people symbolized by the sixty myriads (i.e., the 600,000 mighty battleworthy males) who emerged from Egypt. They are fortified by their allegiance to the Torah, even in exile.

The Midrash comments on this passage: "When a man has yet to sin, his fellow beings on earth stand in awe of him, but once he has sinned he himself is overcome by fear and dread of others."

Its inclusion in the bedtime *Shema,* and its juxtaposition with the verses of the Priestly benediction (see below) is based on the Midrash *(Bamidbar Rabbah* 11:3).

Behold! The couch of Shlomo — Shlomo refers to God, because he is the Master of *Shalom* [peace] ...

Sixty mighty ones round about it — *God's couch* is figuratively surrounded by the sixty letters contained in *Bircas Kohanim;* **of the mighty ones of Israel** — for the blessings strengthen Israel.

All gripping the sword, learned in warfare — these blessings protect Israel against all retributions mentioned in the Torah.

Each with his sword on his thigh, from fear in the nights — if one dreams that a sword is cutting the flesh from his thigh, he should hurry to the synagogue and stand before the *Kohanim* to hear their blessing. Then no evil will befall him.

יְבָרֶכְךָ / **Bircas Kohanim; the Priestly benediction** [*Numbers* 6:24-26]

The blessing contains sixty letters; this has significant Kabbalistic meaning in its parallel with the sixty myriads of the previous passage. [For a full exposition of this blessing, see ArtScroll *Bircas Kohanim.* A sampling follows:]

May HASHEM bless you — with long life and wealth *(Rashi; Ibn Ezra);*

And safeguard you — guard you against robbery *(ibid.);*

May HASHEM illuminate His countenance for you — reveal to you the light of the Torah [i.e., endow you with spiritual growth] *(Sifre);* or, grant you children who will be Torah scholars *(Tanchuma);* may He answer your prayers and fulfill your requests *(Ibn Ezra);*

And be gracious to you — may He cause you to find grace [חֵן] in the eyes of others *(Sifre);* ... in the eyes of God *(Ramban);*

May HASHEM lift up His face toward you — i.e., may He always be favorably disposed towards you *(Ibn Ezra).*

And establish peace for you — peaceful relations with everyone *(Midrash);* spiritual eternity and perfection *(Sforno).* Peace is not simply the absence of war ... within man, it is the proper balance between the needs of the body and its higher duty to the soul *(Or HaChaim).*

Beloved is peace, since even the Priestly Benediction concludes with the hope of

warfare, each with his sword on his thigh, from fear in the nights.

Numbers 6:24-26 *May HASHEM bless you and safeguard you.° May HASHEM illuminate His countenance for you and be gracious to you.° May HASHEM lift up His face toward you and establish peace for you.°*

Psalms 121:4 *Behold, the Guardian of Israel neither slumbers nor sleeps.°*

Genesis 49:18 *For Your salvation do I long, HASHEM.° I do long, HASHEM, for your salvation. HASHEM, for Your salvation do I long.*

In the Name of HASHEM,° God of Israel: may Michael be at my right, Gabriel at my left, Uriel before me, and Raphael behind me; and above my head the Presence of God.

Psalm 128 *A song of ascents.° Praiseworthy is everyone who fears HASHEM, who walks in his paths. When you eat the labor of your hands,° you are fortunate° and it is well with you. Your wife shall be like a*

peace, thus teaching that blessings are of no avail unless accompanied by peace *(Midrash).*

[The three-fold repetition of these passages indicated in some Siddurim is Kabbalistic in origin. Occupation of a house for three years or a farm for three seasons constitutes proof of ownership (חֲזָקָה), and an animal's three-time commission of violent, aberrant behavior identifies it as a habitual menace. Similarly, the three-fold repetition of these verses symbolize the hope that these blessings will become permanently Israel's.]

הִנֵּה לֹא יָנוּם / Behold, the Guardian of Israel neither slumbers nor sleeps.

— And therefore you will be able to sleep peacefully without fear of harm *(R' Hirsch).*

לִישׁוּעָתְךָ קִוִּיתִי ה׳ / For Your salvation do I long, HASHEM.

This three-word prayer was originally uttered by the Patriarch Jacob in his blessing of his son Dan [*Genesis* 49:18]. As the commentators explain, it means: "I do not rely on temporary salvation through human agency; I await *Your* salvation — which will be for all eternity." [See ArtScroll *Bereishis* p. 2167.]

R' Bachya writes that the Kabbalists find in this three-word prayer mystical combinations of letters spelling the Divine Name that provides salvation against enemies. In order to arrive at the combination of letters yielding this Name, the three words of this prayer must be recited in different orders. The common custom is to recite it in the *Krias Shma* before going to sleep as follows: לִישׁוּעָתְךָ קִוִּיתִי ה׳, קִוִּיתִי ה׳ לִישׁוּעָתְךָ, ה׳ לִישׁוּעָתְךָ קִוִּיתִי. However, some infer that *R' Bachya* prefers a different order (see *Chavel* ed.), and *Sh'lah* requires six variations of the verse: לישועתך קויתי ה׳, לישועתך ה׳ קויתי, קויתי ה׳ לישועתך, קויתי לישועתך ה׳, ה׳ קויתי לישועתך, ה׳ לישועתך קויתי.

בְּשֵׁם ה׳ / In the Name of HASHEM

God's angels surround you at His command: Michael, performing His unique miracles; Gabriel, the emissary of His almighty power; Uriel, who bears the light of God before you; Raphael, who brings you healing from Him. Above your head is the Presence of God Himself *(R' Hirsch).*

The Kabbalistic connotation of this arrangement, with man in the center, beneath God, is that the righteous act as God's 'chariot,' so to speak, bearing His glory on earth *(Iyun Tefillah).*

שִׁיר הַמַּעֲלוֹת / Psalm 128

This Psalm is recited in the night-prayer, because, according to the Talmud *(Berachos* 57a), the two images depicted in it — the vine and olive shoots — are good omens for those to whom they appear in a dream [*Mateh Moshe* §401] *(World of Prayer).*

At night, we pause from the travail of the day and our hearts can open to yearnings and hopes for something better. This psalm depicts the joy of an ideal Jewish home, the sort of happiness toward which we should dedicate ourselves *(R' Hirsch).*

יְגִיעַ כַּפֶּיךָ כִּי תֹאכֵל — *When you eat the labor of your hands.* Honest labor benefits both

כְּגֶפֶן פֹּרִיָּה בְּיַרְכְּתֵי בֵיתֶךָ, בָּנֶיךָ כִּשְׁתִלֵי זֵיתִים, סָבִיב לְשֻׁלְחָנֶךָ. הִנֵּה כִי־כֵן יְבֹרַךְ גָּבֶר, יְרֵא יהוה. יְבָרֶכְךָ יהוה מִצִּיּוֹן, וּרְאֵה בְּטוּב יְרוּשָׁלָיִם כֹּל יְמֵי חַיֶּיךָ. וּרְאֵה־בָנִים לְבָנֶיךָ, שָׁלוֹם עַל־יִשְׂרָאֵל.

רִגְזוּ וְאַל־תֶּחֱטָאוּ, אִמְרוּ בִלְבַבְכֶם עַל מִשְׁכַּבְכֶם, וְדֹמּוּ סֶלָה.

אֲדוֹן עוֹלָם אֲשֶׁר מָלַךְ, בְּטֶרֶם כָּל יְצִיר נִבְרָא.
לְעֵת נַעֲשָׂה בְחֶפְצוֹ כֹּל, אֲזַי מֶלֶךְ שְׁמוֹ נִקְרָא.
וְאַחֲרֵי כִּכְלוֹת הַכֹּל, לְבַדּוֹ יִמְלוֹךְ נוֹרָא.
וְהוּא הָיָה וְהוּא הֹוֶה, וְהוּא יִהְיֶה בְּתִפְאָרָה.
וְהוּא אֶחָד וְאֵין שֵׁנִי, לְהַמְשִׁיל לוֹ לְהַחְבִּירָה.
בְּלִי רֵאשִׁית בְּלִי תַכְלִית, וְלוֹ הָעֹז וְהַמִּשְׂרָה.
וְהוּא אֵלִי וְחַי גֹּאֲלִי, וְצוּר חֶבְלִי בְּעֵת צָרָה.
וְהוּא נִסִּי וּמָנוֹס לִי, מְנָת כּוֹסִי בְּיוֹם אֶקְרָא.
בְּיָדוֹ אַפְקִיד רוּחִי, בְּעֵת אִישַׁן וְאָעִירָה.
וְעִם רוּחִי גְּוִיָּתִי, יהוה לִי וְלֹא אִירָא.

body and soul. One should always strive to support himself by his own labor rather than live on charity *(Radak)*.

אַשְׁרֶיךָ — *You are fortunate* — in this world; וְטוֹב לָךְ, *and it is well with you* — in the Hereafter *(Avos* 4:1).

Similarly, *Midrash Tanchuma* cautions that one should not rely on miracles or זְכוּת אָבוֹת, *ancestral merit.* Only after one exerts his own efforts at spiritual improvement does God send His blessing.

בְּיַרְכְּתֵי בֵיתֶךָ — *In the inner chambers of your home.* I.e., modestly reserving herself for her husband *(Tanchuma)*.

שְׁתִלֵי זֵיתִים — *Olive shoots.* The olive, unlike other shoots, cannot be grafted *(Rashi).* [This metaphorically describes Israel's determination not to intermarry with the nations.]

סָבִיב לְשֻׁלְחָנֶךָ — *Surrounding your table.* The entire family together under your own loving care *(R' Hirsch)*.

וּרְאֵה בְּטוּב יְרוּשָׁלָיִם — *And may you gaze upon the good of Jerusalem.* May you be redeemed from exile, *and gaze upon the good of Jerusalem* as you return to the Holy City *(Radak)*.

וּרְאֵה בָנִים לְבָנֶיךָ — *And may you see children born to your children.* A blessing of longevity; may you enjoy the company of grandchildren *(Radak)*.

שָׁלוֹם עַל יִשְׂרָאֵל — *Peace upon Israel!* ''The Holy One, Blessed is He, found no vessel that could contain blessing for Israel except that of peace'' (last Mishnah in *Uktzin)*.

רִגְזוּ וְאַל תֶּחֱטָאוּ / Tremble and sin not [*Psalms* 4:5].

Tremble [in awe and fear] before the Holy One, Blessed is He, and do not sin *(Rashi)*.

Homiletically, this verse exhorts Israel to tremble so much at the thought of sin that the very idea of transgression becomes disturbing and traumatic. The phrase would mean: *'be distressed and upset'* by the prospect of sin. Furthermore, be distressed over your previous sins and thus you will not sin again (Shaarei Teshuvah 1:4).[1]

1. The Talmud *(Berachos* 5a) interprets this verse homiletically. 'A person should constantly provoke his יֵצֶר טוֹב, *good inclination,* to battle against his יֵצֶר הָרַע, *evil inclination,* as it says, רִגְזוּ וְאַל תֶּחֱטָאוּ, literally, *provoke* or *agitate and do not sin.* If he succeeds in defeating the evil inclination, all is well. If

fruitful vine in the inner chambers of your home,° your children like olive shoots° surrounding your table.° Behold! — so shall be blessed the man who fears God. May HASHEM bless you from Zion and may you gaze upon the good of Jerusalem° all the days of your life. And may you see children born to your children,° peace upon Israel!°

Psalms 4:5 *Tremble and sin not.° Reflect in your hearts while on your beds, and be utterly silent. Selah.*

Siddur Shacharis *Master of the universe,° Who reigned*
before any form was created,
At the time when His will brought all into being —
then His Name was proclaimed as King.°
After all has ceased to be,°
He, the Awesome one, will reign alone.
It is He Who was, He Who is,
and He Who shall remain, in splendor.
He is One — there is no second
to compare to Him to declare as His equal.
Without beginning° and with no end° —
He is the power and dominion.
He is my God, my living Redeemer,
Rock of my pain in time of distress.
He is my banner, and refuge° for me,
the portion in my cup on the day I call.
Into His hand I shall entrust my spirit
when I go to sleep — and I shall awaken!°
With my spirit shall my body remain,°
HASHEM is with me, I shall not fear.

אֲדוֹן עוֹלָם — Adon Olam.

This beautiful *zemer* has been attributed to R' Shlomo ibn Gabirol, one of the greatest early *paytanim*. It praises God as the King, Creator, Infinite, and All-Powerful. It is especially appropriate for the night because of its closing stanzas: "Into His hand I shall entrust my spirit when I go to sleep ..."

The following commentary has been selected from the ArtScroll *Siddur* by Rabbi Nosson Scherman.

אֱזַי מֶלֶךְ שְׁמוֹ נִקְרָא — *Then His Name was proclaimed as King.* Although God was Master and reigned before anything existed, there were, as yet, no beings who could proclaim His majesty. Only when He desired to bring *everything into being* could His title of *'King'* be proclaimed *(ibid.)*.

וְאַחֲרֵי כִּכְלוֹת הַכֹּל — *After all has ceased to be.* The universe will not be destroyed, because God promised that Israel is His eternal nation. But *wickedness* will cease to be. As long as the wicked hold sway, they prevent universal acknowledgment of His

not, he should engage in Torah study, as it says, אִמְרוּ בִלְבַבְכֶם, *'reflect in your hearts.'* If he is victorious, all is well. If not, he should recite the portion of *Shema* [through which one accepts the yoke of God's sovereignty] when he lies down to sleep, as it says, עַל מִשְׁכַּבְכֶם, *'while on your beds.'* If he conquers, all is well. If not, he should remind himself of the awesome day of death, as it says, וְדֹמּוּ סֶלָה, *'and be utterly silent, selah.'*

The Sages vividly emphasize that life is a constant struggle to curb our base lusts and desires. *Chovos haLevavos (Yichud haMa'aseh,* 5) records that a pious man once encountered a band of soldiers coming home from battle. He said to them: 'The war from which you return was only a relatively minor skirmish. Prepare yourselves now for normal, daily living which is a truly great war against the evil inclination and his agents' (see *Overview* to ArtScroll *Tehillim).*

sovereignty. With them gone, *He will reign alone,* in the sense that none will doubt Him *(Etz Yosef).*

בְּלִי רֵאשִׁית — *Without beginning.* God is not a physical being and is totally independent. He is unbounded by time or space *(Etz Yosef).*

בְּלִי תַכְלִית — *And with no end.* Since He exists forever, by definition, God can have infinite patience. Unlike a human king who may feel constrained to carry out his policies while he still has the energy and dominion to do so, God knows that His plan can proceed unhurried and uninterrupted. This strengthens our faith immeasurably, for we know that His promises and purposes will be fulfilled, even though that may take many human lifetimes *(ibid.).*

נִסִּי וּמָנוֹס — *My banner, and refuge.* In triumph He is the *banner* that guides me, *(R' Hirsch);* in defeat He is my protecting *refuge (Etz Yosef).*

וְאָעִירָה — *And I shall awaken!* [Though I deposit my spirit into God's safekeeping every night when I go to sleep, I do so with confidence that He will restore it to me in the morning, *I shall awaken!* — refreshed and ready for a new day of accomplishment.]

וְעִם רוּחִי גְּוִיָּתִי — *With my spirit shall my body remain.* I know that God will reunite my body and my spirit, so I have no fear *(Etz Yosef).*

תם ונשלם שבח לאל בורא עולם

Meir Zlotowitz
Rosh Chodesh Shevat, 5742 / January, 1982
Brooklyn, New York

◆§ Shema and the Ten Commandments

The Talmud *(Tamid* 32a) relates that the Ten Commandments were recited in the Temple as part of *Shema* liturgy, because, like the *Shema,* they are a basic declaration of the Jewish faith. The Sages once considered following this practice as part of the regular daily service, but the proposal was withdrawn because of the מִינִים, *heretics,* who would have maliciously cited the practice as proof that only the Ten Commandments were given by God at Sinai but not the rest of the Torah *(Berachos* 12a). Nevertheless, *Yerushalmi (Berachos* 1:5) demonstrates how each of the Ten Commandments is alluded to in the words of the *Shema* itself:

□ *I am HASHEM your God* is echoed in שְׁמַע יִשְׂרָאֵל ה׳ אֱלֹהֵינוּ — *Hear O Israel, HASHEM is our God;*

□ *You shall not recognize the gods of others* is paralleled by ה׳ אֶחָד, *HASHEM is One* — the only One;

□ *You shall not take the Name of HASHEM your God in a vain oath* coincides with וְאָהַבְתָּ אֵת ה׳ אֱלֹהֶיךָ, *You shall love HASHEM, your God* — for one who truly loves his king will not swear falsely in his name;

□ *Remember the Sabbath day* is alluded to in לְמַעַן תִּזְכְּרוּ, *so that you shall remember and do all My mitzvos* — for Scripture equates Sabbath observance with the fulfillment of the totality of all *mitzvos; 'Your holy Sabbath did You make known to them, and mitzvos, decrees and Torah did You command them' (Nehemiah* 9:14).

□ *Honor your father and mother so that you may live a long life* is found in לְמַעַן יִרְבּוּ, *that your days and the days of your children may be increased.*

□ *You shall not kill,* if transgressed, will be punished by וַאֲבַדְתֶּם מְהֵרָה, *you will be swiftly destroyed* — for he who kills shall be killed.

□ *You shall not commit adultery* can be adhered to only if you obey לֹא תָתוּרוּ, *you shall not be led astray after your heart and eyes* — for these organs are the *agents provocateur* of sin [the eyes see and the heart desires];

□ *You shall not steal from another* is reflected in וְאָסַפְתָּ דְגָנֶךָ, *you will gather 'your' wheat,* — your own wheat and not your neighbor's;

□ *You shall not bear false witnesss,* rather you shall follow in the paths of ה׳ אֱלֹהֵיכֶם אֱמֶת, *HASHEM, your God, Who is truth;* and

□ *You shall not covet your neighbor's house* is implied in the *mitzvah* of *mezuzah,* which is on the doorpost of 'your' house, — your own house, not your neighbor's.

Thus, whoever recites the *Shema* is, in effect, affirming the Ten Commandments as well (ArtScroll *Aseres HaDibros*/Ten Commandments, by Rabbi Avrohom Chaim Feuer, pp. 63-46).